Lynched

Lynched

THE VICTIMS OF

SOUTHERN MOB

VIOLENCE

Amy Kate Bailey & Stewart E. Tolnay

The University of North Carolina Press
CHAPEL HILL

*Published with the assistance of the Fred W. Morrison Fund of the
University of North Carolina Press*

Designed and set in Merlo with Archive Antiqua display by Rebecca Evans
Manufactured in the United States of America

The paper in this book meets the guidelines for permanence and durability of
the Committee on Production Guidelines for Book Longevity of the Council on
Library Resources. The University of North Carolina Press has been a member
of the Green Press Initiative since 2003.

Cover illustration: "Paul Reed; Will Cato; Negroes lynched by being burned alive
at Statesboro, Georgia"; published in Ray Stannard Baker, *Following the Color Line*
(1908). Courtesy of General Research & Reference Division, Schomburg Center
for Research in Black Culture, The New York Public Library, Aston, Lenox and
Tilden Foundations.

Parts of chapter 2 are based on Amy Kate Bailey, Stewart E. Tolnay, E. M. Beck,
Alison Renee Roberts, and Nicholas H. Wong, "Personalizing Lynch Victims:
A New Database to Support the Study of Southern Mob Violence," *Historical
Methods* 41 (2008): 47–61. Used with permission.

Library of Congress Cataloging-in-Publication Data
Bailey, Amy Kate.
Lynched : the victims of Southern mob violence / Amy Kate Bailey and
Stewart E. Tolnay.
pages cm
Includes bibliographical references and index.
ISBN 978-1-4696-2087-9 (pbk : alk. paper)
ISBN 978-1-4696-2088-6 (ebook)
1. Lynching—Southern States—History. 2. Victims of violent crimes—Southern
States—History. I. Tolnay, Stewart Emory. II. Title.
HV6464.B35 2015
364.1'34—dc23   2015003804

This book has been digitally printed.

CONTENTS

TABLES AND FIGURES

This book is dedicated to all of those before us who managed to recognize oppression and injustices in this world before they were commonly recognized by their contemporaries.

PREFACE

The era during which lynchings in the American South were frequent enough to play an instrumental role in that region's regime of racial control is long past. By the 1930s, lynchings had become relatively uncommon. Once occurring on an average of one lynching each week, the annual total of incidents plummeted to the single digits in most years after 1930 and eventually grew even less common. What, then, accounts for the continued interest by social scientists and historians in the five decades, 1880 to 1930, that spanned the turn of a new century? Among the many possible answers to that question, we will consider two. First, that thousands of American citizens (and a few noncitizens) were routinely slaughtered by other Americans, most without the benefit of due process, is shocking and seemingly contradicts our national creed. Therefore the phenomenon begs for greater documentation and convincing explanation.

Second, the social and political winds that are blowing in the twenty-first century carry a faint scent of that shameful past. The challenge of racial difference continues to flummox a nation that has grown significantly more racially and ethnically diverse during the last several decades. At the risk of some exaggeration, the current political map of "red" and "blue" states approximates reasonably closely the division of the country into states where lynching was common and states where it was not. W. E. B. Du Bois famously wrote in 1903 that "the problem of the twentieth century is the problem of the color line." Will the "problem" of the twenty-first century be the same?

Certainly the emotional impact of the echoes of our nation's history of lynching—evident in the persistent power that the image of a noose holds within our culture—suggests that the racial conflicts of the past centuries have not been fully resolved. Notwithstanding the election of the nation's first mixed-race president, the current subtly racialized discourse surrounding social welfare policies, mass incarceration, voting restrictions, and immigration strongly suggests that we are not yet living in a postracial society. Alas, the United States is not alone. Race and ethnic tensions and conflict roil the planet, from the debate surrounding immigration in Europe to the perennial instability in the Middle East. Perhaps a fuller understanding of America's lynching era will provide useful insights into the larger phenomenon of racial and ethnic conflict.

It was our broader interest in the history of southern racial violence that brought us to the project that forms the basis for this book. We were well aware of the significant contributions of recent scholarship on lynching that adopted comparative cross-sectional and intensive case study approaches. The comparative studies instruct us about the macrostructural correlates of the intensity of lynching activity over time or across space. The case studies shine a spotlight on specific lynching incidents, revealing in-depth information about the specific victims, the mobs, and the communities in which the lynching occurred. Despite these important contributions, major gaps remained in our understanding of the lynching era, including almost total ignorance of the personal characteristics of the vast majority of the thousands of victims of southern mob violence. It is that gap that we hope to fill, at least partially, in the following chapters.

As we first considered a number of possible sources that might be mined to construct a profile of lynch victims, the daunting challenges facing us became painfully obvious. Most historical newspaper articles reporting on a lynching incident contained too little information about the victim to serve as our primary source. Death certificates and coroners' reports, when available at all, are scattered across the South, gathering dust in archives of state or county governmental offices. Police reports and court proceedings were an implausible source because most lynch victims were never tried and few mob members were ever arrested. That left the decennial U.S. Census as a possible source. In principle, everyone residing in the country on a specific date is enumerated in the decennial census. In principle, all enumerators' manuscripts from historical censuses have been archived and preserved by the federal government and are publicly available seventy-two years after the census was taken. In principle.

Our original exploration of the census manuscripts as the primary source for our project was not encouraging. We found that we would first need to search for each victim's name using a "soundex" code, just to identify the location on a reel of microfilm that *might refer to* the victim. This procedure would have to be repeated for every possible individual that would need to be considered as a possible match for the victim. And it would have been necessary to conduct all of this work at a U.S. National Archives location. Our projections of the time and cost required for this approach convinced us that the project was not feasible. Furthermore, the original census enumerators' manuscripts for the 1890 U.S. Census had been destroyed in 1921 by a fire in the U.S. Commerce Building.

Eventually, technology and religion came to our rescue. The Church of Jesus Christ of Latter-Day Saints (Mormon) places a strong emphasis on locating information about ancestors and tracing the historical connections among family members. When we conducted our exploratory work in the Seattle branch of the U.S. National Archives, most of the microfilm reader stations were occupied by elderly individuals conducting genealogical searches, many of them Mormons, we assume. To assist in this process, the Mormon Church eventually made scanned and electronically searchable copies of the original census enumerators' manuscripts available through the commercial website Ancestry.com. What would have taken days to accomplish in the bowels of the National Archives building in Seattle could be accomplished in minutes on Ancestry.com, from any location with Internet access. We purchased multiple subscriptions to Ancestry.com to allow members of our research team to search for over 2,400 southern lynch victims. We were able to link to the census records of more than 900 of these victims, and the amount of individual-level and household-level information was increased dramatically. Unfortunately, not even the Church of Jesus Christ of Latter-Day Saints could resurrect the 1890 census manuscripts.

The massive trove of information we had located on such a large number of lynch victims was extraordinarily valuable in its own right. It would allow us to construct the first-ever profile of victims of southern mob violence. Now, if we could only have access to a large sample of contemporary southerners *who were not lynched* to compare with the more than 900 lynch victims in our study, the scientific potential for our project would be magnified considerably. Fortunately, we were rescued once again—this time by the Integrated Public Use Microdata Series (IPUMS) project located in the Minnesota Population Center at the University of Minnesota–Twin Cities. The IPUMS project was originally conceived of by the visionary historian Steven Ruggles and continues to be expanded and maintained by his very talented, loyal associates at the Minnesota Population Center. The IPUMS project, with substantial support from the National Institutes of Health and the National Science Foundation, has made available public use samples of the individual- and household-level information from all historical U.S. Censuses between 1850 and 1940—again, with the unfortunate and regrettable exception of the 1890 census. It is from those samples that we obtained information about southerners who were not lynched.

The database that supports our study was roughly five years in the making. We believe that our patience and persistence were worthwhile. Using those data, we have significantly reduced the mystery surrounding the individuals who were killed by southern lynch mobs. Furthermore, we have been able to determine in what ways they were similar to, or different from, the general southern population. And we have been able to illuminate the ways in which the nature of the local community shaped victimization. We hope that, in some small way, the evidence that we present in the following chapters will advance our understanding of this disgraceful episode of U.S. history. Perhaps it will even shed some light on those social and political winds that are blowing in this modern America and, more broadly, on the continuing difficulty that our species has in confronting peacefully the racial and ethnic differences that continue to divide us.

WE HAVE INCURRED a number of debts during the long life of this project—some in tandem, others individually. While a cliché, it is also true that this book never would have been written without the support we received from others.

Let us begin with the financial assistance. Our effort to link the victims of southern lynching to their census records benefited enormously from two awards, roughly two decades apart, from the Sociology Program of the National Science Foundation (NSF). The first award in 1986 (SES-8618123) supported the creation of the original Beck-Tolnay inventory of lynch victims, which represented the starting line for our record linkage project. The second award in 2005 (SES-0521339) supported the record linkage effort itself. We are especially grateful to Dr. Patricia E. White, Sociology Program Director at NSF, for her early recognition of the potential contribution of our project. Partial support for this research came from a Shanahan Endowment Fellowship, a Eunice Kennedy Shriver National Institute of Child Health and Human Development training grant (T32 HD007543), and a Eunice Kennedy Shriver National Institute of Child Health and Human Development research infrastructure grant (R24 HD042828) to the Center for Studies in Demography and Ecology (CSDE) at the University of Washington. Awards from the Mary Gates Undergraduate Research Fellowship Program and the Institute for Ethnic Studies in the United States at the University of Washington made it possible for us to complete this marathon.

Chapter 2 of our book describes the incredibly time-consuming, tedious, and detail-oriented work that was required to create the database that has allowed us to construct profiles for more than 900 southern lynch victims. More than 90 percent of that work was performed by undergraduate research assistants. Diverse in every possible way, these undergraduate RAs were phenomenal employees and wonderful people. Working with them was truly one of the most enjoyable experiences of our careers. It hardly seems adequate only to list them by name as our expression of appreciation, but that is what we must do in this venue: Molly K. Callaghan, Nate Cermak, Haley Gindhart, Fidel Mahangel, Raeanna Mason, Christopher McBride, Serena Alexis Mitchell, Tanya Murray, Pearlita Price, Allison Renee Roberts, Christine E. Rubery, Timothy Thomas, Jessica Van Horn, Brady Weeks, Nick Wong, and Robert A. Yuen.

For the construction, management, and statistical analysis of the linked database, we relied on a different set of very talented people. Suzanne Eichenlaub and Jennifer D. Laird assisted with the original data entry and file creation. Patty Glynn drew from her special relationship with the "computing gods" to help with database construction and management and especially with the statistical analyses that are contained in chapters 4, 5, and 6. The Computing Core at CSDE, especially Core Director Matt Weatherford, generously provided space for data storage and a state-of-the-art computing infrastructure for data analysis. Jessie Schutzenhofer and the Creative Communications design team at the University of Washington produced the excellent graphics that illustrate and help tell our story. Zina Rhone, archives technician at the National Archives' Atlanta office, located James Clark's original World War I draft registration card for us with amazing speed. David Mandel, Director of Exhibitions and Design at the National Center for Civil and Human Rights, was instrumental in helping us secure permission to use the photograph of Mr. Clark after he had been lynched. Paula R. Dempsey, assistant professor and Research Services and Resources Librarian at the University of Illinois at Chicago's Richard J. Daley Library, helped us locate (literally) dozens of articles from historic newspapers, giving us one more tangible reason to hold an exalted opinion of librarians.

Realizing that our project straddles the disparate disciplines of history and sociology, we sought feedback on our manuscript from practitioners of both. We were fortunate to receive comments from some of the best of both scholarly worlds. Historians W. Fitzhugh Brundage, Michael Pfeifer, Mark Schultz, and Roberta Senechal de la Roche provided extremely valuable insights and suggestions. From the sociology field we benefited from the experience and wisdom of E. M. (Woody) Beck, Rory McVeigh, and Matthias Smangs. All of these colleagues, historians and sociologists, read the entire manuscript, provided detailed suggestions, and asked thought-provoking questions that helped us refine the manuscript. Woody, our good friend and collaborator, also shared data, newspaper clippings, and his unique southern perspective on the topic. The final product of *Lynched* is immensely better because of the advice we received from these brilliant and generous people. Nevertheless, we realize that it is far from perfect, and we fully accept all responsibility for its shortcomings.

Before *Lynched* took book form, we received very useful feedback on our work from the participants in a variety of conferences, symposia, and colloquia. These included the Carolina Population Center at the University of North Carolina, the California Center for Population Research and Economic History Workshop at the University of California–Los Angeles, the Minnesota Population Center at the University of Minnesota–Twin Cities, the Department of Sociology at Washington State University, the Center for Demography and Ecology at the University of Wisconsin, the University of Illinois at Chicago's Sociology Department colloquium, the Northwestern University Sociology Department colloquium, and the Department of Sociology at Western Washington University. Our colleagues at the University of Washington provided us with numerous venues for testing our ideas and getting helpful feedback. These included the Sociology Department's Deviance Seminar and Tri-Lecture Series, the Center for Studies in Demography and Ecology

Seminar, and the West Coast Poverty Center. We are also thankful for the helpful feedback provided by the undergraduate students in Amy's senior seminar on race and inequality at the University of Illinois at Chicago in the spring of 2014. The fresh perspectives they brought to the manuscript and the serious critique they provided helped shape our final set of revisions in material ways.

From the very beginning, we wanted our book to be published by the University of North Carolina Press. During the 1930s and 1940s, UNC Press published several important books that described and analyzed southern society and southern agricultural organization during the Great Depression. These included the seminal works of Charles Johnson, Howard Odum, Margaret Hagood, T. J. Woofter, Rupert Vance, and, most important, Arthur Raper, whose classic book, *The Tragedy of Lynching*, was published by UNC Press in 1933. Raper's book combined social science and social activism to lay bare the horrors of southern lynching and to call for an end to the practice. We would like to think that *Lynched* follows in the general tradition of *The Tragedy of Lynching*. Therefore, we were very pleased when UNC Press decided to publish *Lynched*. We could not have hoped for a better editorial team to work with than Joe Parsons (senior editor) and Alison Shay (editorial assistant). Our copyeditor, Julie Bush, and Paul Betz, UNC Press's managing editor, did an excellent job refining the language in our preliminary manuscript and guiding our project to its completion.

We should also note that the project that created the data on which this manuscript is based, and this written product itself, resulted from a true collaborative partnership. The authors are listed alphabetically but should receive equal attribution for the results of this work.

We would also like to express some individual appreciation.

I (Amy) began work on this project as a graduate student and have continued through a postdoctoral fellowship and two faculty positions. My scholarly trajectory generally, and work on this project in particular, has immensely benefited by generous support from the West Coast Poverty Center, the Harry Bridges Center for Labor Studies, the CSDE, and a National Institutes of Health postdoctoral fellowship spent at Princeton University's Office of Population Research. Through it all, my family has given me unconditional support and inspiration, including my parents, Jerry and Carol Bailey, my entire family of origin, my in-laws, and my family of choice. I am especially thankful to my partner and spouse,

Richard Lintermans, for being both a role model and an advocate and for graciously finding ways to occupy himself while I spent too many nights and weekends working on this project. While Richard was keeping himself busy, Mikey and Mickey provided the most excellent feline companionship and lap-warming services. And of course I thank Stew for inviting me to join him on this journey of inquiry and justice. He is a generous mentor, colleague, and friend. Despite his best guidance, the faults with the work are undoubtedly laid at my feet.

From 2010 through 2015, I (Stew) held the S. Frank Miyamoto Professorship in Sociology at the University of Washington. Frank Miyamoto, who passed away at the age of 100 in 2012, was a sociology professor at the University of Washington from 1945 to 1980. The professorship in Frank's name was created by members of his family to honor his scholarly contributions as well as his impeccable professional and personal integrity. This endowed position has provided valuable and strategic financial support for my work on *Lynched*. Even more important, however, I am extremely grateful to have my name associated with Frank Miyamoto and all that he stood for. Patty Glynn, my spouse, did double duty throughout the project by serving as our "go to" computer analyst and cheerleader. When Patty's energy flagged, the responsibility of boosting my morale fell to three canine beasts—Hank, Merry, and Allie—who were willing to listen to anything as long as their favorite treats were involved.

We cannot say that we hope you will "enjoy" reading *Lynched*. By its very nature, the topic of our book is not something to enjoy. Rather, we hope that, when you finish reading, you will feel that you have a fuller understanding of the ignominious history of southern mob violence and, even more important, that you will view the victims as much more than mere silhouettes or lines in an inventory. We invite you to share your thoughts—both positive and negative—by writing to our e-mail addresses.

Amy Kate Bailey
akbailey@uic.edu

Stewart E. Tolnay
tolnay@uw.edu

Lynched

CHAPTER ONE

The Scholarship on Southern Lynching

On the evening of July 9, 1883, a black man named Henderson Lee was taken from police custody, five miles outside the town of Bastrop, in Morehouse Parish, Louisiana. Mr. Lee had been convicted of larceny and was being moved to Monroe, in Ouachita Parish. He and his police escorts had stopped for the night when a group of roughly twenty men broke into their lodging. The mob took Mr. Lee from the authorities and hanged him (*Daily Picayune* [New Orleans], July 10, 1883). We can only imagine the traumatizing effect that the ruthless murder of Henderson Lee had on his family, his friends, and his community. From the vantage point of more than a century and a quarter in the future, we know virtually nothing about who Henderson Lee was as a man or what sequence of events brought him to the attention of this particular mob, making him the target of such brutality. Given that scenarios like this one—in which black men were denied the rights to both police protection and due process of law—were repeated thousands of times across the American South in the late nineteenth and early twentieth centuries, we could wonder about many men like Henderson Lee. Who were the individuals subjected to this vicious crime? Did they possess specific characteristics that put them at risk, other than being black and male? Were certain "kinds" of men more likely to be targeted in specific "kinds" of communities? For example, did the local context—agricultural economy, political atmosphere, or religious organization—influence the individual profile of lynch victims? This book asks, and answers, some of these questions using newly available information about the victims of southern lynching.

In searching for those answers, this book takes us in a direction that departs significantly from our prior work on the history of southern mob violence. That work, like all comparative studies of lynching, relied on the detection of relationships between *aggregate* characteristics—for instance, the association between racial composition, economic structures, patterns of religious membership, and the intensity of mob violence in local areas, or variation in these relationships over time (see, for example, Bailey and Snedker 2011; Tolnay and Beck 1995; Tolnay et al. 1996). Local context remains an important part of the story that unfolds in the following chapters. With all comparative studies of lynching—whether they have compared time periods or geographic areas like counties or states—the nature of spatial or temporal contexts is most important. In this book, those factors yield the spotlight to the characteristics of individual lynch victims themselves. That shift in focus is necessary in order to answer the foundational questions we have posed. And it is a shift in focus that was impossible for researchers to make before we were able to give fuller identities to several hundred lynch victims by locating their records in the U.S. Census enumerators' manuscripts. We will return to the data that we used in our research later in this chapter and more fully in chapter 2.

During the last thirty years, historians and social scientists have devoted a great deal of attention to a shameful era of American history when it was nearly a weekly occurrence for someone to be lynched.[1] This time period of frequent mob violence, which has been dubbed by some as the "lynching era," runs roughly from the early 1880s through the early 1930s, although many lynchings certainly occurred before and after those dates.[2] Because the vast majority of lynchings took place in the South, scholarly attention to lynching has focused disproportionately on that region and on its most frequent victims, African American men. To be sure, not all lynch victims were southern, black, and male (Gonzalez-Day 2006; Leonard 2002; Pfeifer 2004). Other racial and ethnic minorities, especially Mexicans, American Indians, and Chinese, were victimized elsewhere in the country (Gonzales-Day 2006; Pfeifer 2013), as were some whites and a few women. Still, vastly more research has been devoted to trying to document and understand the typical *lynching* rather than the typical *victim*. That is the relatively unexplored path that we will take in the following chapters as we concentrate primarily, but not exclusively, on black male lynch victims in the American South. But before we embark on that journey, it is important to establish a minimum foundation about the phenomenon of lynching and a basic understanding of what previous studies of lynching have been able to tell us about the lynching era and what remains unknown.

What Is a Lynching?

Most scholars of lynching agree upon a general definition of the lethal practice, drawing from a consensus that was reached during a meeting convened by the National Association for the Advancement of Colored People (NAACP) that took place at the Tuskegee Institute in Alabama on December 11, 1940 (Ames 1942). In addition to the NAACP, the Association of Southern Women for the Prevention of Lynching (ASWPL), the International Labor Defense, and members of the press corps participated in the conference. According to the definition that was produced in this meeting, an incident was considered a "lynching" if

1. there was evidence that a person was killed,
2. the person was killed illegally,
3. a group of at least three individuals was responsible for the death, and
4. the group acted under the pretext of service to justice or tradition.

Although working toward the same general goal—the eradication of southern lynching—the NAACP and the ASWPL had slightly different motivations in arriving at a definition. On the one hand, the NAACP desired to be exhaustive in the enumeration of mob-related deaths of African Americans in order to further its antilynching mobilization efforts. On the other hand, the ASWPL wanted to point to a smaller number of incidents as evidence of the effectiveness of its crusade against lynching (Ames 1942). Reaching some agreement about what constituted a lynching was a necessary prerequisite for the missions of both groups.[3]

Whatever the organizational strategizing and maneuvering that led to this definition, it has facilitated the systematic study of lynching by social scientists and historians and shaped the contours of such scholarship for three-quarters of a century. By focusing on a death, the definition excludes nonlethal forms of violence such as flogging, beating, castration, and tarring and feathering, which were also common but vastly more difficult to document and verify. By requiring that the death be "illegal," it excludes fatal encounters with police, sheriffs, and officially appointed posses, although a substantial body of evidence suggests that law enforcement officials were often complicit in incidents of lynching. In the case of Henderson Lee's murder, for example, it is possible that the police officers charged with his safe transport cooperated with the group of men who ultimately killed him. By requiring that a *group* of people be involved in the killing and that they be motivated by a concern for justice or tradition, the definition excludes simple homicides, even those that might have been racially motivated.

Although useful, this definition of lynching is devilish for its details. For example, in some cases it is impossible to know the exact number of perpetrators who participated in the killing. The legality of "posses" that pursued wanted individuals is often ambiguous, based on the surviving evidence. In many cases the motives of the mob are unknown and must be inferred from limited information about the incident or the mob. For example, consider the following case that was reported in the *Montgomery Advertiser* on April 13, 1894. On April 12 the bullet-riddled body of William Lewis, a black man, was found near Lamison, Alabama. It was known that Lewis had hit another man named "Shields" in the head with an ax. Presumably Lewis had been killed in retaliation for the assault on Shields. But based on the limited information contained in the newspaper article, how can we tell whether there were at least three people involved or what the real motives of the killers were?

Or consider the following case that was reported in the *Atlanta Constitution* on June 19, 1911. A white man named Lawrence Cranford had been accused of raping a young woman in Monticello, Jasper County, Georgia. It was reported by the newspaper that Cranford had been abducted by a "posse" of angered friends and relatives of the female victim and that he would be "summarily dealt with." However, Cranford's body was never found, so it is impossible to know with certainty that he was ultimately killed by the mob.[4]

Fortunately for social scientists and historians interested in studying lynching, problematic accounts such as these are a minority of all incidents. Most scholars recognize the limitations to the consensus definition of lynching that has guided empirical research on the topic. But they are comfortable considering these limitations to be sources of measurement error and not an insurmountable obstacle to systematic evidence-based inquiry into the history of southern mob violence.

How Many Lynchings Occurred?

Armed with a working definition of lynching, social scientists and historians have sought to determine how common they were, why they happened, and why they stopped. The task of providing an accounting of the frequency of lynching might seem like a relatively straightforward undertaking—in principle, yes; in practice, no. Even a simple count of the number of incidents or victims depends on the time period considered, the geographic area encompassed, the racial or ethnic groups included, and the evidentiary requirements imposed. Three primary sources have been used to provide scholars with a sense of the scale of mob violence in the United States after Reconstruction. The Tuskegee Institute in Alabama documented more than 4,700 lynchings nationwide between 1882 and 1964. An inventory compiled by the NAACP includes victims from 1889 through the 1950s, with the first three decades of information published in 1919 in the NAACP's report *Thirty Years of Lynching in the United States, 1889–1918*, and subsequent incidents contained in the association's annual reports. A macabre tradition practiced by the *Chicago Tribune* newspaper has served as the third source for information about lynching incidents. Between 1882 and 1918, near the end of each year, the newspaper devoted one page to an inventory of deaths of different kinds, including legal executions, lynchings, and sporting fatalities. While it is clear that these three sources are not independent, the exact relationship among them remains somewhat cloudy.

Errors and inconsistencies in the Tuskegee, NAACP, and *Chicago Tribune* sources prompted E. M. Beck and Stewart E. Tolnay (2010) to attempt to confirm the incidents contained in these three inventories and to reconcile the inconsistencies for ten southern states[5] for the time period 1882–1930. Each of the lynching incidents included in the Beck-Tolnay inventory met the requirements of the NAACP definition *and* was confirmed by a newspaper article reporting the killing. Their inventory documents a total of 2,805 victims in these ten southern states between 1882 and 1930—a geographic area and time period that correspond quite well with the spatial and temporal concentration of the "lynching era."

We use the Beck-Tolnay inventory as the starting point for our empirical evidence reported in the following chapters.[6] Regardless of which source of lynching information is used, however, it is impossible to know with certainty exactly how many people were lynched in the United States during the nineteenth and twentieth centuries. Many lynchings escaped notice of the press and of the observers upon whom the NAACP, Tuskegee, and *Chicago Tribune* compilers relied for their lists. New evidence of previously undocumented lynchings continues to emerge, so any inventory of victims must be considered incomplete and evolving.

What Were Lynchings Like?

Among the thousands of documented lynchings, it is the more spectacular cases that have received disproportionate attention in historical and popular treatments of the phenomenon (Wood 2009). These are lynchings that match the four definitional criteria without any doubt. They involved hundreds, if not thousands, of mob members and onlookers. In some cases the lynching was advertised well in advance of the actual killing of the victim, allowing interested folks to travel to the location, sometimes from quite far away, by foot, horse, automobile, or even train. Many times the victim was subjected to prolonged torture and mutilation while still alive, and the corpse was plundered for souvenirs in the form of severed body parts. Occasionally photographs were taken of the proceedings and made into postcards. In the overwhelming majority of these spectacular lynchings, the victims were black.[7] A commonly cited example of the "spectacle lynching" is the killing of Sam Hose in Newnan, Georgia, in 1899. The following excerpt from the *New York Times* (April 24, 1899) provides the grisly details of Hose's death on the previous day:

> Sam Hose, the negro murderer and assailant of Mr. and Mrs. Cranford was burned at the stake, in the presence of 2,000 people, near this town this afternoon. Before his death, Hose's body was mutilated with knives, and the torture endured for half an hour. . . . The clothes were torn from the wretch in an instant. A heavy chain was produced and wound around the body of the terrified negro, clasped by a new lock which dangled at Hose's neck. . . . A hand grasping a knife shot out and one of the negro's ears dropped into a hand ready to receive it. Hose pleaded pitifully for mercy and begged his tormentors to let him die. His cries were unheeded. The second ear went the way of the other. Hardly had he been deprived of his organs of hearing than his fingers, one by one, were taken from his hands and passed among the members of the yelling and now thoroughly maddened crowd. . . . The torch was applied about 2:30, and at 3 o'clock the body of Sam Hose was limp and lifeless,

his head hanging to one side. The body was not cut down. It was cut to pieces.

Sadly, many victims of southern lynching suffered similarly horrendous deaths. Yet it would be a mistake to conclude that *most* lynchings were spectacles like the gruesome murder of Sam Hose. In fact, relatively few lynching incidents took the form of the Hose lynching, with very large mobs and massive audiences. It is our impression, based on the examination of thousands of historical newspaper reports of southern lynchings, that most lynch victims were not tortured or mutilated before death and that relatively few incidents were photographed or commemorated with souvenir body parts or postcards.[8] The "typical lynching," if we can claim such a thing, was a less elaborate affair. In one version of the typical lynching, a small mob killed the victim in the presence of no additional onlookers. In some of these cases, but not all, the mob members attempted to clothe their actions with the vestiges of legal proceedings. For instance, the mob might attempt to extract a confession from the victim for whatever alleged offense he was accused of. In others, especially those that involved alleged sexual assaults by black men on white women, the accused was taken before the alleged victim to be identified before being killed. The execution itself in such lynchings was generally conducted in a secluded location by hanging or gunshots.

It was common for local newspapers to express approval for such "orderly" lynchings. Occasionally the press would opine that such incidents were "unfortunate" but would then proceed to explain that they performed an important function in southern society by punishing criminals more efficiently and severely than was possible in the formal criminal justice system. The following case reported in the *Memphis Appeal Avalanche* on August 6, 1893, is an example in which the press clearly approved of the mob's actions as a service to southern society. Will McClendon, a black man from Fair Oaks, Arkansas, was accused of murdering a constable while resisting arrest for burglary. While being transported by the sheriff to the jail in Newport, Arkansas, McClendon was taken by a mob. According to the newspaper account, "The infuriated crowd were quick about their work. No large tree being convenient, McClendon, the murderer, was hanged to a sapling, whose bark was tender and whose years of experience are few. Yet that sapling served as well as a nobler tree and did its country service."

Another version of the typical lynching saw the mob intervening in the criminal justice process itself. Many victims, like Mr. McClendon and Henderson Lee, whose lynching was described at the beginning of this chapter, were snatched from the custody of sheriffs or posses as they were being transported to jail, between jails, or between the jail and the courthouse. Other victims were taken from jails or courthouses before, during, or after a trial. Even individuals who were tried and convicted of their alleged offenses were not immune to mob violence. In these cases, the victim was likely to be carried to a nearby public place and executed, again generally by hanging or gunshots. A prominent place in the black section of town was a popular location for lynchings or the public display of the corpse, most likely to emphasize the threatening message and the lesson that the mob intended for the African American community. Indeed, in some cases, messages of warning were written on paper that was pinned to the victim's body. Generally there were witnesses to such lynchings, in addition to the members of the mob, but the proceedings were not drawn out for entertainment purposes like the spectacle lynching of Sam Hose, nor was torture or mutilation typically involved. The lynching of three men in Tuscumbia, Alabama, in 1894 illustrates this type of incident. Three black men, Fayette Delaney, Emmet Delaney, and Ed Felton, were accused of being the ringleaders of a "barn burning gang." They were arrested and jailed in Tuscumbia on April 22, 1894. As reported by the *Montgomery Advertiser* the next day, the "three negroes were taken from the jail last night at Tuscumbia and lynched by an orderly mob of about 75 armed men for burning a gin at Leighton [Alabama] a year ago last March. They were hanged and riddled with bullets."

What proportion of lynchings can be allocated to spectacle events and what proportion to what we refer to as the more typical forms? Unfortunately, it is impossible to know. We still lack a systematic taxonomy of all known lynchings by the nature of their execution. Some insights can be gained by W. Fitzhugh Brundage's typology of lynchings that occurred in Georgia and Virginia between 1880 and 1930. According to Brundage (1993, 18–19), lynchings can be sorted into five different types based on their "size, organization, motivation, and the extent of ritual": mass mobs, posse, terroristic, private, and unknown. Brundage describes these types of lynchings as follows: "Small mobs, numbering fewer than fifty participants, may be separated into two types. They were either terrorist mobs that made no pretense of upholding the law or private mobs that exacted vengeance for a wide variety of alleged offenses. Posses . . . ranged in size from a few to hundreds of participants and often overstepped their quasi-legal function and were themselves responsible for mob violence. Finally, mass mobs, numbering from more than fifty to hundreds and even thousands of members, punished alleged criminals with extraordinary ferocity and, on occasion, great ceremony" (1993, 19). Brundage estimates that roughly 44 percent of all lynching incidents in Georgia and Virginia between 1880 and 1930 were conducted by "mass mobs" (1993, appendix, Table 1). Only a small fraction of the lynchings carried out by mass mobs would have matched the size, brutality, and publicity of the Sam Hose lynching.

Still, the typical lynching was no less reprehensible just because it did not include the number of people or the same level of torture and mutilation as the spectacle lynching. Both types of lynching resulted in the death of a victim who had not had the benefit of a trial or, if tried and convicted, was punished outside of the formal criminal justice system. In most cases, guilt was not established with nearly the same level of rigor guaranteed to the vast majority of whites who were accused of crimes, and the punishment of death was often more extreme than would have been administered to a convicted white offender. And, as poignantly noted by Arthur Raper in his classic book on the subject, *The Tragedy of Lynching*, "any group which can execute a lynching could place the accused in the custody of peace officers" ([1933] 1969, 36).

Why Did Lynchings Occur?

Most academic studies of lynching seek, in one way or another, to uncover evidence that will help us understand why average citizens would take the law into their own hands to inflict lethal punishment on another person. Exactly how this objective is pursued, however, varies considerably from investigation to investigation. Some researchers dig deeply into the circumstances surrounding a single lynching incident. This "case study" approach is valuable for providing rich detail about the events leading up to the lynching, the cast of characters involved, and the impact of the event on the local community. For example, Claude A. Clegg III's 2010 book, *Troubled Ground: A Tale of Murder, Lynching, and Reckoning in the New South*, focuses on two specific lynching events in

Rowan County, North Carolina, that claimed the lives of three black men and two black boys. Clegg's study focuses on the social and political conditions that allowed these vicious expressions of race hatred to manifest and marshals an extensive array of primary sources, including court records, archival correspondence, and journalistic reports, to accomplish this task. We learn much about the men and boys who were lynched in Rowan County, including their family dynamics, location in the local social and economic hierarchies, and purported relationships with others in town—a level of detail simply not possible for statistical and comparative analyses that are based on many incidents distributed over an extended time period and a wide geographic area. Clegg's history of lynchings in Rowan County is just one example of the case study approach. The same general methodology has been used to excellent effect to study many other lynching episodes, including Howard Smead's (1986) disturbing account of the lynching of Mack Charles Parker in Pearl River County, Mississippi, in 1959 and Laura Wexler's (2003) insightful investigation of the 1946 Georgia lynching of two young black married couples at Moore's Ford Bridge on the border of Oconee and Walton Counties.

The primary limitation of the case study methodology is that information or conclusions gleaned from a single lynching incident are very unlikely to be generalizable to all lynchings, just as we would be remiss in generalizing the circumstances of a single violent crime today to suggest it represents all violent crimes. So, while the case study approach might be able to present definitive information about why a *specific* lynching incident happened and perhaps yield insights that would be helpful in constructing theories about racial violence, it is less useful for telling us why lynchings *in general* occurred. Other researchers rely on limited information about a large number of lynchings, often aggregated within specific time periods or geographic areas. Those temporal or spatial tallies of lynching incidents or victims are then combined with other information about the same time periods or geographic areas in order to infer patterns or relationships that might provide insights into the social forces conducive to lynching. While this comparative approach is limited in the richness of detail that it can offer about specific lynching incidents, it is more likely than the case study approach to yield evidence that is representative of lynchings in general. It is from the comparative

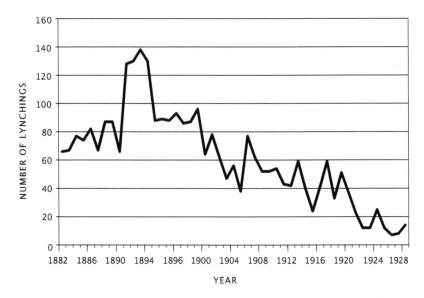

Figure 1.1 Total Number of Lynch Victims, by Year, for Ten Southeastern States, 1882–1930 (Three-Year Smoothed Averages). Source: Beck and Tolnay (2010)

investigative tradition that we draw in order to summarize what prior research has told us about why lynchings occurred.

TEMPORAL PATTERNS OF LYNCHING

The general temporal patterning of southern lynchings has been well documented in the previous literature, especially for the post-Reconstruction period. The number of lynching incidents rose sharply through the 1880s, reaching a peak during the early 1890s when more than 100 lynchings occurred in every year between 1891 and 1894 (see Figure 1.1). From that apex, the frequency of lynchings entered a prolonged period of decline. After 1930, lynching became a relatively rare event, with the total number of incidents reaching only the single digits for most years. There were, however, notable periods of resurgence in the number of lynchings during this protracted decline. Perhaps most notable was the rise in the number of lynchings after World War I when black soldiers returned from service in Europe, where they had witnessed a markedly different racial order. This was also a time when the Ku Klux Klan enjoyed its greatest growth and political influence, not only in the

South but within many parts of the country (McVeigh 2009). For example, on May 21, 1918, a black man named John Womack was accused of attacking a white woman near Red Level, in Covington County, Alabama. The account of his lynching, which appeared in the *Atlanta Constitution*, took pains to note that Mr. Womack had "been called in the draft" (May 23, 1918). Such pulses in overall lynching trends lend credence to the idea that, in addition to the underlying level of racial intolerance and the widespread acceptance of the white supremacy dogma, variation in the number of lynching episodes was at least partially a response to broader social, economic, and political forces.

The effort to explain the temporal pattern of southern lynching has taken two general forms. The first, which we will call the "long-term" strategy, has attempted to account for the overall decline and the eventual demise of lynching. The second, which we dub the "short-term" approach, focuses on shorter time intervals in an effort to explain year-to-year fluctuations in the frequency of lynching. The dominant long-term school of thought argues that lynchings grew less frequent because they were replaced by legal executions (see, for example, Garland 2010; Pfeifer 2004; Vandiver 2006). Pfeifer describes this as the substitution of rational, due process justice for "rough justice." In short, only after the public was convinced that serious criminal offenders would receive official punishment that was swift and severe enough for their tastes were they willing to abandon their practice of extralegal punishment. Important to this substitution process was an implicit assurance that official punishment would continue to be "racialized" in the same way that rough justice had been. That is, by engaging in extralegal lethal violence, the public was not only concerned about punishing criminals but also interested in controlling and subordinating racial and ethnic minorities. The disproportionate application of the death penalty to African Americans throughout the twentieth century and the mass incarceration of black males in the United States after 1980 also would seem to support the notion that there is more to the punishment of African Americans than the desire to control crime (Alexander 2010; Beckett and Sasson 2004; Garland 2010; Wacquant 2000; Western and Pettit 2005).

The substitution explanation for the decline in southern lynching is appealing in many respects—it comports well with the increased professionalization of southern law enforcement and the general long-term trends in capital punishment and lynching. Based on the substitution perspective, we would expect to observe that an increase in the use of legal capital punishment would be associated with a decline in the prevalence of lynching—in statistical parlance, a negative relationship. Yet statistical analyses of the correspondence between the trends in lynching and legal executions have not borne out this prediction. In fact, prior research suggests just the opposite. That is, periods during which there were more legal executions also witnessed more intense lynching activity (Tolnay and Beck 1995). Thus, it seems possible that the intensity of both lynchings and legal executions responded to some of the same antecedent social, economic, and cultural forces rather than served as substitutes for each other.

By focusing on the shifting frequency of lynching from year to year, the short-term approach to studying the patterning of mob violence over time has considered a somewhat different set of possible precipitating factors. The health of the cotton economy has received a good deal of attention by research employing a short-term approach. The possibility that the intensity of lynching responded to cycles in the southern agricultural economy was first examined statistically by Arthur Raper in *The Tragedy of Lynching*. Based on quite limited empirical evidence, Raper claimed that "periods of relative prosperity bring reductions in lynching and periods of depression cause an increase. Mathematically, this relationship is shown by the correlation of −0.532" ([1933] 1969, 30).[9] Subsequent efforts to document an association between the level of economic prosperity, as measured by cotton prices, and lynching have yielded mixed results, prompting John Shelton Reed and colleagues (1987) to claim that the continuing and frequent citation of this relationship between cotton prices and lynching was simply "too good to be false" (p. 1). Beck and Tolnay (1990) used better data and a more sophisticated time-series methodology to explore the issue. According to their evidence, lynchings were significantly more common when the real price of cotton was lower and the rate of inflation was higher, much as Raper claimed. They found the relationship between cotton prices and lynching to be especially strong prior to 1900.

Other studies have considered whether short-term fluctuations in lynching were related to the timing of political disenfranchisement of African American voters in southern states. In general, the evidence suggests that there was no significant relationship between the prevalence or incidence of lynching and political disenfranchisement, either in the

South as a whole or within individual states (Tolnay and Beck 1995). It is our assessment that the combined evidence yielded by studies focusing on the short-term fluctuation in lynching provides stronger support for economic explanations of year-to-year changes in the number of lynchings than for either political or substitution explanations.

SPATIAL PATTERNS OF LYNCHING

The vast majority of lynchings occurred in a relatively small number of states concentrated in the southern region of the country. Of those incidents included in the Beck-Tolnay inventory, Mississippi and Georgia far exceeded the total number of lynchings in any other southern state (see Figure 1.2). Together, those two states alone accounted for 996, or 36 percent, of all documented lynching incidents in the ten southern states covered by the Beck-Tolnay inventory between 1882 and 1930. Drilling down to a finer level of geographic detail reveals concentrations of lynching along the Mississippi River, through the "cotton belt" of Alabama, Georgia, and South Carolina, and in the north-central part of Florida. To a large extent, the distribution of lynching incidents throughout the South followed the contours of the size of the local African American population. Indeed, one of the strongest correlates of the intensity of lynching in southern counties during this time period is the percentage of the population that was black. On the one hand, this association is not surprising because the overwhelming share of lynch victims was African American. On the other hand, it raises the question of whether there were deeper societal structures that contributed to the correspondence between mob violence and the size of the black population. Florida provides a good illustration. Some counties in Florida witnessed very high numbers of lynchings, a fact that comports well with the high percentage of the county's residents who were black. However, the overall population was quite small—the Floridian counties with the highest levels of racial violence were sparsely populated and experiencing rapid agricultural expansion—suggesting that factors other than the sheer number of available "targets" were at play.

Most comparative studies of the history of lynching in the United States that focus on geographic variability have attempted to identify some social, economic, demographic, or cultural antecedent to mob violence—that is, factors that were associated with there being more

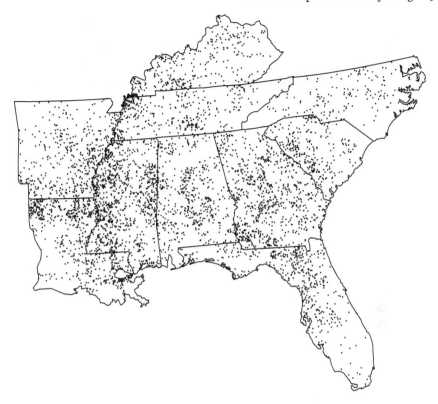

Figure 1.2 Distribution of Lynch Victims across Ten Southeastern States, 1882–1930. Note: Each dot represents one victim. Source: Beck and Tolnay (2010)

lynching incidents in some areas of the South than in other areas. A variety of possibilities have been considered.

One set of correlates of the intensity of lynching in the South suggests that the economic activity and agricultural organization of local areas affected the propensity for mob violence. For example, it has been shown that counties that relied more heavily on cotton production as a cash crop experienced more lynchings than counties with other agricultural specialties (Tolnay and Beck 1995). In a similar vein, there tended to be more lynchings in counties in which fewer whites owned farms and more were farm renters. When combined with the strong association between the frequency of lynching and the percentage of the county population that was black, these relationships are reflective of the greater reliance on mob violence in those parts of the South that were organized around plantation agricultural production rather than around yeoman farmers tilling their own, smaller, parcels of land.

Research by Aaron Gullickson (2010) has documented fascinating, and complex, relationships between inter- and intraracial inequality and the frequency of lynching. Gullickson has shown that, during the 1880s, lynchings were more frequent in counties in which there were smaller differences between the economic standing of blacks and whites, suggesting that whites felt more threatened where the racial caste line was not accompanied by a larger difference between the economic well-being of blacks and whites. Furthermore, Gullickson found that inequality *within* the African American population also was related to the level of mob violence. The existence of a "mulatto" population, with higher status compared with the economic standing of those enumerated as "black" in the U.S. Census, was associated with *more lynchings* in areas that were dominated by *lower-status* whites, again suggestive of economic competition between poor whites and African Americans. In contrast, greater intraracial inequality among African Americans appears to have *reduced mob violence* in areas dominated by *higher-status* whites, indicating that a more successful "mulatto" population served as a "buffer" between poor and well-to-do whites and reduced the potential for a class-based coalition of poor whites and poor blacks.

Although it does not appear that the timing of political disenfranchisement within the South influenced the intensity of lynching activity, southern politics does seem to have played a role. In general, mob violence was more frequent in those southern counties in which the Democratic Party was stronger and the Republican Party was weaker. For example, Tolnay and Beck (1995, chapter 6) found a negative relationship between the frequency of lynching between 1882 and 1889 and the percentage of voters supporting the Republican Party candidate in the 1884 presidential election. In that election, James G. Blaine, the Republican candidate, lost to the Democratic candidate, Grover Cleveland. They found an even stronger negative relationship between the percentage voting for the Republican Party presidential candidate in 1892 and the number of lynchings that occurred between 1890 and 1899. In 1892, Grover Cleveland, again the Democratic Party candidate, defeated the Republican Party candidate, Benjamin Harrison, and the Populist Party candidate, William Jennings Bryant. That a local political environment dominated by southern Democrats was more dangerous for blacks during this time period is consistent with that party's reliance on campaign strategies structured around white supremacy and race-baiting rhetoric (Clegg 2010). Interestingly, to our knowledge, no evidence has been found of a significant relationship between the frequency of lynching and the strength of the Populist Party across southern counties during this time period (see, for example, Inverarity 1976; Soule 1992; Tolnay and Beck 1995, chapter 6).

Even the nature of the southern pulpit has been found to have influenced the intensity of mob violence in the South. Anecdotal evidence suggests that clergy and lay church members were involved in the commissioning and justification of lynchings, as well as in informal and organized efforts to oppose lynching (Brundage 1993, 1997; Hall 1993; McGovern 1982, 67; Miller 1957; Raper [1933] 1969). A systematic analysis by Bailey and Snedker (2011) of the relationship between the local religious environment and the level of racial violence finds a link between the kinds of religious organizations available in a local community and the risk to its black citizens. More lynchings occurred in counties in which a larger number of religious organizations competed for members, and fewer blacks were lynched when a larger share of church members belonged to organizations that included both black and white members.

Much remains to be learned about the explanations behind the substantial spatial variation and temporal fluctuations of southern mob violence during the lynching era. However, the evidence yielded by the comparative research that has been conducted clearly demonstrates the potential of considering the correspondence between the intensity of lynching and a wide variety of social, economic, demographic, and cultural characteristics in local areas or during specific time periods. The findings from comparative studies have led to a much better understanding of southern mob violence than we had just thirty years ago. But this progress has been made by aggregating many lynching events within areas (usually counties) or within time periods (usually years or decades). In the process of this aggregation, the individual victims who compose the temporal or spatial totals are obscured, if not lost entirely.

Why Did Lynchings End?

In the early 1890s southern mob violence peaked at more than 120 lynch victims per year. By the early 1930s there were fewer than 10 lynchings per year. After 1940, lynchings occurred only infrequently and were no longer such an integral part of the southern racial order, even though blacks remained terribly disadvantaged within that social hierarchy. What accounts for this dramatic change? Relatively little systematic research has been aimed at answering that specific question. Yet possible explanations have been proposed.

Proponents of the substitution explanation mentioned above argue that extralegal lethal violence eventually became an unnecessary component of white efforts to subordinate the black population when lethal violence in the form of state-sponsored executions performed the same functions of punishing serious criminals sufficiently swiftly and severely, while also remaining a racialized form of social control (Garland 2010; Pfeifer 2004). Despite the logical appeal of this explanation, it suffers from a variety of weaknesses. First, as noted earlier, it is not supported by the statistical evidence with respect to either the temporal or the spatial correspondence between the levels of lynching and legal executions (Tolnay and Beck 1995).

Second, we believe that the formal criminal justice system in most southern jurisdictions typically functioned as a reliable partner for the white citizenry in punishing black defendants with haste and severity. After all, many lynch victims were grabbed from the custody of sheriffs, posses, and jailers, which suggests that the formal wheels of justice were fully engaged at the time the lynching occurred. To be sure, unlike lynching, a legal execution or a sentence of life in prison did not provide local whites an opportunity to humiliate, torture, or mutilate the accused. But, precisely because those opportunities were sacrificed when convicted criminals were marched off to the state-sanctioned gallows, we also know that there is an imperfect correspondence between legal and extralegal executions in the expressive functions they performed.

Third, a substantial proportion of lynch victims were not accused of capital crimes that would have resulted in the death penalty (Tolnay and Beck 1995, 48). Many victims were lynched for allegedly committing theft, arson, simple assault, or even relatively minor violations of the racial caste system. Greater use of the state's gallows or electric chair could not have substituted for mob violence as punishment for such transgressions as offending a white man, as was the case for George Paul, a black man who was lynched in Pointe Coupee Parish, Louisiana, on May 23, 1894 (*Daily Picayune*, May 29, 1894). Still, despite these weaknesses, we do not dismiss the importance of the formal criminal justice system as a factor influencing the frequency of lynching. Rather, we believe that any substitution effect of the death penalty for lynchings was more nuanced and conditional in ways that have not yet been adequately explored (see Vandiver 2006 for a notable exception).

Another explanation for the demise of lynching emphasizes the increasing efficiency and technical capabilities of southern law enforcement and state militias, including the use of motorized vehicles and radio dispatch of officers (Ames 1942). An assumption behind this explanation is that southern sheriffs, policemen, and state militia commanders had long desired to do a better job of preventing lynchings but were impeded in doing so by logistical limitations. On the one hand, this seems like a dubious assumption, considering the many lynching incidents in which local legal authorities were so obviously complicit in the mob's efforts. Some statements by southern governors, who directed the assignment of state militia forces, would also seem to contradict this assumption. For instance, Benjamin "Pitchfork" Tillman, who served as governor of South Carolina from 1890 to 1894, later made the following comments from the floor of the U.S. Senate, where he represented the state of South Carolina: "We of the South have never recognized the right of the negro to govern white men, and we never will. We have never believed him to be equal to the white men, and we will not submit to his gratifying his lust on our wives and daughters without lynching him."[10] Such expressions by the white elite of southern society do not suggest a strong commitment to control mob violence, regardless of the technical ability of law enforcement.

On the other hand, many cases have been documented in which determined efforts were made by state or legal authorities to prevent or abort an attempted lynching. Recent research by E. M. Beck (2015) has located more than 3,000 references in historical newspaper articles to such incidents between 1877 and 1950. Some interventions ultimately failed, but many efforts to thwart would-be lynch mobs succeeded. In many of the successful cases, local law officers or state militia mobilized to head off potential mob violence. Beck concludes that mob violence would have claimed roughly 2,000 additional victims during this time period, and, of course, most of those victims would have been African American men. A good example of one type of intervention discovered by Beck occurred in Union, South Carolina, on August 7, 1888, as described by the following article in the *Charleston Observer Journal* on August 9:

> Tuesday [August 7] a mob of over a hundred horsemen rode up to the jail at Union and demanded a negro who was accused of the rape of a white woman. The sheriff refused their demand and warned them not to attempt to break into the jail. He guarded the approach to the entrance with the assistance of his brother. They held repeating rifles pointed at the mob and begged them to leave. In the meanwhile a child had slipped out of the back door and given notice to the captain of the local military company. The alarm was given, and soon the mob was galloping out of Union before the double-quick charge of the Johnson Rifles. A guard is now placed over the jail every night, and the citizens of Union are determined the accused negro shall have a fair trial. This is the first instance in this State of a negro accused of rape being saved from the mob by white men.

Considering the sheer number of cases in which legal authorities risked their lives to prevent lynchings and the high likelihood of success when their numbers and weaponry were sufficient to intimidate the mob, it is feasible that improvements in transportation and communication technology did contribute to the sharp reduction in the frequency of mob violence after 1920.

The activity of antilynching organizations within the South, and beyond, likely helped to mobilize opposition to mob violence and possibly hastened its demise. The NAACP, the ASWPL, and the Commission on Interracial Cooperation all pursued active agendas to publicize the horrors of mob violence and to present the case against it. While the role of these groups in bringing an end to the lynching era has not been systematically documented, it is reasonable to assume that they helped to increase public opposition to lynching within the South and possibly were influential in eventually turning the southern press against the practice. Outside of the South, the ghastly and embarrassing messages conveyed by these organizations represented a threat to the effort by southern captains of industry, businessmen, and politicians to create an image of a "New South" that portrayed an attractive and safe location for investment and commerce.

Armed resistance by the black community and by potential lynch victims represented a different type of opposition to southern mob violence. Many incidents have been documented by historians in which blacks threatened to respond violently to whites who were intent on physical or financial harm, and in some cases they carried through with that threat (see, for example, Schultz 2005; Shapiro 1988; Sitton and Conrad 2005). Lacking a systematic accounting of such incidents, it is difficult to characterize the overall scale and intensity of black resistance to potential lynch mobs with any degree of confidence. Was it rare? Occasional? Frequent? Given the severe racial imbalance of power of all kinds in the South during the lynching era, for blacks to fight back against white mobs was a risky and dangerous gamble. The potential for violent retribution from local whites was substantial, and the potential consequences ensuing from African American resistance appears to have varied by the characteristics of the individuals involved and the racial climate within the local area. On this point, historian Mark Schultz (2005, 168) concludes that, "considering the risks for blacks[,] the best-case scenario in a standoff with whites was to threaten violence but not resort to it. Knowing when and how far to push involved a good deal of brinkmanship." On balance, it is difficult to know whether armed resistance by blacks resulted in a net reduction or a net increase in the number of southern blacks who were victimized by white mobs. And it is doubtful that a trend of increasing armed resistance from southern blacks can account for the sharp decline in lynching by 1930.

Most likely, a complex combination of factors was responsible for the virtual disappearance of lynching from southern life by the early 1930s. In addition to the more proximate mechanisms mentioned above, we believe that it is useful to also consider more distal forces, some of which may have triggered the proximate mechanisms, or at least made them possible. As mentioned earlier, the barbaric behavior of southern lynch mobs contradicted the image of a New South that southern capitalists and politicians wanted to project to other regions of the United States and to Europe. Most poor whites probably perceived little reason to change their behavior in an effort to attract outside investment to the region. However, wealthy boosters of the New South grew more sensitive to the potential impact of negative publicity of mob activity (Clegg 2010). Tolnay and Beck (1995) argue that, when the class interests of southern whites diverged in this way, blacks were generally safer from mob violence. More generally, Senechal de la Roche (2001) suggests that a decline in the level of solidarity among southern whites reduced the frequency of lynching.

The increasing migration of southern blacks to the North that began with the onset of World War I also had different consequences for poorer and wealthier whites. On the one hand, lower-status whites stood to benefit from the exodus of southern blacks with whom they competed for tenant farms and unskilled jobs. On the other hand, white planters and employers worried about losing their plentiful and inexpensive pool of unskilled laborers (White [1929] 1969). As the out-migration of blacks intensified, the southern press complained about the loss of cheap workers and even called for improvement in the southern racial order to entice local blacks to remain. Indeed, it appears that the volume of out-migration of blacks was greater for counties that had experienced more lynchings, and in turn, counties from which more blacks fled were less likely to experience subsequent lynchings (Tolnay and Beck 1992, 1995).

Fundamental shifts in the organization of southern agriculture introduced during the Great Depression also may have played a part in preventing the resurgence of mob violence to pre-1930 levels, despite the difficult economic conditions. The New Deal's Agricultural Adjustment Act induced landowners to increase the amount of fallow acreage in order to restore the fertility of the exhausted southern soil. There also were incentives for farmers to invest more heavily in mechanized farming, especially the use of tractors and tillers for preparing the soil and, eventually, mechanical cotton pickers to harvest the crop. One effect of these innovations was to displace millions of sharecroppers, black and white, which fueled even more intensive migration to the North during World War II as northern industries dramatically expanded the production of the armaments and matériel that would eventually overwhelm the German and Japanese militaries.

In sum, the explanation for the demise of southern lynching can be likened to a jigsaw puzzle. Scholars have identified many important pieces, but as yet no one has successfully assembled the pieces into a coherent and compelling story that combines both proximate and distal forces. That remains an important objective for social historians, but it is not the purpose of our research in this book.

Who Were the Victims of Lynching?

Previous research on southern lynching has contributed significantly to our understanding of this dark period of American history. It has been especially successful at revealing the sheer magnitude of the phenomenon and at documenting the distressing details of thousands of lynching incidents. It has also provided valuable insights into the underlying reasons for the lynching era and for its demise. To be sure, there are many questions that remain to be answered, and there is still a need for additional research into the temporal circumstances or contextual conditions that created a social environment in which average citizens felt justified in orchestrating and completing an execution beyond the reach of the formal criminal justice system. But one of the greatest gaps in our knowledge about the lynching era concerns the identities of the victims. By "identities" we do not mean simply the victims' names. For most documented lynchings, we *do* know the names of those who were killed. Beyond their names, however, we typically know only the victims' race and sex. We do not know, for example, if they were married, if they had children, what they did for a living, where they were born, if they could read and write, or even how old they were. Some of these details are known for lynch victims who have been the subject of intensive case studies, but they represent a very small percentage of all lynch victims. What has been missing, until now, is a source of information about the personal characteristics of a large cross-section of all lynch victims. In the following chapters we make significant progress toward filling this gap by utilizing a new database for the study of southern lynchings, which includes extensive information about the victims and their households. This data source is described in more detail in chapter 2. Here, we offer a very brief synopsis.

We were able to resurrect the identities of roughly 900 southern lynch victims by locating their personal and household records in the U.S. Census that immediately preceded their deaths. For example, if a victim was lynched in 1883, we attempted to find the information that was recorded for him or her in the 1880 census. If we were successful, then we learned everything about the victim that was contained in the original census enumerators' manuscripts. This includes, for example, the victim's age and state of birth, literacy or school enrollment status, occupation, and family and residential situations.

Furthermore, for those victims who were successfully matched to their census records, we had access to this same information for everyone who resided in the same household as the victim. So, for victims who were living with families, we could also determine the characteristics of the victim's spouse and children, if they were present. For victims who were not living with families, we could describe their relationship to the head of the household. Equipped with this information, we are able to present a profile of lynch victims that was simply impossible to construct prior to the creation of this linked database. In addition to describing the individual and household characteristics of a large number of lynch victims, we have been able to compare them to a sample of non-victims from the same locations by drawing extracts from the Public Use Microdata Samples that exist for all historical U.S. Censuses during the lynching era, with the unfortunate exception of the 1890 census. (The original 1890 census enumerator manuscripts were lost to all researchers when they were destroyed by a fire in the U. S. Commerce Building in Washington, D.C., in 1921.)

Theoretical Contribution

The information that we have harvested from the rich material obtained by linking lynch victims to their census records has value beyond pure discovery. It also allows us to gauge the extent to which this new body of evidence supports conceptual or theoretical perspectives that might be used to derive alternative predictions about the characteristics of lynch victims. Stripped of the often obscure language of social science theories, the objective at stake here is really quite straightforward. It is motivated by an interest in answering the following simple question: "Compared to the general black male population, how, if at all, were lynch victims different?" There are three possible answers to this question. One possibility is that they did not differ at all. In other words, lynch victims were essentially drawn at random from the general population. A second possible answer is that, on average, lynch victims were selected disproportionately from the lower-status, more socially marginal population of black males. And finally, we must consider the possibility that southern lynch mobs were more likely to target higher-status black males from the general population. We briefly consider these three possibilities here and reserve more in-depth discussion for chapters 4, 5, and 6, in which we directly evaluate these alternative perspectives.

That lynch victims were likely to be lower-status black men with weak ties to the local community is consistent with Senechal de la Roche's (1997) description of the "sociogenesis of lynching." Senechal de la Roche offers the following four propositions regarding the relationship between lynch victims and the larger community, including those against whom they allegedly offended: (1) lynching varied directly with relational distance, (2) lynching varied inversely with functional interdependence, (3) downward lynching was greater than upward lynching, and (4) lynching varied directly with cultural distance. The full importance, and nuance, of these propositions for understanding the nature of mob violence is greater than we shall consider in this book. Directly relevant for us, however, is that they imply that lynchings were more likely to occur when potential victims had lower socioeconomic standing within the community and when they were transients, strangers, or marginal individuals who were unable to draw upon the support and protection of local residents, black or white.[11]

Support for the notion that lynch victims were of lower status than the general black male population also can be found in theories of deviant behavior and social control. Nearly all victims of lynching had been accused of some sort of social transgression—frequently a crime. In most cases, their alleged offenses were quite serious, involving murder, physical assault, or sexual assault. On the one hand, it would be naive of us to believe that all such allegations were legitimate and that the accused would have been convicted if they had been given the benefit of good legal counsel and a fair trial. On the other hand, it would be equally naive to believe that all lynch victims were innocent of the crimes of which they were accused. Of course, what proportion was innocent and what proportion was guilty will never be known. But the profile of those who were guilty was likely shaped and influenced by the same general behavioral and structural forces that make up the explanatory foundation for many theories of criminal behavior. At least for those crimes that were instrumental in nature and in which the offender was motivated by potential financial gain, criminological theory tells us that the offenders were likely disproportionately drawn from the lower socioeconomic stratum of the general population (Cloward and Ohlin 1960; Merton 1957). More generally, Social Control Theory of deviant behavior (Hirschi 1969, 1977) contends that norm violations are more likely to be committed by individuals with weaker attachments to the "conventional order," which includes most traditional social institutions such as the family, school, and church. Consistent with the propositions offered by Senechal de la Roche, Social Control Theory would predict a higher probability of being lynched for black men who were transients, strangers, or less embedded within the local community.

Shifting our emphasis from lynch victims as possible criminal offenders to the lynch victims themselves as the victims of a crime (that is, the behavior of the lynch mob), the Routine Activities Theory of crime would also predict greater vulnerability for black men who were more socially marginal. According to Routine Activities Theory, three conditions are required for crime to occur: (1) motivated offenders, (2) suitable victims, and (3) the absence of capable guardians against a violation (Cohen and Felson 1979, 589). Black men with newer or weaker ties to other members of the community, white or black, were less likely to be protected from a lynch mob than were men with longer and stronger social or economic connections. That is, relative outsiders lacked "capable guardians" to thwart the efforts of a potential lynch mob. And the likelihood of negative community reactions to a "successfully" executed lynching was lower for those incidents in which strangers, transients, or socially marginal individuals were the victims.

In contrast, theoretical justification is also available for predicting that lynch victims were drawn disproportionately from higher-status, well-established members of the black community. Such a prediction is consistent with, though not necessarily a requirement for, the various threat models of southern lynching discussed earlier (Bailey and Snedker 2011; Brundage 1993; Gullickson 2010; Raper [1933] 1969; Tolnay and Beck 1995). To recap, those models contend that southern whites were motivated to mob violence where and when they felt threatened by economic, political, or status competition from southern blacks. Although they typically are framed and tested as the operation of structural forces, based on macrolevel conditions, threat or competition models do have a microlevel counterpart. Put simply, in a society that was sharply divided into superordinate and subordinate racial castes, as was the American South during this time period, any signal of social, economic, or political success by individual blacks could have been perceived as a transgression against the accepted racial order. Witnessing the relative success of individual southern blacks would have been especially troubling for lower-status whites whose racial status presumably guaranteed them a position in the social hierarchy that was superior to that of all blacks. As a result, it is possible that individual black men were singled out for mob victimization specifically because of their success, or that more successful individuals served as convenient scapegoats when other precipitating events led to vigilante violence.

Because, until now, we have lacked information about the individual characteristics of lynch victims, it has been impossible to systematically evaluate these alternative theoretically driven predictions about the targeting of black men by southern mobs. Anecdotal references have been made to the low socioeconomic status and social marginality of victims as well as to the greater vulnerability of higher-status and successful blacks. By constructing a profile of lynch victims and comparing it to the characteristics of black men who were not lynched, we will be able to adjudicate between contrasting theoretical perspectives. Or, perhaps, we will conclude that the evidence fails to support any theoretical prediction about the characteristics of victims and that southern mobs selected their victims essentially at random from the larger population of black males. These are the issues that we address in chapters 3, 4, 5, and 6.

We should be clear about the nature of the research that appears in those chapters—that is, what we attempt to do and how we do it and, conversely, what we leave to other scholars of southern mob violence. Our training is in sociology. More specifically, our mode of inquiry involves the articulation of theoretically driven research questions and hypotheses that can be investigated and tested with quantitative data and enlightened by qualitative evidence. That approach differs considerably from the more humanistic, narrative investigative tradition that characterizes most research on southern mob violence done by historians. We draw selectively from the large and valuable historical literature on the topic, but it is impossible to fully engage that literature while also using a sociological rudder to steer us along the course that is required for our own discipline's logic of inquiry and rules of evidence. We firmly believe that important contributions can be, and have been, made by research on southern racial violence from both scholarly traditions. This is not an intellectual competition. Rather, we view it as a collective effort by researchers using different kinds of evidence and tools to help us better understand a particularly horrific and shameful chapter in American history.

Why Do Lynching and Its Victims Matter in the Twenty-First Century?

Thankfully, lynch mobs and their terroristic activities are a part of the American South's distant past. The United States of the twenty-first century has adopted laws that punish crimes of hate, even those that pale in severity when compared with the horrible events of the South's lynching era. For decades, federal law has prohibited discrimination against groups or individuals based on race or ethnicity, in addition to other individual characteristics. In 2005 the U.S. Senate passed legislation that issued an official apology for its sorry history of blocking the passage of federal antilynching legislation during the early to mid-twentieth century, when southern Democrats held disproportionate influence in that body. In 2008 Americans elected Barack Obama, a man of mixed racial heritage, as their forty-fourth president, even though his electoral opponent, Senator John McCain, was a white Vietnam War hero. Obama was then reelected in 2012, soundly drubbing Mitt Romney, a white man from a wealthy family with a storied political history, in both the electoral and popular votes. Opinion polls reveal that Americans now hold significantly more enlightened and progressive views about racial issues and civil rights than was true in the past, despite the persistence of very high levels of racial economic disparities and social segregation. Given these and many other social changes, surely it is time to leave the past behind and focus on the vast improvements in civil rights, race relations, and social tolerance that have occurred in this "postracial" nation rather than dwell on the horrors of the late nineteenth- and early twentieth-century American South. Or is it?

It is certainly true that Americans should take pride and comfort in the dramatic improvements in race relations and civil rights that have occurred during the last six decades. But we would caution against a collective historical amnesia that ignores why those changes were made and leaves us vulnerable to repeating our past mistakes. For example, one only needs to consider the racialized discourse that lies behind modern-day debates over capital punishment, mass incarceration, welfare, and immigration to understand that America continues to struggle with its racial and ethnic divisions. More to the point, however, there is ample evidence to suggest that a "legacy of lynching" persists in the twenty-first-century United States and that it continues to influence a variety of modern-day social phenomena.

Recently, social scientists have identified a number of consequences of the legacy of lynching. The results of sophisticated statistical analyses have shown that the number of lynchings that occurred in a geographic area (usually counties, but sometimes states) during the late nineteenth and early twentieth centuries *is significantly and positively* related to the following:

- number of homicides in southern counties in the 1990s (Messner, Baller, and Zevenbergen 2005)
- use of the death penalty by states in the 1990s (Jacobs, Carmichael, and Kent 2005)
- strength of the Ku Klux Klan in North Carolina counties in the 1960s (Cunningham and Phillips 2007).
- church burnings in the late 1990s (McAdam, Snellman, and Su 2013)
- levels of incarceration between 1972 and 2000 (Jacobs, Malone, and Iles 2012)
- the rise of white segregationist academies in southern counties during the 1950s (Porter, Howell, and Hempel 2013).

In addition, King, Messner, and Baller (2009) have shown that the history of lynchings within southern counties is *significantly and negatively* related to the propensity for local jurisdictions to enforce federal hate crime laws. Three qualities of this body of research deserve special emphasis. First, all of the modern-day phenomena occurred at least three decades after the end of the lynching era, in some cases much longer. Second, the modern-day outcomes studied are very diverse in nature, spanning the spectrum from the behavior of individuals (for example, murders) to the behavior of local police jurisdictions (for example, enforcement of federal hate crimes laws) to the behavior of states (for example, use of the death penalty). Third, in every case, the impact of the legacy of lynching has been robust to the inclusion of an extensive set of control variables that account for innumerable alternative explanations. How is it possible that events that occurred so far in the past can continue to influence American society in so many different ways, so many decades later?

Although social scientists have successfully documented the relationship between the intensity of historical lynching and several modern-day phenomena, they have struggled to account for the mechanisms through which the history of mob violence operates. Very few living people ever witnessed a lynching or participated in one. Public support for and state tolerance of extralegal violence have vanished. White supremacy groups have grown increasingly marginalized, even within the South, so the rhetoric of racial hatred is relatively muted when compared with the speeches of politicians and newspaper editorials of the past. Yet that significant relationship between historical lynchings and modern-day outcomes is found again and again and persists through rigorous efforts to "wash out" the effect of lynching and explain variation in these current phenomena with other social and economic factors. We are left, then, with the unsatisfying conclusion that the modern relevance of lynching is due to some kind of "historical legacy" of mob violence. Historical legacies are easy to claim but difficult to operationalize for quantitative analyses.

The work of sociologist David Garland may help to demystify the origin and impact of historical legacies in America. In his book *Peculiar Institution*, Garland explains why the death penalty has persisted in the United States when all other Western democracies have abandoned it. Historical conditions figure prominently in Garland's story, and lynching is a central feature of that history. Garland writes,

> The American state's historic failure fully to disarm the population and fully to monopolize violence continues to shape present-day events. This distinctive state formation, together with America's history of inter-racial hostilities, is the underlying source of several linked phenomena. These include high rates of homicide; widespread lynching and vigilantism; a masculine culture of honor-violence; widespread gun ownership; and a cultural fascination with violence. Rather than view these phenomena in isolation we ought to think of them as elements in an adaptive pattern, a cultural complex formed around the nation's high rates of violence and victimization (2010, 189).

Garland goes on to conclude that "history matters. Aspects of the historical past are reproduced in the present. . . . The effects of path dependency carry the past into the present and give history continuing force" (2010, 205). It must remain an objective for future research to expand upon Garland's basic point about the relevance of history to tell us more about why mob violence that occurred so long ago continues to influence modern-day events. That goal is beyond the scope of our efforts in this book. For our purposes, it is sufficient to recognize that there are important connections between what happened then and what happens now. For that reason, it is important to know as much as possible about what happened then, why it happened, and *who it happened to.*

Lynching was not unique to the American South during the late nineteenth and early twentieth centuries. Mob violence occurred in other regions of the United States and during other time periods (see, for example, Carrigan 2006; Evans 2009; Godoy 2006; Gonzales-Day 2006; Leonard 2002; Pfeifer 2004, 2013; Rushdy 2012; Senechal de la Roche 2001, 2004). It continues to this day in diverse settings across the globe. To some extent, the evidence that we present in the following chapters regarding the characteristics of southern lynch victims and their selection from among the general African American population might be broadly applicable to furthering the understanding of lynching in other places and times. At the same time, we caution against the uncritical assumption that lynching behavior was the same whenever and wherever it occurred. Rather, as will become very clear in the following chapters, the local context of mob behavior must also be considered carefully.

A final reason why the history of lynching in America still matters in the twenty-first century concerns the victims themselves. For far too long, the thousands of men, women, and even children who died at the hands of lynch mobs have been little more than names in an inventory. Yet each of these victims was much more than a name. They had jobs, parents, spouses, and children. Linking lynch victims to their census records not only opens doors and creates opportunities for social scientists to know more about these victims; in a small way it also honors the memory of all those people who died without the benefit of due process in a land that takes pride in being a nation of laws.

CHAPTER TWO

Resurrecting the Identities of Lynch Victims

Late in the fall of 1914, after the crops would have been harvested and put in storage, trouble hit Marshall County, Mississippi. Marshall County sits just south of the state line separating Mississippi and Tennessee. Its county seat, Holly Springs, is roughly fifty miles southwest of Memphis. In November of that year, a barn on a plantation owned by the sheriff's brother caught fire. A married black couple, Fred and Jane Sullivan, were suspected of lighting the blaze and were arrested. While the sheriff was transporting the Sullivans to the tiny hamlet of Byhalia on November 25, the day before Thanksgiving, the group was intercepted by a mob reported to include more than 100 people. The mob wrested the Sullivans from the sheriff's custody, took the couple into the woods, and hanged them (*Times-Picayune* [New Orleans], November 26, 1914).

A major obstacle for scholars interested in studying the lynching era has been the frustrating lack of information about the thousands of victims, like Fred and Jane Sullivan, who were claimed by the lethal practice. The various inventories that have been compiled, including the Beck-Tolnay inventory (2010), include very few of the victims' personal characteristics, generally limited only to their name, race, and gender. This is likely because most of the original newspaper articles that reported about lynchings offered scant description of the victims. Without more personal information about the people who were killed by lynch mobs, most statistically based lynching research has been forced to rely on counts of victims or the number of incidents within specific time periods or geographic areas, as we summarized in chapter 1. The victims themselves have remained figurative silhouettes. The major exceptions, of course, are case studies of specific lynching incidents, which provide very rich, detailed information about the focal victims. Because only a tiny percentage of all lynching incidents has been the subject of an in-depth case study, however, the personal characteristics of the overwhelming majority of lynch victims remain a mystery.

In this chapter we describe our effort to acquire personal information about a large cross-section of lynch victims and their families. Broadly speaking, our goal has been to learn more about the individuals who died at the hands of southern lynch mobs so that their identities can be incorporated into scholarship on the lynching era. More specifically, we have attempted to link more than 2,400 lynch victims included in the Beck-Tolnay inventory to their person and household records in the U.S. Census that immediately preceded their deaths. Why use the census for this purpose? We have relied primarily on the census records for information about lynch victims and their families because they are the only repository of such information that is centralized, comprehensive, and relatively accessible. Recall that most newspaper articles that reported on mob violence contained very limited information about the victims—certainly not enough for historical newspapers to serve as the primary archival resource for our purposes. Likewise, death records[1] or coroners' reports included minimal personal information and, when available at all, typically are housed at geographically dispersed state capitals or county seats, making widespread access difficult, if not impossible. Police or court records are even less useful because many lynch victims were never arrested, tried, or convicted. And very few lynchings were thoroughly investigated as crimes, which means that official documents that might have included details about the people killed by lynch mobs simply do not exist. We are thus extremely fortunate that most original enumerators' manuscripts for historical U.S. Censuses have survived, are publicly available, and are electronically searchable. Without these census records, the characteristics of lynch victims likely would have remained permanent mysteries.[2] That does not mean, however, that relying primarily on census information to obtain a portrait of a large number of lynch victims does not have its own challenges and limitations. It definitely does, as we will detail below.

In the discussion that follows, we offer a rather detailed description of the record linkage process we have conducted. We provide such a comprehensive account for three important reasons. First, and most important, the evidence that we will present in the following chapters relies heavily on information that was gathered during the record linkage effort. Thus, we feel an obligation to provide the reader with enough information to instill a reasonable level of confidence in the quality of these data. Our record linkage effort drew evidence from a variety of primary sources and faced a number of significant challenges. Readers deserve to know what those sources were and how we confronted the difficulties that we faced so that they can judge for themselves where the strengths and weaknesses lie in the linked data file we have constructed. Second, a systematic description of our record linkage procedures may prove instructive for other scholars who undertake a similar data collection effort in the future. And third, we believe that the process we used to construct the linked lynch victim–census record database is an interesting story in its own right.

That said, readers who are less interested in how the record linkage effort was completed can proceed directly to the profile of lynch victims that begins in chapter 3 and still understand both the presentation of evidence that is based on the new database and the substantive conclusions that we draw from that evidence. However, we discourage taking that shortcut because we are convinced that a general familiarity with the methods and materials that were used to produce the linked data file will enrich and reinforce a fuller understanding of the empirical evidence presented in the chapters to follow.

Where Our Search Begins and Ends

Our record linkage effort to connect more than 2,400 lynch victims in the Beck-Tolnay inventory with their census records might best be described as "forensic social science." That is, it shares much in common with careful detective work. Working with frustratingly few clues, we searched for each victim through the millions of pages of the original enumerators' manuscripts from the U.S. Population Censuses of 1880, 1900, 1910, 1920, and 1930. Let us begin with the clues. Figure 2.1, an excerpt from the Beck-Tolnay inventory for some of the lynchings that occurred in Florida during the 1920s, shows that the useful information available for us to conduct a search for the victims' census records was limited to the date and location of the lynching, as well as to the victim's name, race, and sex. The *date of the incident* directed us to the correct census—for example, we searched in the 1920 census records for the victims included in this excerpt for Florida. The *location of the incident* directed us to the correct state and county to begin our search. The *name, race, and sex of the victim* served as our only search filters as we considered possible matches for the victim in census enumerators' manuscripts for the correct census and within the proper geographic area.

YEAR	MO	DAY	VICTIM	COUNTY	RACE	SEX	MOB	OFFENSE	ALT NAME
1925	5	13	John West	Seminole	Blk	Male	Wht	Criminal assault (rape)	Jack West
1925	11	27	Arthur Henry	Orange	Blk	Male	Wht	Shooting Officer	
1926	1	11	Nick Williams	Marion	Blk	Male	Wht	Attacked woman (rape)	Chandler Colding, Cohen Pickney
1926	4	27	Charles Davis	Hernando	Blk	Male	Wht	Murder	
1926	5	17	Wm. McKinley	Marion	Wht	Male	Wht	Reported moonshiners	Gilliam McKinley
1926	5	11	Henry Patterson	Lee	Blk	Male	Wht	Frightening woman	
1926	5	9	Parker Watson	Pinellas	Blk	Male	Wht	Robbery	
1926	7	11	James Clark	Brevard	Blk	Male	Wht	Unknown	
1926	12	27	George Buddington	Alachua	Blk	Male	Wht	Extorting debt	George Buttington
1929	2	18	Buster Allen	Hernando	Blk	Male	Wht	Criminal attack (rape)	
1929	5	18	E. R. Romeo	Columbia	Wht	Male	Wht	Altercation	E. R. Romer, N. G. Romey
1929	5	.	Jim Mobley	Hamilton	Blk	Male	Wht	In company of white woman	
1929	11	9	Will Larkins	Gadsden	Blk	Male	Wht	Criminal assault (rape)	
1930	4	27	John Hodaz	Hillsborough	Wht	Male	Wht	Dynamiting house	

Figure 2.1 Excerpt from Beck-Tolnay Confirmed Inventory of Lynch Victims. Source: Beck and Tolnay (2010)

Note that in this sample of victims from Florida, about one-third had at least one alternate name. For example, Nick Williams, who was lynched in Marion County, Florida, on January 11, 1926, was also associated with the names "Chandler Colding" and "Cohen Pickney" somewhere in the chain of evidence that led to the creation of the Beck-Tolnay inventory. This is true for about three out of every ten victims in the Beck-Tolnay inventory and generally results from differences in the names reported by the various source inventories (that is, that of the NAACP, Tuskegee University, or the *Chicago Tribune*) or in different newspaper articles. Many of these differences in a victim's reported name reflect a difference in spelling—as is the case for the man listed in the inventory from Florida, lynched in Alachua County on December

27, 1926, who is recorded as both George Buddington and George Buttington. Still other victims who were identified in media reports by more than one name had more and less formal versions of their first names used. This is the case in the Florida inventory for the man lynched in Seminole County on May 13, 1925, who was listed as both John West and Jack West in various sources. Having more than one name for a victim complicates significantly the search for matches in the census records, although cases that merely reflect variations in spelling or in the use of both formal names and nicknames do not pose a particularly difficult challenge for the search process. The small proportion of victims with substantially different names, however, such as the person identified by the names Nick Williams, Chandler Colding, and Cohen Pickney, are more difficult to resolve with confidence. One might liken this to the search for a criminal suspect who has several aliases.

Before we describe the actual searching process in more detail, let us preview the benefits we obtained from a successful record linkage by considering the case of James Clark. Mr. Clark was lynched on July 11, 1926, in Eau Gallie, in Brevard County, Florida (see Figure 2.1). Today, Eau Gallie has been absorbed by the city of Melbourne. On modern maps, it is a neighborhood in Melbourne's northern section, bordered to the south by the Eau Gallie River and to the east by the Indian River and lying roughly midway between Cape Canaveral and Vero Beach. All we know about James Clark from the Beck-Tolnay inventory and the original research notes used to construct that resource is that he was a black male and that he was lynched by a white mob for an unknown reason.[3] Clark's lynching was one of the relatively few for which there is photographic evidence, which we reproduce in Figure 2.2.[4] It is, of course, troubling for us to view such graphic images of victims, and we expect that many of our readers will find it troubling as well. It is our belief, however, that the lasting consequences of our country's history of racial violence are more easily discounted if we gloss over its grotesque horrors. We decided to include this photograph of James Clark only after careful consideration.

From the information in our initial inventory, we know only that James Clark was a black man. Newspaper reports tell us that he had been in police custody when he was taken by the mob that killed him, and we see in the photograph that he remained handcuffed at the time of his death. If one were to judge only from his clothing at the time he

Figure 2.2 James Clark, Lynched in Brevard County, Florida, July 11, 1926.
Source: The Without Sanctuary Collection, Center for Civil and Human
Rights, Atlanta, Georgia

was lynched, it would seem unlikely that Mr. Clark was an agricultural worker or an unskilled laborer, but that would be pure speculation. After all, in 1926, July 11 fell on a Sunday. If the police had arrested him on that day, it is possible that James was dressed to attend church rather than for work when he was killed. If he was being transported for a court appearance, he may have been dressed for court.

After locating Mr. Clark in the 1920 census, we learned much more about him. He was thirty-eight years old when he was killed. His wife, Mary P., would have been twenty-seven years old. They had three children: Charlie May would have been eleven years old, Elizabeth nine, and James Jr. six when their father was killed. Both James Sr. and Mary could read and write. James was a laborer in a foundry. Mary and her parents were born in South Carolina; James and his parents were born in Florida. They rented their home. The neighbors on one side of the Clark residence were Richard and Viola Ridley, another African American couple, also with three children. In 1926 Marie would have been age sixteen, Louis age fifteen, and Mose age thirteen. On the other side of the Clarks lived Philip Wynn, a black widower who would have been fifty when James Clark was killed, with his two daughters, whose ages in 1926 would have been eighteen and twenty-two.[5]

Through this example of successful record linkage, James Clark becomes much more than a line in an inventory of lynch victims. In a very real sense, his individuality is restored. This man, this lynch victim, was a middle-aged husband and a father to three young children, one of whom shared his name. He was a blue-collar worker. He could read and write. His family rented a home in a neighborhood with other black families, with children just a few years older than their own. The case of James Clark illustrates the additional information that we gained for the 935 lynch victims whom we successfully matched to their census records during the lynching era.[6] By using the case of James Clark to highlight the benefits of locating the census records of lynch victims, we do not mean to suggest that all, or even most, victims were married men with children. Rather, this case simply represents the potential of census data to augment the paucity of information that we had about victims before this record linkage project was completed.

We obtained the additional personal and household information about James Clark from the original census enumerators' manuscripts. The specific content of the census manuscripts varied modestly from census to census as a few questions were added or deleted and the wording of some questions was changed (see Appendix Table A.2.1). For example, the 1920 census manuscripts in which we located James Clark include a question about home ownership. That question was also included in the 1900, 1910, and 1930 censuses but not in the 1880 census. Also, possible responses for the "race" question in the 1880, 1910, and 1920 censuses included the category "mulatto," the term commonly used in the late nineteenth and early twentieth centuries for people with both African and European ancestry. "Mulatto" was not included as a possible racial category in the 1900 or 1930 censuses. Aside from a relatively small number of differences like these, the census manuscripts for this time period share a core set of sociodemographic characteristics, such as the geographic location of the household and each individual household member's name, age, sex, race, and relationship to the head of the household. Each census also records whether individuals were literate, as well as their marital status, birthplace, occupation, and their parents' birthplace. An important consequence of finding lynch victims in the census manuscripts was that we also learned about all individuals who resided in the same household—whether or not they were members of the victim's family. Our goal with this record linkage project was to locate the enumerators' manuscript pages on which each lynch victim is recorded. In principle, the objective of finding the census records for lynch victims was simple and straightforward. In its execution, however, it was anything but simple, as we explain below.

The Record Linkage Procedure

Our attempt to locate lynch victims in the U.S. Census that preceded their deaths was jeopardized by two types of potential errors. These errors are the scourge of all record linkage efforts. On the one hand, there was the risk of "false positives," in which we might mistakenly identify an individual who was enumerated in the census as the lynch victim when, in fact, he or she was not the victim. On the other hand was the risk of the "missed match," in which we might fail to link the victim to his or her individual census records, even though the records actually were contained in the original census manuscripts. These errors can be likened to a jury's risks of convicting an innocent person (false positive) or acquitting a guilty defendant (missing match).[7] And, as in the jury analogy, efforts to reduce the likelihood of one type of error can increase the risk of the other. Every step in the record linkage procedure we describe in this chapter was designed to minimize the likelihood of committing these two errors. But, of course, we recognize that striving too hard to reduce one type of error can increase the likelihood of committing the other mistake. It would be naive to believe that we were completely successful in avoiding these errors. And while we cannot quantify the extent to which our linked data file suffers from false positives or missed matches, we are confident that our careful detective work has kept them at a reasonable minimum.

Searching for Victims: The Methods and Materials

Because most of the original census enumerators' manuscripts for the 1890 census were destroyed in 1921 by a fire in the U.S. Department of Commerce Building, they were unavailable for searching for victims who were lynched during the 1890s. This was an unfortunate limitation because it was during the 1890s that southern lynchings reached their peak. Rather than sacrifice the ability to search for all of the people who were lynched during the 1890s, we used the 1880 census manuscripts to search for victims who were lynched between 1890 and 1895.[8] We decided against using the 1880 census to search for victims lynched after 1895 because the extended period of time that elapsed between the census and those lynchings reduced both the likelihood of a successful match and the value of the census information obtained for successful matches. For instance, a twenty-year-old victim who was lynched in 1898 would have been only two years of age when enumerated in 1880, and any victims younger than eighteen would not have been born.

We began the record linkage effort with a total of 2,483 lynch victims from the Beck-Tolnay inventory.[9] It was not possible to search for the roughly 10 percent of victims with no known name reported. For victims with more than one name, like Nick Williams, the victim who was killed in Florida in 1926, we conducted searches for all reported names. The number and percentage of victims in our "searchable" time frame who had only a single name, a partial name, or multiple names reported or who were unnamed are presented in Table 2.1. In addition to the information contained in the inventory itself we also utilized the original notes on each case that were recorded in the prior phase of this work, as the

Table 2.1 Lynch Victims with a Single Name, a Partial Name, or Multiple Names, or Who Were Unnamed, 1882–1930

	Single Name	Partial Name	Multiple Names	Unnamed	Total
Number	1,426	155	659	243	2,483
Percent	57.4	6.2	26.5	9.8	100

Source: Beck-Tolnay Inventory (2010)

Beck-Tolnay inventory was being constructed. The original purpose of those notes was to record the most important information contained in the original newspaper articles that were used to confirm every incident in the inventory. These notes typically focused on facts associated with the *lynching incident* but sometimes included additional personal information about the *lynch victims* that was helpful in locating the victim's census records, such as reference to the victim's age, occupation, or the name of another family member. In many instances, we referred to additional supplementary materials to inform our linkage effort, including World War I draft registration cards, accounts of the lynching published in major newspapers,[10] and death certificates. We were sometimes able to ascertain details from these additional materials that proved useful in matching records from the lynching inventory to the census records, such as age, occupation, marital status, or community of residence.

One valuable auxiliary source was World War I draft registration cards. These cards were collected for more than 24 million men of draftable ages, roughly between the ages of eighteen and forty, in 1917 and 1918 and are available online and in a searchable format.[11] Although they were useful only for the male victims of lynchings within a selected age range that occurred during a very limited time period, the draft registration cards sometimes contained personal information that assisted in the location or confirmation of a victim's census records. For example, the image of James Clark's draft registration card is shown in Figure 2.3. It tells us that at the time he registered for the draft on June 5, 1917, Mr. Clark lived in Jacksonville, Florida, and worked as a boilermaker's helper. We also learn that James Clark was born on August 6, 1888, which could have proven useful if multiple possible matches for Mr. Clark were found in the census manuscripts but of differing ages. He is listed as being married and having two children in 1917—a time when Charlie May would

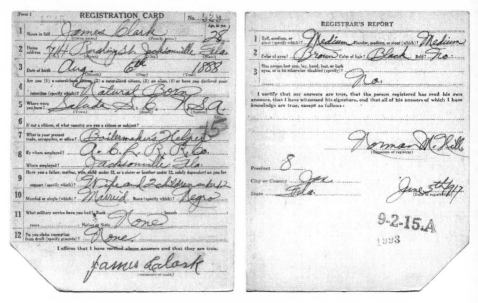

Figure 2.3 World War I Selective Service Registration Card for James Clark. Source: The National Archives at Atlanta, Record Group 163: Records of the U.S. Selective Service System (WWI), Draft Registration Cards, Records of Local Boards 1917–1918, Florida, Duvall County, James Clark

have been around two years old, Elizabeth would have been an infant, and James Jr. would not yet have been born. James Clark's draft card also includes an inconsistency when compared to his census record. The place of birth listed for James Clark on his draft card is Saluda, South Carolina. In the 1920 census, his birthplace is listed as Florida, but his wife, Mary, and her parents are listed as having been born in South Carolina.

In this version of the World War I draft registration card, there is a line allowing the recording of each registrant's race, and James Clark is listed as "Negro." However, instructions to the draft board specified that the corner of the registration form should be clipped off for black men. There were three separate forms used for World War I draft registration, two of which used only the "clipped corner" approach to identify black men and the third of which recorded the applicant's racial category in writing. Apparently, James Clark's local draft board also clipped off the corner of his draft registration card to be sure that he and other black men considered for admittance into the racially segregated armed forces would be clearly identified as such.

We relied on Ancestry.com's scanned, searchable census records to conduct the initial search for victims, limiting our search to individuals who were the same race as the victim.[12] We used soundex[13] codes to identify individuals with names similar to those reported for the lynch victim and with common nicknames or other variants of the victim's reported name(s). We documented all possible matches identified during this initial search procedure, including the victim's age, race, and name as identified in the census. We also noted the state and county in which the victim was located and the relative distance of this location to the site of the lynching, measured in number of counties. For victims with more than one reported name, separate searches were conducted for each possible name.[14]

Geography was a key element of the search. We began each search in the county in which the lynching occurred. From there we expanded our search outward to contiguous counties for all victims. If no possible matches were located within either the target county or in contiguous counties, we conducted a statewide search. For counties bordering a state line, the spatial criterion includes counties from both states. For a very small number of cases in which the victim had a name that was considered to be especially unusual, we even conducted national searches. This sequential strategy for expanding the geographic scope of our search was based on the reasonable (though certainly not unchallengeable) assumption that most migrants moved short or modest distances during this historical period (Tolnay 1999). We used this logic to restrict the number of potential "matches" without excluding nearby areas due to the arbitrary nature of political boundaries. Counterbalancing the advantages conferred by relying on this systematic logic for locating candidate matches were a variety of limitations that these methods imposed. These disadvantages included the possibility that the restrictions might have selectively eliminated more transient victims from being linked with their census records, that more transient victims who shared a name with a resident member of the community would be inappropriately matched with our target lynch victim, and that some true matches would be missed by the restricted geographic scope.[15]

Potential census matches who were the same gender and race as the victim and in a range of ages most likely to have been lynched were recorded for each lynch victim. In most cases, we identified ten to seventy years as the age range most likely to encompass lynch victims. However, for lynch victims who were accused of rape or murder, we increased the minimum age to fourteen years, unless additional information from the original case file, newspaper article, or supplementary sources indicated that the victim was unusually young. Lynch victims for whom we identified too many plausible matches, or for whom we located no possible matches, were considered unmatchable. To this point in the record linkage effort, we were most interested in limiting the number of "missed matches"—that is, in reducing the likelihood that we overlooked existing census records for one of the lynch victims. In our next phase of research, case selection, we shifted our focus to identifying which, if any, of the possible matches was in fact the person who was lynched.

Estimating Confidence in Potential Matches

Once we recorded the possible matches who were identified in the original census enumerators' manuscripts, the complete list of potential matches was then subjected to "sifting" and "sorting" procedures. Through sifting we attempted to eliminate from further consideration any potential matches who were extremely unlikely to be the lynch victim for whom we were searching. By sorting, we used all available information to rank the potential matches according to the likelihood that they actually were the lynch victim in question. During this stage of the process we were primarily motivated by a desire to reduce the chances of false positives—that is, apparent matches who were not lynch victims.

During the sifting process we used the enumerators' manuscripts and all relevant supplementary material employed in the search process to winnow from the list of possible matches those who seemed very unlikely to be the lynch victim. For each person who remained in the list of possible matches, we searched in the subsequent census records to determine whether the individual in question could be located—a "forward search."

For example, if "Bob Smith" was located in the 1910 census as a possible match for Bob Smith who was lynched in 1915, we then searched the 1920 census records for the Bob Smith who was found in 1910. If we found him in 1920, then it was impossible for Bob Smith from the 1910 census records to be the person who had been killed in 1915. This type of forward linkage process cannot confirm that any individual was, in fact, the lynch victim; however, it does allow us to eliminate potential false positives. The case of Lee Green, lynched on August 17, 1923, in Houston County, Georgia, provides a good illustration. The original search revealed three possible matches in the 1920 enumerators' manuscripts. One of the possible matches was located during the forward search into the 1930 census, reducing the possible number of matches from three to two.[16]

Information on family members—particularly the spouses—of potential matches was also used in forward searching and frequently yielded information that increased our level of confidence in a particular match. For example, in the case of Sam Williams, lynched January 6, 1921, in Talbot County, Georgia, the original search yielded too many possible name matches—only one in Talbot County itself and several in its contiguous counties. Through subsequent searching we located a short newspaper article in the January 8, 1921, edition of the *Atlanta Constitution* that explained that the Sam Williams who was lynched had recently moved from Talbot County to contiguous Meriwether County in Georgia. There were no black men named Sam Williams enumerated in Meriwether County in 1920, indicating that the Sam Williams from Talbot County was the most likely of the nine potential matches to be the lynch victim. We had particular confidence in this match since not even a year had passed between the census enumeration date (January 15 and 16, 1920) and the date of the lynching (January 6, 1921).

The Sam Williams enumerated in Talbot County was listed as being forty-six years old. His wife, Mandy, was forty-two years old, and they had six children. We requested and obtained the death registration for a Sam Williams who died on January 6, 1921, from the Talbot County archives. The death record confirmed that the deceased's name was recorded as "Sam Williams," in contrast to the more formal "Samuel Williams," the name under which some alternative potential matches were enumerated. Through a forward match, we identified possible matches for Sam Williams's widow, Mandy, in 1930. Only three black women named Mandy Williams in the age range of Sam Williams's wife were enumerated in the entire United States in 1930. The "Mandy Williams" located in the 1930 census within the closest geographic proximity to Talbot County, Georgia, and with the closest age match to Sam Williams's wife was found in prison in Baldwin County (four counties away from Talbot County) in the following census. Her marital status was listed as "Widowed."

Not all possible matches located in the census were of the same quality. Based on all of the evidence compiled during the search process, it was clear that we could have greater confidence in some matches than in others. Such variation in our level of confidence was often due to differences in the name of the victim and the distance of his or her residence in the census from the location of the lynching. This was true whether the victim was linked to only one possible matching individual in the census or to more than one. So the final critical step in the record linkage effort, the sorting process, consisted of assigning "subjective estimated probabilities" for each possible match that was found in the census.

This was done in a meeting that included at least three members of the research team and during which all of the census records and supplementary material located during the search were examined carefully, including efforts at forward linkage in a subsequent census. In most cases, there was strong consensus about the level of confidence that could be placed in the potential matches. When there was disagreement, we took a vote. We used this very labor-intensive approach to assigning confidence levels, rather than employing some kind of statistical algorithm, because of the multiple issues involved in selecting between potential candidate matches, the variation in information available for each case, and differences in the weight we deemed appropriate to give to specific kinds of information, depending on the circumstances. For example, exact name matches were accorded more weight for unusual names as compared with relatively common names. Geographic distance received greater emphasis when we had additional information from draft registration cards or newspaper accounts regarding the location of the victim's residence. Age became more informative when the newspaper article cited the victim's age or life stage, when multiple people were lynched for supposed joint participation in criminal activity or social transgressions, or if the victim was accused of attacking someone with whom he or she had an interpersonal dispute. While we certainly applied search and selection criteria scientifically, the "art" of adjudicating between matches seemed, to us, to require a humanistic rather than a statistical approach.[17]

For cases in which a single individual was identified as a possible match, we assigned a "high" or "medium" probability. A rating of high probability indicated a level of confidence in excess of 75 percent. For example, we assigned the single match we identified in the census enumerators' manuscripts for James Clark a high probability of being the person who was lynched outside of Eau Gallie, in Brevard County, Florida, in 1926. We identified one black man named James Clark living in Orange County, Florida, during the 1920 census enumeration, the only black man by this name identified in Brevard or any of its contiguous counties. Based on strong similarities in family structure, age, occupation, and literacy, we also believed that the James Clark enumerated in Orange County was the same person who registered for the World War I draft in Jacksonville in 1917. Jacksonville is roughly 150 miles north of Brevard County, but a direct route between the two areas was served by the Atlantic Coast Line Railroad during this time period (Dozier 1920), making travel and migration less onerous. We were unable to locate James Clark, his wife, or any of his three children in the 1930 census, lending credence to the idea that Mr. Clark had been lynched in the intervening time period.

A medium probability reflected our belief that there was a 50–75 percent likelihood that the individual located in the census was the lynch victim. For example, we identified a single match for Henderson Lee, the black man whose 1883 lynching in Louisiana was mentioned in chapter 1. Mr. Lee was lynched while in transit between Morehouse and Ouachita Parishes. Our search of the 1880 census manuscripts identified a Henderson Lee living in Madison Parish, two parishes away, and we were unable to locate the same individual in the 1900 census records. Because Henderson Lee was lynched only three years after the enumeration, however, and was located in a parish somewhat farther afield, we reduced our level of confidence that the person residing in Madison Parish was the man who was lynched.

When we identified only one possible match but had serious doubts that the individual found in the census was in fact the lynch victim, we considered the victim to be "unmatched." For example, in the case of Andrew Cassels, a black man accused of robbery and arson who was lynched in Franklin County, Mississippi, on September 20, 1884, we found only one black male in the entire country with a similar name. However, that potential match was named Anderson Cassels, not Andrew Cassels, and he was enumerated in distant Chester County, North Carolina. It is certainly possible that the fellow who lived in North Carolina in 1880 was lynched four years later in Mississippi. However, we concluded that the probability of that being true was too low to consider North Carolina's Anderson Cassels to be a successful match for Andrew Cassels, the Mississippi lynch victim—at least with any reasonable level of confidence. Rather, the more likely possibility is that the Andrew Cassels who was lynched in 1884 was one of many black men who were not enumerated in the 1880 census.

For cases with more than one possible match in the census, we retained only those cases for which there were two, or at most three, possible matches after the "sifting" process, from all combinations of reported names, and we had at least a medium level of confidence (that is, at least 50 percent) in one of the possible matches that the individual located in the census was the lynch victim. For cases with multiple possible matches, we assigned each census-linked individual a subjective estimated probability, all of which added up to 1.0 for each case. For example, we located three possible matches for the victim James King, who was accused of grave robbing for the purpose of witchcraft and lynched in Hinds County, Mississippi, on September 4, 1883. One possible match was "James King," enumerated in Hinds County in 1880 at the age of sixty. A second possible match was "J. King," enumerated in contiguous Yazoo County at age forty. The third possible match was "Jimmie King," who was seventeen years of age when enumerated in Madison County, which is also contiguous to Hinds County.

After considering all of the information gathered during the search process, we concluded that James King from Hinds County was most likely to be the lynch victim. We based this decision on a number of important factors, including these: (1) he was the only one of the three possible matches whose name was recorded in the census manuscripts exactly as reported in the newspaper article that confirmed his lynching; (2) he was also the only one of the three who was enumerated in the same county in which the lynching occurred; and (3) it seemed more plausible that an older person would have been accused of a crime with a spiritual dimension such as witchcraft, compared with a man who was barely out of his teens (Jimmie King would have been just twenty at the time of the lynching). Still, we concluded that it would be inappropriate to eliminate the other two potential matches, J. King and Jimmie King. Therefore, we assigned a confidence level of 0.80 to James King from Hinds County and a confidence level of 0.10 to both J. King and Jimmie King (0.80 + 0.10 + 0.10 = 1.0).

In other cases with multiple possible matches, we were unable to locate information that would have allowed us to have greater confidence in any particular match versus the other possible matches. For example, in the case of William Buckley, who was lynched on April 21, 1925, in Walthall County, Mississippi, the search procedure yielded four possible matches, two of whom were eliminated from further consideration through forward searching in the 1930 census. One of the two remaining possible matches was "Will Bucklay," who resided in Marion County, Mississippi, which is contiguous to Walthall County. The other possible match was "Willie Buckley," who lived in Jefferson Davis County when enumerated in the 1920 census. Jefferson Davis County is not contiguous to Walthall County, but their county seats are less than fifty miles apart. We located no additional information during the search process that could allow us to place greater confidence in one of these two possible matches. Therefore, we assigned equal probabilities of 0.50 to both Will Bucklay and Willie Buckley (0.50 + 0.50 = 1.0).

Challenges to Successful Record Linkage

Like all historical record linkage projects, ours faced a number of difficult challenges—some of which were shared with those of earlier record matching efforts and some that were unique to the types of records that we attempted to match. Here we briefly describe the primary challenges we faced and the strategies that we employed to deal with them.

CENSUS UNDERENUMERATION

If a lynch victim had not been included in the census immediately prior to his or her death, then it was impossible to locate that individual in the enumerators' manuscripts. The historical decennial censuses varied in the completeness with which they enumerated the U.S. population. In general, African American males were more likely than other groups to be missed by the enumerators (see, for example, Rosenwaike, Preston, and Elo 1998), and this may have been especially true within the South during the decades of the lynching era. Demographers Ansley Coale and Norfleet Rives (1973, 21) have constructed estimates of the extent to which black males were undercounted by the census for the ages and decades (though not the geographic locations) that were of special interest to us. Their estimates indicate that the probability that black men were missed by census enumerators varied considerably across the decades between 1880 and 1930, as well as by age group. In some cases the undercount was substantial. For example, for men between the ages of thirty and thirty-four, nearly one in five of all blacks was unaccounted for in the census in each of the five decades we examined. That level of census underenumeration would mean that, at best, the hypothetical maximum rate of successful linkages for black men of those ages in those decades would be 80 percent rather than 100 percent.

In a few cases, we were able to use supplementary sources to find information about the lynch victim to partially substitute for the absence of census records. Most helpful in this regard were the World War I draft registration cards. Information available from the draft registration cards generally included name, age, race, occupation, home address, employer, marital status, physical disability, and, in some cases, next-of-kin and parents' names. Clearly this source provided information only for individuals who were lynched in the later years covered by our research (among the named victims from the Beck-Tolnay inventory, this included a total of 326 black males and 23 white males who were lynched between 1918 and 1930, not all of whom would have been of age to register for the draft in 1917 and 1918).

We were also aided in locating information for unenumerated victims by material that was available in local and state death records. Because of the relatively late adoption of vital registries in southern states and because rural areas within the region were the last to maintain public records of births and deaths (Shapiro 1950), death records also were available for only a small minority of the victims who were killed during the latter years of our investigation. Legal restrictions on access to death certificates also vary geographically, so in many states or counties where records might have been kept, they are by statute released only to family members.

Newspaper accounts of a lynching and its aftermath were available for all victims. Occasionally these articles provided information that would help us to more successfully identify victims, such as the names of family members, a general age range for the victim, a specific place of residence, or an occupation or employer. However, evidence from these supplementary sources was not always available and, even when found, was not a perfect substitute for the missing census information. Still, by drawing from non-census sources to obtain at least partial information for unenumerated victims, we were able to retain a few additional linked cases in the data file.

In the case of John Lee "Eberhardt," for example, accused of murder and lynched February 16, 1921, in Oconee County, Georgia, both the World War I registration cards and newspaper stories proved to be very useful—even though the victim himself appears to have been missed by census enumerators in 1920. In our original search, we identified two men with this exact name, both in their forties and both enumerated in the county of lynching. However, in reviewing the case, we located numerous newspaper reports as well as an article by University of Georgia law professor Donald E. Wilkes Jr. (1997) that all described John Lee "Eberhart" as a "young man." In addition to the age discrepancy, this spelling is somewhat different from that reported in the Beck-Tolnay inventory. A search of the World War I registration card database identified John Lee Eberhart, twenty-one years old, living and working in the county of lynching. The Wilkes article also mentions that Eberhart's father helped police to find him. John Lee Eberhart's father—listed by name as his next-of-kin in the draft registration records—was found enumerated in the Oconee County census records in 1920.

Although we were unable to locate John Lee Eberhart in the 1920 enumerators' manuscripts, we had sufficient information from these supplementary sources to locate him—as a child, living in his father's home—in both 1910 and 1900 in Clarke County, which is adjacent to Oconee County and where the police said they were familiar with him as a sort of criminal character. Conducting a forward search into the 1930 census, we were unable to locate John Lee Eberhart, although we found his father and his father's family living in Detroit. Thus, although John Lee Eberhart was apparently not enumerated in the 1920 U.S. Census, we were able to identify him as the lynch victim and to obtain useful information about him from other sources and from other census years. In general, we would expect the challenge of census underenumeration to be more severe for lower-status and geographically mobile members of the southern population because they were more likely to be missed by census enumerators. It is possible, then, that higher-status, more residentially stable lynch victims were more likely to be linked to their census records.[18]

DESTRUCTION OF 1890 CENSUS RECORDS

As mentioned earlier, most of the original enumerators' manuscripts for the 1890 census were destroyed by fire. This prohibited us from matching victims lynched during the 1890s—the bloodiest decade in the lynching era—to their 1890 census records. However, a disproportionate share of the lynchings that occurred during the 1890s were committed in the earlier years of the decade, and lynching rates declined over the later years (see Figure 1.1 in chapter 1). By using the 1880 census records and restricting our search to the first half of the 1890s (1890 through 1895), we substantially increased the number of potential matches with only a small decrement to our confidence in each individual match. Given the extended time frame between census enumeration and the date of lynching for all of these victims—between ten and fifteen years—we also relaxed somewhat the geographic restrictions associated with these cases. We further required a somewhat higher level of evidence to determine that a match for a victim from the 1890s had been successfully identified.

An example of a victim lynched in the 1890s is Newton Jones, a black male accused of murdering a prominent white farmer and subsequently lynched in Floyd County, Georgia, on November 29, 1893. Initial searching of the 1880 enumerators' manuscripts generated two possible matches, both named "Newton Jones": the first man was twenty-two years of age, enumerated in Floyd County, Georgia, and the second was thirty-one years of age, found in (somewhat distant) Muscogee County, Georgia, and married to a woman named Sophie. Utilizing the information on both men from the 1880 census, we conducted a forward search into the 1900 census and were able to find the older "Newton Jones" and his wife, Sophie, once again enumerated in Muscogee County, Georgia. Additionally, the 1880 census reports both the husband's and wife's ages as thirty-one while, by the 1900 census, their ages increased to fifty-one, as would be expected. Although none of the children living in Newton and Sophie Jones's household of the 1880 census was found living with them in the 1900 census, by 1900 these "children" would have been of common age to establish independent households. By triangulating the 1880 and 1900 census records and utilizing information on the victims and their families, we were able to identify the younger Newton Jones from Floyd County as the likely lynch victim—even without the benefit of the original enumerators' manuscripts for the 1890 census.

NAME IRREGULARITIES AND COMMON NAMES
The historical records we relied on—both the census enumerators' manuscripts and the newspaper accounts used to construct the Beck-

Tolnay inventory of lynch victims—were created in an era when a sizable proportion of adult blacks in the South were illiterate. The names of county residents and individual lynch victims were recorded not by the individuals themselves but by a census worker or a newspaper reporter. Census workers often obtained names for all household residents from one member, who may or may not have been the eventual lynch victim, a relative, or even a permanent member of the household. On occasion, when the census worker was unable to contact a member of the household directly, information would be gathered from a neighbor. At the same time, reporters may have received victims' names from members of the lynch mob, the local black community, or local authorities. There is no guarantee that any of these sources knew the victim's true name or its correct spelling. The incorrect recording of a name for a given person in the inventory, the census, or both made a successful match more difficult. Additionally, in many lynchings, different newspaper articles reported different names—particularly variations on the first name—for a single victim. For example, for a black man lynched in Campbell County, Tennessee, on October 26, 1926, three different newspaper accounts agreed on his last name—Bell—but variously reported his first name as "Nip," "Rip," and "Herbert."

Common names and nicknames posed a similar problem. For example, a search for Wilbur Smith, lynched in Montgomery County, Alabama, in 1920, yielded no Wilbur Smiths but twenty-three black men named "Will," "Willie," or "William" Smith. In some cases, because of the individual's common name or the reporting of multiple names, we compiled a very long list of potential matches for the lynch victim, greatly complicating our effort to identify the correct match in the census. In this instance, because of the large number of possible matches for Wilbur Smith from Alabama, we were forced to consider his to be an unresolved case, although the man who was lynched may very well be included among the twenty-three we were able to identify.

Neither inconsistent name reporting nor multiple possible matches necessarily doomed our search effort to failure, however. The case of James Johnson, lynched September 28, 1922, in Johnson County, Georgia, provides a good example. We determined, based on information gleaned from newspaper articles, that the victim was taken from police custody in Sandersville, in Washington County, into the neighboring county of Johnson, where he was lynched. We therefore focused our search on

Sandersville, where two men named James Johnson were enumerated in the 1920 census records. We were able to successfully eliminate one of these possible matches by locating him through a forward match in the 1930 census manuscripts. Additionally, utilizing a death record from Johnson County, we confirmed that on the same date as the lynching, the death of a man named "Jim Johnson" was recorded in Johnson County. Although it is not an exact name match, "Jim" is a common nickname for "James." A subsequent search of the 1920 census records identified no black men named Jim Johnson enumerated in Sandersville, strengthening our confidence in this link.

GEOGRAPHIC MOBILITY

There is no guarantee that lynchings occurred in the county in which the victim resided when he or she was enumerated in the previous census. Individuals who migrated across county lines generally were more difficult to link to their census records than those who were residentially stable. However, while geographic mobility was common during the period under investigation, most moves involved exchanging residences within the same county rather than migrating between counties (Tolnay 1999). Still, the length of time between census enumeration and the lynching, which in some cases was fully fifteen years (for lynchings that occurred in 1895), introduces the possibility that victims had relocated and therefore could not be found in the census records within the county in which they were lynched.

Our strategy for dealing with geographic mobility was to incrementally expand the geographic parameters for the search. For example, Garfield Burley was a black man accused of murder and lynched, together with Curtis Brown, on October 8, 1902, in Dyer County, Tennessee. We were unable to locate Garfield Burley in the 1900 census enumerators' manuscripts in the county of lynching or its contiguous counties. Because "Garfield Burley" is an unusual name, we conducted a statewide search. This search yielded only one black man in all of Tennessee named Garfield Burley. He was enumerated in the 1900 census living in a railroad construction labor camp in Tipton County, only two counties away from Dyer County. There was one other black male in the entire country with the name of Garfield Burley enumerated in the 1900 census, and he was only five years old and living in Texas. These circumstances led us to conclude with a high level of confidence that the Garfield Burley we identified in Tipton County in 1900 was very likely to have been the Garfield Burley who was lynched two years later in nearby Dyer County.

UNNAMED VICTIMS

We do not know the names of all of the victims in our initial inventory, a fact that is disappointing both for the way it limits our scientific efforts as well as for what it tells us about the value of black human life in the Jim Crow–era South. Apparently not all southern newspapers found it necessary to identify *exactly which* black man had been killed when publishing an account of a local lynching. Although our recent efforts have enabled us to identify additional newspaper sources and reclaim the names of a few of the victims, most of the 243 unnamed victims remain unknown. For an additional 155 victims, we have incomplete names—a given or surname only, or a person's first initial and last name—and a handful of "complete" names that appear to have been local nicknames. For example, on January 2, 1908, in Brookhaven, Lincoln County, Mississippi, a mob took a black man from police custody and shot him. The name of the victim, who was accused of shooting two police officers, was reported as "Coot" Autman (*Daily Picayune* [New Orleans], January 3, 1908). Although Autman appears to have been a common surname in the local area, we were unable to locate any men with a name similar to Coot Autman, even conducting a national search. Without this basic shred of identifying information—the victim's name, as it would have been recorded in the census—we were unable to search for Mr. Autman or any of the men and women who were unnamed in the newspaper articles that reported their deaths.

The cultural convention of women adopting their husbands' surname upon marriage also posed a challenge to our efforts to identify female victims in the census records. It meant that for female victims who married between the year of census enumeration and the time of their death, we would either find no matches (if there were no women living in the area who shared the victim's "maiden" name) or would incorrectly select someone whose name was the same as the victim's before her marriage. For example, a black woman named Emma Hooper was accused of shooting and wounding a police officer while she resisted arrest. On February 28, 1917, in Tangipahoa Parish, Louisiana, as she was being transported to the Amite City jail, she was taken from police custody and hanged (*Times-Picayune* [New Orleans], March 1, 1917). The only potential matches we were able to locate were recorded in the census as living more than ten counties away in the neighboring state of Mississippi. While it is possible that one of these women was, in fact, the Emma Hooper who was lynched early in 1917, it is also possible that the victim had been recorded in the 1910 census with a surname other than Hooper. If, during the seven years between the census enumeration and the date of Emma Hooper's lynching, she married and changed her last name, correctly locating her in the census manuscripts is not possible.

The Outcome of the Record Linkage Effort

After restricting our record linkage effort to those victims for whom we had a complete enough name and after omitting victims who were lynched between 1896 and 1899, we searched for a total of 2,164 victims in the census manuscripts. Of those, 1,898 were black, 222 were white, and 44 were either recorded as a different race/ethnicity or had no recorded race/ethnicity.[19] Overall, we achieved a 42.3 percent rate of successful matches, with a statistically nonsignificant difference between black and white victims (42.9 percent and 46.2 percent, respectively). We were considerably less likely to locate the census records for victims whose race/ethnicity was unknown or for those who had a recorded race/ethnicity other than black or white (22.4 percent). The overall level of successful linkages, as well as those for blacks and whites, compare favorably with other historical record linkage projects, most of which have had the benefit of more information with which to initiate the search and to evaluate potential matches (see, for example, Ferrie 1996; Guest 1987; Rosenwaike, Preston, and Elo 1998; Steckel 1988).

Considering temporal variation in the rate of successful matches reveals that we were most likely to find the census records of victims who were lynched between 1920 and 1929 (51.7 percent). This relatively high level of success is likely due to the significant contribution of World War I Selective Service records and death certificates to searches for this later time period. It is also possible that greater detail about victims in newspaper reports of lynching during the 1920s provided more information with which to conduct the search of census manuscripts (for example, if age, occupation, or other detail was included in the article). We were least likely to find those killed between 1890 and 1895 (36.0 percent). This lower level of success is undoubtedly due to the longer

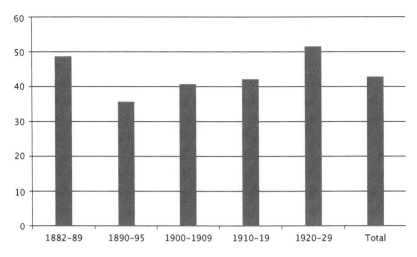

Figure 2.4 Percentage of Lynch Victims Successfully Linked to Their Census Records, by Decade

period of time that had elapsed between the 1880 census and the lynchings that occurred in the early 1890s, as well as to the increased level of scrutiny we applied to these cases. For the remaining time periods, the rate of successful matches varied modestly from 40.3 percent for 1900–09 to 48.5 percent for 1882–89 (see Figure 2.4).

In all but one of the southern states included in the Beck-Tolnay inventory, we were able to successfully match more than 40 percent of lynch victims with their census records. We were most successful in finding victims who had been lynched in North Carolina (49.5 percent) or Tennessee (44.6 percent) and least successful in locating those killed in Florida (39.6 percent). Success rates for the remaining seven states varied only from 40.0 percent for South Carolina to 44.6 percent for Tennessee (see Figure 2.5).

There were only 63 females among the more than 2,100 lynch victims included in our record linkage effort. Of those 63 women, all of whom were either black or white, we were successful in finding census records for 35 (54.7 percent). That this is somewhat higher than the success rates for black and white males (43.0 percent) is a bit surprising, given that record linkage efforts are typically made more difficult by the common practice of women changing their surnames when they marry, as we have discussed. It is possible that the lynching of women was such a

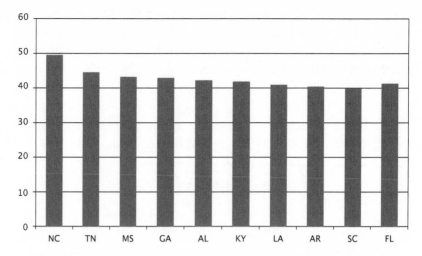

Figure 2.5 Percentage of Lynch Victims Successfully Linked to Their Census Records, by State, 1882–1929

rare event that it resulted in the reporting of more detailed information about the victims, which would facilitate the search for census records. It is also possible that women in the age range most likely to be newly entering a marriage and experiencing a name change were less likely to have been lynched.

Comparison Sample of Non-lynch Victims

A multidimensional profile of southern lynch victims will answer many questions that were simply unanswerable prior to the construction of the linked database described in this chapter. By comparing the characteristics of lynch victims to the characteristics of black men who were not lynched, we can answer many important questions. For example, as mentioned in chapter 1, there are alternative theoretical perspectives regarding the identification and selection of lynch victims. Were southern mobs more likely to target higher-status individuals whose success violated the southern racial hierarchy? Or were lower-status, socially marginal black men more likely to be targeted for lynching? In order to answer these questions, we needed detailed information about those black men who were not lynched—a type of "control group" to compare to our "treatment group" of victims. Any significant differences between the victims and non-victims provided valuable clues about the types of characteristics that increased southern black men's vulnerability to mob violence. Note that because of the small number of victims who were women or white men, we were only able to compare the characteristics of black and mixed-race men with those of others in their communities.

For a comparison sample of non-victims, we drew from the historical Public Use Microdata Samples (PUMS) of the U.S. Census that have been created, cleaned, and "harmonized"—or made comparable across decades—by the Minnesota Population Center at the University of Minnesota (Ruggles et al. 2008). The PUMS files that we used were created from the original enumerators' manuscripts for the 1880, 1900, 1910, and 1920 U.S. Censuses—the same enumerators' manuscripts we used to locate the records for lynch victims. Therefore, we had access to the same individual- and household-level information for both victims and non-victims. Each PUMS file represents a 1 percent nationally representative sample of all households that were enumerated in the United States for a given census.

We constructed separate samples of non-victims for each decade, again using the 1880 PUMS to substitute for the 1890 PUMS, which is not available. We first determined the county within which each victim had been lynched. We then identified all black (or "colored" or "mulatto") males between the ages of ten and seventy years who resided *within the same counties in which lynchings occurred AND in which we were successful in linking victims to their census records* during the decade. Finally, we extracted all available information for the individual non-victims and all co-residents of his household. The restricted age range for non-victims was used to approximate the parallel extremes in age for all victims.

We used counties as the geographic catchment area to approximate the population of black males who lived in the same general vicinity of a lynch victim but themselves escaped victimization. Evidence derived from the comparison sample of non-victims, in conjunction with the information for the lynch victims who were successfully linked to their census records, allows us to describe simple differences between the characteristics of victims and non-victims (chapter 3) as well as to model the likelihood of being lynched as a function of various combinations of individual, household, and contextual characteristics (chapters 4, 5, and 6).

Concluding Comments

Through our record linkage effort, we have successfully resurrected the identities of 935 victims of southern lynching. In the following chapters, we analyze the personal and household information we have gained about these individuals to present the first thorough sociodemographic profile for a substantial segment of all southern lynch victims. In addition, we take advantage of this large number of successfully linked cases to describe how the characteristics of lynch victims varied over a broad sweep of time and across several southern states. We compare the information for victims with corresponding information drawn from the samples of non-victims to determine whether the likelihood of being lynched was related to the individual-level characteristics of African American men. For example, were socially marginal men or men with higher socioeconomic standing more likely to be targeted by lynch mobs? Finally, we determine whether the personal dimensions of vulnerability to mob violence were themselves a function of the social setting within which black men were embedded.

CHAPTER THREE

The Characteristics of Black Male Lynch Victims

In the 1880 census, an African American teenager named Daniel Oliver was enumerated in Webb City, part of Middle Township in Franklin County, Arkansas. Franklin County straddles the Arkansas River, and Middle Township occupies a peninsula directly south of and across the river from the town of Ozark. With no real population centers of its own, and dotted with tiny lakes, the area where Daniel Oliver lived as an adolescent might appear idyllic. When he was enumerated in the census, Daniel was fifteen years old, was able to read and write, and was listed as working as a farm laborer. His father, Charles, was a farmer, and his mother, Belle, kept house. Both of Daniel Oliver's parents were literate, and both were enumerated as "black" rather than as "mulatto." The Oliver household also included a twenty-four-year-old black woman named Margaret Smith, who appears to have been the Olivers' servant, and two black children, a three-year-old girl named Lee Smith and a four-month-old boy named John Smith. Both of these children were listed as orphans. In the summer of 1884, when he would have been just nineteen years old, Daniel Oliver was accused of attempting "to rape the daughter of one of the best citizens of Logan County" (*Daily Arkansas Gazette*, June 30, 1884). He was lynched in the town of Roseville on July 28, 1884. Logan County is adjacent to Franklin County, lying due east, and fewer than ten miles separate Middle Township and Roseville.

In the previous chapter we were able to provide an identity for James Clark, who was lynched in Brevard County, Florida, in 1926. By locating Clark's personal and household information in the original enumerators' manuscripts for the 1920 U.S. Census, we learned that when he was killed, he was a thirty-eight-year-old husband, father, and neighbor. But it would be naive of us to believe that all, or even most, black southern lynch victims shared Mr. Clark's personal and family characteristics, or those of Daniel Oliver—just as we could not select a single homicide victim to represent the thousands of individuals who are murdered every year in the United States. Rather, it is by combining information for a large cross-section of lynch victims that we can gain a better understanding of their "typical" personal profile, as well as gain a sense of the degree of variation in individual and family characteristics within the set of victims. For example, learning that the average (median) lynch victim was twenty-nine years old when killed would be a useful summary of the typical victim. Knowing that the ages of victims ranged from ten years to seventy years would tell a different story about the pool of black and mixed-race men who were lynched.

We have two primary objectives for this chapter. First, we provide an overview of the individual and family characteristics of roughly 900 black and mixed-race male victims of southern lynching.[1] Although descriptive and somewhat simple, this objective is also pathbreaking. The evidence presented in the following pages offers the first available portrait of the persons and lives that were affected by the deadly violence of southern lynch mobs. Second, we conduct an initial comparison between the characteristics of lynch victims and a sample of black men residing in the counties where lynchings took place, but who were not lynched. These comparisons offer preliminary clues about the identification, or targeting, of victims by southern mobs. Were these victims more likely to be lower-status men who were marginal within their communities? Were they disproportionately drawn from among the higher-status, successful members of the black community? Or were victims essentially a random cross-section of the black male population?

Demographic Characteristics

AGE

All of the lynch victims considered in this chapter were males and African Americans—including men who were of mixed-racial heritage.[2] The gender and race of the vast majority of southern lynch victims are two demographic characteristics that have been well known for several decades. The brutal practice was disproportionately applied to black males, as previously constructed inventories of lynch victims have convincingly documented (Brundage 1993; Carrigan 2006; Pfeifer 2004). Beyond gender and race, however, we know very little about the demographic profile of these people. Even something as basic as the victims' ages has remained elusive. Some hints have been provided by the small proportion of newspaper accounts of specific lynching incidents that mention the victim's age, or in which he was referred to as a "young man" or an "old man," for example. One might also infer a rough age range for victims based on the types of offenses they were alleged to have committed. For instance, the most common accusations leveled against lynch victims were murder, physical assault, and sexual assault (Tolnay and Beck 1995; see also Brundage 1993). The criminological literature tells us that violent crimes such as these are committed primarily by older adolescents and young adults, with the likelihood of offending dropping off sharply with increasing age (Blokland and Nieuwbeerta 2005; Farrington 1986; Gottfredson and Hirschi 1990; Wilson and Herrnstein 1985). Of course, we have no way of knowing whether any of the victims were actually *guilty* of the crimes of which they were accused. To the extent that the justifications lynch mobs used to explain their brutal acts were meant to seem plausible to other members of the community, however, it is likely that victims' ages fell within the reasonable range for those most likely to have committed the crime.

We were able to determine the ages of 913 black and mixed-race male victims at the time they were lynched.[3] The average (median) age of lynch victims in our sample was twenty-nine years—meaning that half of all victims were younger than twenty-nine and half were older.[4] The oldest victim was seventy-six and the youngest victim was eleven. Benjamin Smith, the seventy-six-year-old victim,[5] was lynched on Sunday, May 21, 1911, in Swainsboro, Georgia. Swainsboro is located roughly midway between Macon and Savannah. On the modern map it lies just north of Interstate 16, which runs east and west through the state of Georgia. According to the census information for 1910, Smith was a widowed man who lived as a boarder in a farm household along with the John Dock family, which included Dock, Dock's wife, Amelia, and their four children. Although Smith's occupation was recorded in the census as "laborer," he was also referred to as a "preacher" in the newspaper stories that reported his death. According to his census record, Smith was illiterate. The incident in which Smith was killed was reported in the May 25, 1911, *Abbeville Chronicle* as follows: "Ben Smith, an old negro preacher, shot and fatally wounded Neal Canady, deputy marshal of Summit, last night, and soon afterwards was hanged and his body riddled with bullets. . . . Smith had been discovered hiding in a swamp nearby. A posse gathered and he was strung quickly up to a limb and his body filled with bullets, after which the crowd dispersed. Smith, although a preacher, was a notoriously bad negro. He was an old man with hoary head and was toothless. He was somewhat of a leader among the negroes, being a little above the average in intelligence."[6]

In addition to summarizing the bare details of the lynching of Benjamin Smith, this report contains a number of revealing clues for the student of southern mob violence. For example, we learn that even an old, toothless, white-haired black man was not exempt from the summary justice meted out by lynch mobs. In addition, the mob that captured and executed Smith is described in the article as a "posse," demonstrating the ambiguity of that term when determining whether such killings were carried out by official or unofficial groups (as discussed in chapter 1). Finally, we learn that an illiterate laborer and part-time preacher was considered to be "above the average in intelligence" among African Americans and a "leader" in the black community.

The eleven-year-old victim was named James Gillespie. James was lynched, along with his thirteen-year-old brother, Harrison, in Salisbury, North Carolina, during the early morning hours of Wednesday, June 11, 1902. Salisbury is located in Rowan County, roughly fifty miles north of Charlotte and just west of Interstate 85. The Gillespie boys had been accused of murdering a twenty-seven-year-old white woman named Cornelia Benson a few days earlier by bashing in her head with a rock. Although it perhaps stretches the limits of credulity to imagine two young boys being able to accomplish such a brutal murder, particularly absent a compelling motive or convincing evidence, the white community in Rowan County demanded swift and vicious punishment for the accused.

Against minimal resistance from the sheriff, the Gillespie brothers were extracted from the jail in Salisbury by a mob that then escorted the two boys to a point just beyond the Salisbury city limits. There, the mob hanged these children, James and Harrison, from a large elm tree and riddled their bodies with bullets. In a macabre twist of fate, two additional members of the Gillespie family, John Gillespie and Nease Gillespie, would be lynched in the same location only four years later.[7] The *Asheville Citizen* (June 11, 1902) reported the lynching of the Harrison boys as follows:

The mob formed a line and marched half a mile to a big elm tree outside the corporate limits. They held up a switch engine along the way and at the point of a pistol forced the engineer to give them packing for a light. Then they made the youngest of the two boys climb a tree, where the master of ceremonies was waiting. A rope was placed around his neck and tied to the limb and the boy pushed off.

One end of the rope was tied around the older boy's neck, the other end thrown to a man in the tree and the boy pulled up. Both died from strangulation, after which two volleys were fired at their bodies.

The boys were allowed to hang until 10 o'clock this morning when Coroner Dorsett held an inquest. He said that they came to their deaths at the hands of unknown parties. . . .

The mob was composed chiefly of farmers, but it is believed that several Salisburians were among the masked members of the party. There is no clue to any of the lynchers. [emphasis added]

A separate account of this incident published in the *Charlotte Observer* (June 11, 1902) claimed that no members of the mob that murdered the Gillespies were from Salisbury—a common refrain in many newspaper stories about a nearby lynching that might have been an attempt to direct blame for the vigilante violence away from the community where the event occurred.

When he was enumerated in the 1900 census, James Gillespie was nine years old and resided on a rented farm with his uncle and aunt, Stokes and Anna Cowan, a black married couple in their early thirties. Stokes Cowan, a farmer, was enumerated in the census as illiterate, but his wife, Anna, was able to both read and write. Also in the household were Stokes's sister-in-law, Sarah, a twenty-two-year-old single mother, and her three-year-old daughter, Susana. Harrison, the older brother, was age eleven when the census was taken. Harrison was literate and had attended school for four months during the prior year, probably the length of the entire school term for African American children during the early twentieth century. James could neither read nor write at the time the census was taken, and he had not been attending school.[8]

The lynching of the Gillespie boys in North Carolina complements the lynching of Benjamin Smith in Georgia to bookend the age distribution of victims in our data set. Together, they demonstrate that black males of nearly all ages were vulnerable to violence at the hands of the

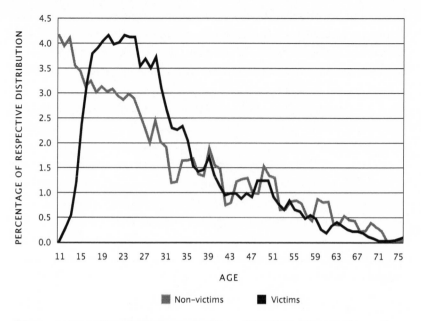

Figure 3.1 Ages of Lynch Victims at the Time of Death and Non-victims at the Time of Census Enumeration, 1882–1929

southern lynch mob. Furthermore, the details of each of their killings, including hanging and gunshot wounds, were repeated again and again throughout the lynching era, suggesting a type of "script" for the accomplishment of a lynching.

Turning our attention away from the extremes in age and to the overall age distribution of the victims we successfully located, the evidence shown in Figure 3.1[9] comports generally with our expectation, based on the slim evidence from newspaper stories and the nature of their alleged offenses. That is, most victims were teenagers or young adults at the time they were murdered. Nearly seven in ten (69.1 percent) of all victims were between the ages of sixteen and thirty-five. It was relatively uncommon for victims to be younger than sixteen years (3.9 percent) or over fifty-five years (4.6 percent). The proportion of victims at ages older than twenty-five years decreased sharply with increasing age. In contrast, the age distribution for non-victims is representative of a typical "age pyramid" in which the relative size of the population declines with increasing age. This pyramid shape results from high levels of fertility, which creates a wide base of younger people, and a reduction in the number of people alive at older ages, as general mortality, unrelated to lynching, takes its toll. The most obvious divergence between the age distributions of victims and non-victims occurs during the ages of late adolescence and early adulthood, where lynch victims are more heavily concentrated.

While the age profile for lynch victims does resemble the well-known age distributions for violent criminal offenders, we stress that the vast majority of these men were never arrested, tried, or convicted of the crimes of which they had been accused. And there are many alternative reasons that could account for this age profile of victims, other than their violent criminality. Importantly, the age distribution of our victims also mirrors the general age distribution for *victims* of violent crime (Hashima and Finkelhor 1999; Truman, Langton, and Planty 2013), so at least in terms of this characteristic, it appears that lynch victims resemble the victims of other types of violent crimes.

RACIAL CLASSIFICATION

It is true, as mentioned above, that the large majority of southern lynch victims, and all victims considered in this chapter, were African Americans. Due to southern whites' obsession with racial purity, however, the category "black" included people with a variety of racial heritages—a practice of racial categorization that largely continues to the present day. Three different censuses administered during this time period included the designations of "white" and "black," as well as the additional racial category of "mulatto." The inclusion of both black and "mulatto" racial categories allows us to examine a finer-grained distinction of race for the victims we were able to link to the 1880, 1910, and 1920 census manuscripts. In 1880, the federal government's instructions for census enumerators regarding the recording of an individual's race were quite detailed, both in their intent and potential value for historical researchers: "Color.—It must not be assumed that, where nothing is written in this column, 'white' is to be understood. The column is always to be filled. Be particularly careful in reporting the class 'mulatto.' The word is here generic, and includes quadroons, octoroons, and all persons having any perceptible trace of African blood. *Important scientific results depend upon the correct determination of this class in schedules 1 and 5*" [10] (emphasis added).

The quality of the "important scientific" analyses associated with this detailed measurement may have been somewhat attenuated since the census enumerators relied in large part on their own perceptions of in-dividuals' racial membership (rather than the categories people assigned to themselves). The invocation of science in the enumerators' instruction to justify the careful recording of racial membership, however, suggests that the prevailing thought believed strongly in inherent differences between the races. Different assumptions regarding the relative location of mixed-race individuals in the historical southern stratification system are available in the literature. On the one hand, it was argued by some that individuals of mixed black-white racial heritage were biologically and genetically inferior to those of "pure" racial ancestry, possessing what were considered to be the "worst" qualities of both races. As a result, it was believed that they were destined to socioeconomic failure at best and social degeneracy and depravity at worst. This claim is encountered in the historical writing of eugenicists and other authors who subscribed to the dogma of scientific racism that was popular, possibly dominant, within intellectual circles and that eventually metastasized to (especially white) members of the general public during the late nineteenth and early twentieth centuries (Frederickson 2002; Hoffman 1896; Hofstadter 1955).

On the other hand, more recent work by social scientists has argued that mixed-race individuals enjoyed a status advantage over blacks in the historical South. Perhaps their lighter skin, and possibly stronger familial and friendship connections to the white community, provided some social and economic advantages in southern society, which was divided sharply along racial lines during this time period. Certainly, historical accounts identify familial relationships between blacks and whites that included close social as well as biological connections (Schultz 2005, 119–24). Racial status may also have been linked to vulnerability based on its correlation with other kinds of advantage and disadvantage. For example, Aliya Saperstein and Aaron Gullickson (2013) have used linked census records for 1870, 1880, 1910, and 1920 to provide fascinating evi-dence that the "mulatto" racial identity served as a sort of "escape hatch" from a generally disadvantaged and denigrated black southern popu-lation during the late nineteenth and early twentieth centuries. That is, for those people enumerated as "black" in an earlier census, if they subsequently experienced upward occupational mobility, census enu-merators were more likely to list their racial identification as "mulatto" in the later census manuscripts. Conversely, those who were identified as "mulatto" in an earlier census were more likely to be classified as "black" in the later census if they experienced downward mobility between the enumerations.

Scholarly opinion about the relative status afforded by mixed racial heritage seems to have settled on agreement with the implications of work like Saperstein's and Gullickson's. Eugenicist arguments of the late nineteenth and early twentieth centuries seem to be a better reflection of theory than of fact. The evidence suggests that, despite cultural rhetoric about the biological degradation associated with "race mixing," people from mixed African and European heritage did, indeed, appear to occupy a higher social and occupational status than did people who were considered to be black. This disjuncture between attitude and behavior is much like the persistence of traditional attitudes about the gendered division of labor long after the social and economic reality created opportunities for large numbers of mothers and married women to actively participate in the paid labor force.

The evidence shown in Figure 3.2[11] reveals that roughly one in every nine of the lynch victims successfully linked to their census records during these decades was recorded in the census manuscripts as "mulatto" rather than as "Negro" or "black." There was little variation in the percentage of victims who were recorded as "mulatto" across decades, with 11 percent in 1880, 10 percent in both 1890 and 1910, and 12 percent in 1920. In contrast, one in every seven black men in the comparison sample of non-victims was enumerated as "mulatto."[12] To the extent that people with both African and European ancestry enjoyed a privileged social station within the African American population of the South during this time period, it appears that lynch victims, on average, were selected disproportionately from among the lower stratum.

RELATIONSHIP TO HEAD OF HOUSEHOLD

Every southern lynch victim who was enumerated in the censuses between 1880 and 1920 was embedded within a "household."[13] Within each household a single individual was designated as the "household head." In the vast majority of cases, the household head was a patriarchal figure— generally a husband and father to other individuals enumerated within the household. The relationship of every enumerated individual to the head of the household was recorded in the enumerators' manuscripts. For example, a woman married to the household head was enumer

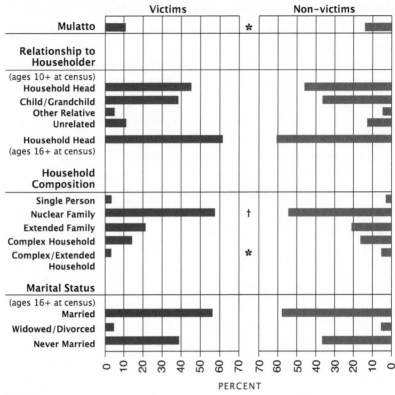

Figure 3.2 Demographic Characteristics of Southern Lynch Victims and a Random Sample of Non-victims, 1882–1929

ated as "wife." The children of the head were enumerated as "son" or "daughter." A sibling of the household head was recorded as "brother" or "sister." It was possible for a single household to contain multiple families. With multiple co-resident families, the composition of households could become quite complex. To illustrate, a man living with his wife and children in a household headed by his own father would have been recorded as the "son" of the head of household—even though he would have been considered the traditional head of his own nuclear family. An individual's position within the household might be reflective of his or her embeddedness or marginality within the local community and, therefore, perhaps related to his or her vulnerability for selection as the target of a lynch mob. For example, heads of households might be considered more firmly connected to the local community—black or white—than those who were enumerated as nonrelatives, such as boarders, lodgers, and laborers, especially if householders resided with other family members.

We have used the information recorded by the census enumerators for "relationship to household head" to gain a general understanding of the residential situations of lynch victims. Specifically, we have distinguished among the following four different statuses: (1) the victim himself was the head of household, (2) the victim was the child or grandchild of the head of household, (3) the victim was another relative of the household head, and (4) the victim was not related to the householder. It is important to note that these categories refer to the victim's relationship to the head of his household at the time he was enumerated in the most recent census before his death. It is, of course, possible that his residential situation had changed by the time he was lynched—especially for younger victims and in those cases in which the lynching occurred several years after the census (for example, lynchings in the early 1890s, which were linked to the 1880 census manuscripts). This limitation should be kept in mind as the evidence regarding relationship to the head of household reported in Figure 3.2 is discussed.

Most victims were recorded at the time of census enumeration as being either the head of the household or the child of the household head. Combined, these two relationships account for roughly eight out of every ten victims—45 percent of all victims were heads of their own households and an additional 37 percent were the sons of the householder. Before concluding that more than a third of lynch victims were children when they were killed, it should be recalled that in many cases, several years had elapsed between the date of the census and the date of the lynching. For victims lynched during the early 1890s, this gap could be as long as fifteen years. In many other instances, older adolescents and young adults remained living in their parental home until they were financially able to establish independent households. This often meant that even young adults who had married and were the parents of young children were enumerated living with their parents. Thus, the relatively large share of victims who were *recorded as the children* of household heads reflects the young age profile of victims shown in Figure 3.1, the length of time between the census and the lynching, and the practice of young adults residing with their parents. For instance, the share of victims during the 1880s and early 1890s who were enumerated as children was 53 percent, compared to only 30 percent of those lynched during the first decade of the twentieth century. If only those victims who were at least sixteen years of age when enumerated are considered, then the overall percentage recorded as children of the household head drops to 19 percent.

Roughly one in every nine victims was unrelated to the head of the household at the time of census enumeration. Within this category, most men were listed as "boarder," "servant," "roomer," "lodger," or "laborer." The relatively few victims who were recorded as "other relative" included a diverse set of relationships, including "nephew," "son-in-law," and "brother-in-law." We observe a very similar profile for non-victims in their relationship to the household head. None of the differences in category-by-category comparisons of the relationship to the householder between victims and non-victims is large enough to attain statistical significance.

HOUSEHOLD COMPOSITION

We now "zoom out" a bit to consider the larger household context within which the lynch victims were embedded. That is, we move beyond a singular focus on only the victim and his relationship to the head of the household to consider all members of the household and its overall structure. To accomplish this, we draw from the roster of all individuals enumerated within the same household as the victim to construct a classification of household types that reflects the diversity of living arrangements during this historical period. Family historians have documented the greater frequency of more complex family structures and household composition in the past (Alderson and Sanderson 1991; Engerman 1977; Tolnay 2004).

The nuclear family, consisting of parents and their children, has always been a central feature of American family structure. However, in the late nineteenth and early twentieth centuries, it was common for the "core" nuclear family to be augmented, within the same household, by co-resident nonnuclear family members and even by nonfamily members. Higher mortality and the virtual absence of social welfare programs, other than those provided by church congregations, meant that widows, widowers, orphans, and other potentially dependent individuals relied on their families for support, as was true for the two young children living with Daniel Oliver's family in Arkansas in 1880. In addition, some families took in boarders and lodgers to supplement their incomes. Still others absorbed child and adolescent relatives, such as nieces, nephews, and cousins, to supplement household labor or provide informal occupational apprenticeships and to relieve employed parents—particularly mothers in "live-in" domestic employment—of the daily responsibilities of parenting. At the other end of the spectrum, the relatively few wealthy families might have had servants or other household employees living with them. Death, penury, wealth, geographic mobility—all worked to create a diverse array of household environments within which the lynch victims might reside.

By examining every resident in the victim's household, we have constructed a typology of household composition that consists of the following five categories: (1) single persons living alone (that is, the lynch victim himself); (2) nuclear family households (parents and children only); (3) households in which at least one additional family member was present to supplement the nuclear family ("extended family" households); (4) households in which at least one additional nonfamily member was present to supplement the nuclear family ("complex" households); and (5) households that included at least one additional family member *and* at least one additional nonfamily member ("complex/extended" households).[14] The distribution of lynch victims by the type of household in which they lived when they were enumerated in the census prior to their deaths is shown in Figure 3.2.

The majority of lynch victims, 58 percent, resided in nuclear family households, with only a co-resident spouse and/or children. Only 3 percent of lynch victims lived alone when they were enumerated in the census. Still, the complexity of southern households is clearly evident, with nearly four in every ten victims residing in households that included at least one additional family member or nonmember. Harrison and James Gillespie, the young brothers lynched in Rowan County, North Carolina, for example, were enumerated living in an extended family household. The household was headed by their aunt and uncle, Stokes and Anna Cowan, and included the Gillespie brothers as well as their uncle's sister-in-law, Sarah, aged twenty-two, and her three-year-old daughter, Susana. Elderly Benjamin Smith, conversely, lived in a complex household. He was a boarder in a household that included John and Amelia Dock and their four children.

Pearson King, a young "mulatto" man who was accused of attempted sexual assault and lynched in Franklin Parish, Louisiana, in the fall of 1887, lived in a complex and extended household. When he was enumerated in the 1880 census, King lived in the rural First Ward of Tensas Parish with his mother, Kitty, and her husband, Mick Davis, as well as their adopted daughter, six-year-old Ellen French, and Mick's two-year-old granddaughter, Sophia Clark. The household also included sixteen-year-old Oscar Bowles, a black teenager listed as being a laborer, and thirty-two-year-old Ada Hickman, a "mulatto" woman listed as the local schoolteacher.

A comparison of the household composition for victims and non-victims reveals few notable differences. Victims were somewhat more likely than non-victims to be members of nuclear families and to be living alone, although the latter difference is not statistically significant, even at the $p < .10$ level. In contrast, victims were less likely to reside in households that we define as complex and extended. This statistically significant difference might suggest the greater vulnerability for individuals with smaller, or more socially homogeneous, local personal networks from which to draw support in the event they were threatened with lynching. To be sure, these differences in household composition between victims and non-victims are quite small, so any conjecture about their connection to the vulnerability of being targeted by lynch mobs is largely speculative. Furthermore, the differences that do exist tend to tell conflicting stories. On the one hand, the higher percentage of victims living in nuclear families would suggest that more established members of the community were more likely to be victimized. On the other hand, the differences related to single persons and complex/extended households imply the opposite.

MARITAL STATUS
Marital status is another important dimension of the lynch victim's family-related situation, and one that is rather closely tied to his age and relationship to the household head, both of which were described above. In general, we would expect older victims to have been more likely than younger victims to be married and to be the head of their household. Recall that the average (median) age of the victims at the

time they were killed was twenty-nine years and that many victims were twenty years old or younger (Figure 3.1). Like the victim's relationship to the household head, marital status might be considered an indicator of his embeddedness within the community, and also to social status. Marriage is most common among higher-status people and least common among lower-status people. Basic requirements for a man to enter the institution of matrimony in the Jim Crow–era South probably included sufficient economic and social status that a woman would be willing to view him as a reasonable "provider" and her family would at least nominally accept him into their graces. It is also possible that married men were less likely than single men to engage in activities—such as drinking, gambling, or inappropriate sexual behavior—that could lead to accusations of criminal offenses that were typically lodged against lynch victims (Horney, Osgood, and Marshall 1995; Piquero, MacDonald, and Parker 2002; Sampson and Laub 1990; Theobald and Farrington 2009). Both of these possible correlates of marital status could have been related to the likelihood that an individual was targeted for mob violence.

Figure 3.2 describes the marital status of all victims who were at least sixteen years of age at the time they were enumerated in the census. Of adult victims, 56 percent were married at the time they were enumerated in the census. Roughly four out of every ten adult victims were single and had never been married. Only 4.7 percent were divorced or widowed. The latter figure likely reflects the rarity of divorce in the United States during this time period and the propensity for widowers to remarry.[15] Only very small differences are observed between the distributions by marital status for victims and non-victims, with none of the contrasts attaining statistical significance.

Social and Economic Characteristics

There is little question that race served as the most important source for social stratification in the American South during the late nineteenth and early twentieth centuries. The virtual racial caste line assured, at least in principle, that everyone who was white was socially superior to all who were black. Yet within both white and black populations, southerners were further divided by social class. As with all societies, education, occupation, and income were important dimensions of social class in southern society. But because the South was primarily an agricultural economy during this time period, a key indicator of success, or privilege, was ownership of land—preferably lots of land.

Access to land ownership was severely restricted for southern blacks during this era, as a system of plantation agriculture emerged following the Civil War (Mandle 1992; Ransom and Sutch 2000). The South faced an economic crisis with the cessation of hostilities and the loss of involuntary labor extracted from an enslaved labor force four million people strong. White southern landowners still needed the labor of the freedmen to produce their crops and, thereby, their profits. But they no longer *owned* their workers, as they had before emancipation. The former slaves enjoyed their freedom, but they owned no land, and most lacked any occupational training, other than as agricultural workers. This dilemma for southern capital and labor led to the rise of the sharecropping or share tenancy system[16] in which white landowners allowed black families to cultivate a small section of their land in exchange for a percentage of the harvest. This arrangement for agricultural production was especially dominant in those areas of the South that were most dependent on cotton production and where slavery had been most common—and, by extension, in those areas that experienced the largest share of lynchings between 1880 and 1930.

The rise of agricultural production based on the tenancy system after the Civil War had several consequences for the African American population that are particularly important for our consideration of the social and economic characteristics of lynch victims. First, it replicated the plantation structure that had developed under slavery, including its functioning to "lock" the black labor force into the agricultural sector of the southern economy and to bind them geographically via annual labor contracts to specific employers and tracts of land. Indeed, during this time period, vagrancy laws were widely adopted across the South. These laws allowed the imprisonment of any black man who lacked a current labor contract. White planters needed the labor of black workers in their fields and simply could not abide their movement, in large numbers, out of the rural South. At this time, the southern economy also lacked significant opportunities for nonagricultural labor, given the retarded industrial development of the region, so transitioning into the nonagricultural labor force would have been difficult for most African Americans to accomplish *without* migrating out of the region.

The tenure-based plantation system also rationalized formal and informal barriers to farm ownership for black families, even as they remained in the rural, agricultural economy. It would not have bene-fited the white agricultural elite if sizable numbers of rural blacks were able to become independent farm owners. Furthermore, such upward economic mobility was inconsistent with the strong southern cultural prescription for the economic subordination of African Americans. The potential for upward socioeconomic mobility by southern blacks, in general, was further constrained by the usurious conditions for borrow-ing that developed in the postbellum plantation South. Sharecroppers and share tenants received their earnings when the crop was harvested and sold to market. In the meantime, they bought household supplies from local merchants (or the plantation owner) on credit at extremely high rates of interest (Grant 1975; Ransom and Sutch 2000). At the end of the year, the family's accumulated debt often surpassed their share of the harvested crop, leading to the infamous economic trap of "debt peonage" (Daniel 1972), which contributed significantly to rural black penury while also anchoring the family from year to year to the same white planter to whom they owed money.

This "new" plantation system stifled the development of educational opportunities for southern blacks (Anderson 1988; Margo 1990; Tolnay 1999). Many southern whites saw no need for blacks to be educated because their well-defined niche in the agricultural economy did not require it. This sentiment was clearly expressed by Georgia governor Hoke Smith, whose 1907 inaugural address stated, in part, that "the negro race was improved by slavery, and . . . that the majority of negroes have ceased to improve since slavery. Few have been helped by learning from books. All have been helped who have been taught or made to work" (*Washington Post*, June 30, 1907). Indeed, even when progressive white leaders supported public provision of education for blacks, they urged that "the kind of education best suited for negroes . . . [was] manual training" and disparaged "the ordinary [black] country school, where children are repressed, bound down all day long to dull old books and made to stand examinations" (*Washington Post*, January 17, 1903). In sev-eral states, white citizens mounted campaigns to restrict public provision of funding for black schools to the amount blacks contributed to public coffers via taxation, a move that would effectively "deprive the colored people of education" (*Washington Post*, September 11, 1900). Southern governments seemed to agree with this sentiment, as indicated by their decisions to fund black schools at a small fraction of their support for white schools. As a result, despite their generally strong desire for schooling, many southern blacks lacked the institutional support to realize their educational dreams.

This very brief overview of the social and economic circumstances faced by southern African Americans during the late nineteenth and early twentieth centuries is intended to frame the socioeconomic profile of lynch victims that follows. It paints a picture of a population that was severely disadvantaged in its share of the region's property, power, and prestige—each of which was in short supply for southern African Americans compared to those in states in the North and West. Not only were blacks assigned to the inferior category in a rigid racial caste system, but also, within that subordinate caste position, they were denied access to the avenues of social advancement that were available, at least in principle, to poor whites—education, land ownership, and a political voice.[17] Indeed, the economist Jay Mandle (1978, 1992) has drawn an intriguing and plausible link between the plantation economy in which southern blacks were mired during this era of American history and the perpetuation of black poverty into the second half of the twentieth century. Despite this extremely discouraging overall picture, however, it is important to recognize that variation within the southern black population did exist. There were black landowners. There were well-educated African Americans. Some African Americans were engaged in skilled occupations. Our purpose here is to determine how common this kind of economic and social class advantage was among lynch victims and to compare their social standing with that of black male non-victims.

TYPE OF RESIDENCE

According to the census information we have located for the victims of lynching, slightly more than one-half (54 percent) resided on a farm when they were enumerated (see Figure 3.3). In contrast, farm residence was substantially more common among the sample of non-victims, with fully 62 percent living on farms. It is possible that this difference represents a greater degree of protection from lynching offered to black men who were disengaged from the local agricultural economy. Alternatively, victims who were engaged in agricultural employment may have been more likely to have been sharecroppers or hired laborers than farm owners, living in homes that were near the fields they tilled but not living on

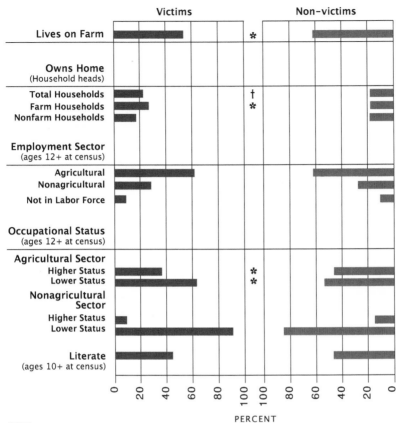

Figure 3.3 Social and Economic Characteristics of Southern Lynch Victims and a Random Sample of Non-victims, 1882–1929

the farm itself. The higher concentration of farm residence among non-victims could also reflect the confounding influence of other differences between victims and non-victims that are not accounted for in the simple bivariate contrasts included in Figure 3.3.[18] It should be noted that the evidence for farm residence is restricted to the 1900, 1910, and 1920 censuses because farm residence was not recorded in the 1880 census.[19] Our examination of the occupations reported by lynch victims will provide additional information with which to assess the extent to which they were divided between agricultural and nonagricultural employment.

OWNERSHIP OF DWELLING

We can also use the census information located for lynch victims to determine whether they resided in a dwelling that was "owned" or "rented."
In general, as is true today, families that owned the dwelling in which
they resided enjoyed higher socioeconomic status than families that
rented. However, it is important to acknowledge certain limitations to
this census information. First, like farm residence, information about
housing tenure was not recorded for 1880. Second, in the 1900, 1910, and
1920 censuses, information regarding ownership was recorded only for
the head of the household. This should not pose serious problems for
us if the victim was the head of the household or closely related to the
head of the household. For individuals recorded as "boarders," "room-
ers," "laborers," and the like, however, housing tenure status is not a
useful indicator of their own socioeconomic status but rather provides
information about the economic circumstances of their employers or
landlords. As noted earlier, only about 11 percent of the victims were not
related to the householder. With these caveats in mind, the evidence in
Figure 3.3 indicates that, at the time of their census enumeration, three
out of every four lynch victims who were heads of their own household
resided in a dwelling that was rented rather than owned.

To put this proportion in some historical perspective, it is important
to keep in mind that as recently as 1865, virtually no southern African
Americans owned property.[20] According to information from the 1860
U.S. Census, roughly 94 percent of blacks living in the South were slaves
(Gibson and Jung 2002),[21] who had been prevented from owning property. Only the relatively tiny 6.2 percent of southern blacks who were
not slaves before the Civil War *could* own land—and it is unlikely that
many of them did. Therefore, the levels of ownership described in Figure
3.3, while seemingly low, represent a rather impressive achievement of
property acquisition during the half century of freedom encompassed
by the data—especially in light of the legal and institutional barriers to
upward economic mobility faced by southern blacks during this era.

We can combine the information regarding *type* of residence and
dwelling *ownership* to gain a better idea of the extent to which farm
households and nonfarm households differed in housing tenure. According to Figure 3.3, ownership was somewhat more common among the
farm households than for nonfarm households in our sample of lynch
victims. While more than one in four farm households occupied by lynch

victims was owned rather than rented, less than two out of every ten nonfarm households were owned.

Both overall home ownership (17.9 percent) and ownership of farms (17.7 percent) were somewhat less common within the sample of non-victims than the rates we observed for victims. These differences are consistent with theoretical perspectives that describe the disproportionate targeting of higher-status, more successful black men by southern lynch mobs. The larger difference between victims and non-victims for farm ownership is especially intriguing because it could suggest that the same characteristics were associated with differing levels of risk in different kinds of communities. In the case of home ownership, it may be that economically successful and upwardly mobile blacks were particularly vulnerable within the agricultural economy. Again, however, caution must be exercised when interpreting the bivariate comparisons reported in Figure 3.3. It is possible that the observed advantage in home ownership for lynch victims was actually the result of other differences between victims and non-victims that have not been accounted for by viewing this characteristic in isolation.

EMPLOYMENT AND OCCUPATION

The occupations available to black men in the Jim Crow South were restricted by both the structure of the southern economy and the prevailing racial hierarchy. Farming provided the productive foundation of the former Confederate states, so most workers—both black and white—were concentrated in agricultural jobs. Because the region was slow to mechanize its plantation system, these jobs tended to be quite labor intensive and, as we have discussed earlier, often tied workers and families to specific plantations and employers through the vicious practices of sharecropping and debt peonage. But, as described in the preceding section of this chapter, some black farm families were successful in achieving landowning status despite the odds working against them.

Black men who were able to find work away from the fields faced the harsh reality of a society ruled by whites. The restricted opportunity set encountered by all workers in the southern economy weighed especially heavily on the region's African American population. A small professional class of blacks and "mulattos" did exist, primarily to serve the needs of the black community, and some black men were able to secure skilled or semiskilled jobs in the nonagricultural sector. Still, blacks who were able to escape farm labor were consigned largely to unskilled labor or to jobs that focused on serving whites. For example, early in December 1887, three black men named Joe Tribble, Monroe Harris, and Charles Taylor were jailed in Charleston, Mississippi, accused of attempting to murder a white man. On December 3, a mob of between twenty-five and seventy-five masked individuals took the three prisoners from the jail to a spot half a mile out of town and killed them (*New Orleans Times-Democrat*, December 5, 1887). In the vicinity of Charleston, we identified too many black men named Charles Taylor and Monroe Harris to allow us to say with any certainty which—if any—of them might have been the men who were killed by the mob.

We were able to locate just one man named Joe Tribble, however, and believe that he was the man who was lynched in 1887. In the 1880 census, Joe Tribble was twenty-two years old, living about thirty miles southeast of Charleston in a town called Grenada. In 1880 Mr. Tribble was living with his sixteen-year-old wife, Lara, and their newborn daughter, Susan. Both Joe and Lara were able to read and write, and both had been born in Mississippi. Despite being literate and living in an urban environment, however, Joe Tribble was enumerated as working as a "laborer." Constrained by the twin forces of an anemic southern economy and a rigid racial caste system, the occupational opportunities available to black men were stymied.

Thus, although the proportions of black and mixed-race men distributed among occupations outside of agricultural sharecropping were somewhat anemic, the gainful employment of southern black men during this era can be examined along two general dimensions—agricultural versus nonagricultural sector and lower-status versus higher-status occupations.[22] An important *disadvantage* of using simple dichotomies to identify employment sector and to measure the status associated with particular occupations is that it obscures the greater detail that would be revealed by using finer-grained categories. An important *advantage* of this approach is that it likely suffers from less measurement error, in the form of misclassification. Fully aware of the crudity of the metrics, we use these two dimensions to profile the occupational status of victims and non-victims in Figure 3.3.[23]

Roughly six out of every ten lynch victims (62 percent) were employed in the southern agricultural sector. Among that large majority of workers, a similar percentage (63 percent) held what we consider to be lower-status positions. Within the agricultural sector, most higher-status individuals had occupations that were reported as "farmer" or "planter." Most lower-status individuals were recorded as "farm laborer," someone "working on farm," or "farm hand." A roughly similar share of non-victims was engaged in agricultural pursuits; however, a much larger percentage of the non-victims had occupations that we have classified as higher-status—46 percent versus 37 percent for victims. Just over one-quarter of both victims (29 percent) and non-victims (27 percent) were employed in the nonagricultural sector. Higher-status occupations were considerably less common among nonagricultural workers than among agricultural workers. But we find, once again, that non-victims were more likely than victims to be represented in higher-status positions—14.9 percent and 9.1 percent for the two groups, respectively.

These occupational profiles for victims and non-victims suggest the possibility that lynch victims were selected disproportionately from among the lower-status segment of the black population. Within both the agricultural and nonagricultural sectors, non-victims were more likely than victims to hold higher-status occupations. This gradient, by victim status, appears to contradict the evidence that we presented earlier regarding home ownership, which indicated that victims were more likely than non-victims to own their homes, especially if they resided on farms. Again, however, it would be premature to draw strong conclusions regarding the differential selection of lynch victims by occupational status without the benefit of a more sophisticated analysis that considers the potentially complex relationships among the many individual- and household-level characteristics examined in this chapter.

LITERACY

Typically, no provisions were made for the schooling of slaves. In fact, in nearly all Confederate states it was illegal to teach a slave to read and write (Elkins 1959). After the Civil War, the freed African American population of the South sought to reverse the effects of this historical wrong. In the face of substantial obstacles, including race-based educational segregation, woefully inadequate state funding of African American schools, and racist beliefs about the intellectual capacity of their race (Anderson 1988; Margo 1990; Spiro 2009), southern blacks rapidly gained the ability to read and write. In 1870 only one in every ten southern blacks was literate; by 1930 that proportion had risen to six out of every ten. During that same sixty-year period, the level of literacy among white southerners rose a more modest ten percentage points, from 64 percent to 74 percent.[24] Although still trailing their white counterparts, southern blacks had reduced significantly the racial differential in literacy—again, in the face of miserly public funding and strong social and philosophical headwinds. To provide a national perspective for the southern educational condition, the level of literacy for whites outside of the South rose from 68 percent to 80 percent between 1870 and 1930 while the percentage of non-southern blacks who could read and write jumped from 42 percent to 79 percent during the same time period.

Regrettably, the U.S. Census Bureau did not begin to collect information about educational attainment until 1940. Therefore, it is impossible to know how many years of schooling lynch victims had completed. In lieu of that information, however, a distinction between those who were and were not able to read and write is a useful dimension of social standing within this bucolic society. As shown in Figure 3.3, a minority (44.8 percent) of the lynch victims we were able to link to their census records reported that they were able to read and write.[25] The comparable figure for the sample of non-victims is 46.9 percent, comprising a difference in the level of literacy between the two groups that is not statistically significant. These relatively modest levels of literacy are consistent with the generally rural and agricultural profile of the southern African American population that we have described thus far.

Geographic Mobility

One of the very important benefits of freedom for southern African Americans was the ability to move—from one residence to another, from one county to another, from one state to another, or even to leave the South entirely. Geographic mobility for slaves, of course, was not an option, unless it was arranged and sanctioned by the slave owner. Indeed, the punishment for unauthorized geographic mobility by slaves could be very severe. Great effort was made by owners and local authorities to capture "runaway" slaves. Those who dared to violate this rule risked being flogged, mutilated, or even killed (Rushdy 2012). In principle, freedom changed all of this.

Following the Civil War, many freed people took advantage of their ability to move about as they searched for family members from whom

they had been separated or as they sought simply to put distance between themselves and their former circumstances of servitude. Most of
this movement involved short distances, and relatively few newly freed
former slaves crossed state lines or left the region. However, once the
South's new arrangement for agricultural production was in place, based
largely on a system of farm tenancy for blacks, the freed people faced
new restrictions even on their local geographic mobility.

The pernicious system of debt peonage bound farm tenants to the
same landowner through financial dependency and legal obligation.
When the sharecropping family's balance sheet dipped into the red,
they were forced to borrow at exorbitant rates of interest, with their
next cash crop serving as collateral. Landowners were disinclined to
allow families that owed them money to leave the county or to move to
a different plantation. Furthermore, for most of the year, the family's
primary financial asset (the maturing crop) was in the ground and could
not be realized for months into the future, if then. This made it virtually
impossible for many sharecroppers to make the economically rational
decision to seek better arrangements with a different landowner or to
exit the quagmire of farm tenancy altogether. They had few assets, and
they were in debt. Local jurisdictions assisted white landowners in this
effort to tie tenant families to their land by adopting "anti-transient"
laws that gave sheriffs the power to arrest unemployed individuals who
were moving through their counties (Blackmon 2009; Mandle 1978). In
this "hand-in-glove" fashion, the southern criminal justice system and
the white economic elite cooperated to maintain an adequate supply of
labor with few alternative options. And, of course, the financial interests
of white landowners could also be protected through the threat of mob
violence.

Our ability to describe the geographic mobility of lynch victims is
constrained by the information that is available in the census enumerators' manuscripts for this time period. Unfortunately, the U.S. Census
asked no questions about recent migration or residential mobility until
1940. However, we are able to glean two measures of geographic mobility
from the data at our disposal. First, we can compare the state in which the
victim was lynched to his state of birth, as reported in the census. This
measure allows us to describe the level of *lifetime* interstate migration
for the victims. We distinguish between those who were lynched in the
same state in which they were born from those who were lynched in a

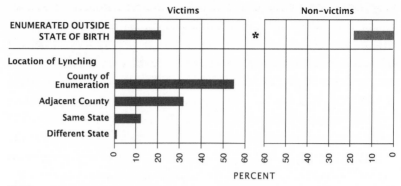

Figure 3.4 Geographic Mobility of Southern Lynch Victims and a Random Sample of Non-victims, 1882–1929

different state. Second, we can compare the county in which the victim was lynched to the county in which he resided when he was enumerated in the census. For the latter measure we consider the following four possibilities: (1) the victim was lynched in the same county in which he was enumerated; (2) the victim was lynched in a county that was contiguous to his county of enumeration;[26] (3) the victim was lynched in another county in his state of enumeration;[27] and (4) the victim was lynched outside of his state of enumeration.[28]

The evidence in Figure 3.4 reveals that the overwhelming majority of lynch victims—roughly eight of every ten—were killed in their state of birth. This number is slightly higher than the percentage of men in the comparison sample who were enumerated outside of their state of birth—21.1 percent of victims compared to 18.4 percent of non-victims. This small but statistically significant difference could simply reflect the modest level of interstate migration for the southern black population during most of this time period. Among those who did move outside their state of birth, migration to nearby states predominated. Among victims, two of every three interstate migrants moved to a state that shared a border with their birth state. The only states to which a relatively large percentage of lynch victims appear to have moved from more distant locations are Florida, Arkansas, and Louisiana—each of which experienced rapidly expanding economies and heavy in-migration (Lee et al. 1957) during the lynching era. It should also be noted that interstate migration is a behavior most often associated with higher-status individuals and families. Relocation is financially costly, and settling in a new community is made easier if one has social or professional contacts in the destination community. The modestly higher migrant concentration among victims may reflect *either* weak social ties and a marginal status *or* a generally higher level of socioeconomic status among this group.

While the comparison of birth state to the state of lynching offers some insight into the lifetime history of interstate migration for the victims, it is less useful for inferring patterns of more recent geographic mobility. Given that the average (median) lynch victim was about twenty-nine years of age when he was killed, the period of time considered by our measure of lifetime migration was typically more than two decades. Nor does the history of interstate migration tell us about moves that covered a shorter distance, such as moves between counties within the same state.

For a finer-grained picture of geographic mobility that focuses on more recent moves and moves of a shorter distance, we compare the county where the lynching occurred and the county in which the victim was enumerated in the census.[29] The time that elapsed between the victim's death and his enumeration in the prior census was limited to a maximum of fifteen years—for those individuals who were lynched in 1895 and linked to their 1880 census records. For the vast majority of cases it was much shorter—sometimes less than a year. According to Figure 3.4, most victims were lynched quite near to the place in which they were enumerated. Over one-half of all victims (54.8 percent) were lynched in the same county in which they were enumerated in the census; an additional one-third (31.9 percent) were lynched in a contiguous county. In contrast, only about 1 in every 100 victims was lynched in a different state.[30]

Overall, the patterns of geographic mobility described in Figure 3.4 reinforce the conventional image of a southern black population that was relatively immobile during this time period. For the most part, it appears that lynching was a "local affair." The large majority of victims were lynched in their birth states, and quite close to home. On the one hand, this is probably exactly what most scholars of lynching and southern history would have predicted. On the other hand, we emphasize, once again, that this is information that was simply unavailable before these victims were linked to their census records. It is obviously impossible to present comparable information for more recent geographic mobility for the sample of non-victims, since we have no comparable event—a lynching—to use to identify their location at a specific date subsequent to the census enumeration. Based on the disparity in the percentage of each group that was born out of state, however, it may be that victims were more likely to have been relative newcomers in their communities.

Concluding Comments

By linking southern lynch victims to their census records, we have been able to construct a profile that is unique in its scope and level of detail. As a result, a simple inventory of victims that includes only names, races, genders, and the date and location of their demise yields to a much richer resource—one that transforms the lynch victims into actual persons. The same process that gave James Clark an age, a family, an occupation, and neighbors[31] has been implemented for over 900 southern lynch victims to also give them the routine characteristics of personhood.

In many ways, the profile of lynch victims that we have constructed comports quite well with what prior research and common sense would have suggested. That is, the black men who were killed by southern mobs were, for the most part, older adolescents or young adults who resided in rural areas and were engaged in unskilled work, generally within the agricultural sector. And they were a relatively geographically immobile population. But there was also considerable diversity among the victims, especially with respect to their ability to read and write, their marital status, and the structure of the households in which they lived.

The comparison of the victims' profile to that for a sample of non-lynched black men who resided in the same counties where these lynchings took place paints a preliminary and tentative picture of how the targets of southern mobs were similar to, and different from, the general population. The image that emerges includes somewhat contradictory streams of evidence. On the one hand, we have shown that victims were *less likely* than non-victims to be enumerated as "mulatto" and to have higher-status occupations. These differences are consistent with theoretical perspectives that predict that lynch victims were selected disproportionately from among the lower-status, more marginal segment of the local African American community. On the other hand, our evidence suggests that lynch victims were *more likely* than non-victims to own their homes rather than to rent, and the difference in ownership was concentrated among those living on farms. The differential in home ownership suggests the possibility that higher-status black men were more likely to be targeted by lynch mobs, as hypothesized by many scholars.

The profile of lynch victims presented in this chapter advances significantly our basic understanding of who the victims of southern lynching were. And the comparison of victims to non-victims offers some useful hints about the selection of victims by southern mobs. But the content of this chapter also begs for answers to additional important questions. First, do the initial differences between victims and non-victims hold up to greater analytic scrutiny that accounts for the correlations between the various characteristics that we have examined in this chapter? Second, do the basic profile for victims and the differences between victims and non-victims vary by the socioeconomic and demographic characteristics of the local area in which they resided? And finally, what can we say about the characteristics of those victims who were not black males? These are among the many important questions for which we seek answers in the following chapters.

CHAPTER FOUR

Victims as Marginal Men?

In the 1880 census, Gus Knight was enumerated as an illiterate fourteen-year-old, Georgia-born black teenager living in the rural Eighty-Fifth District of Jefferson County, Georgia. Jefferson County lies southwest of the city of Augusta, roughly midway between Interstate 16 to the south and Interstate 20 to the north on today's maps. In 1880 Gus Knight was working as a servant. He did not stay with his own family but with a white man who was his employer, along with two other black adolescents. Despite living in a different household from his family, Gus and both of his parents are reported to have been born in Georgia, and evidence suggests that he may have had other familial connections in the area. The enumerator's manuscript page that includes the household in which Gus Knight lived also contains two black families who shared the surname Knight, including the only literate blacks on the page—a young married couple named Tom and Rose Knight. Two years later, when Gus would have been sixteen years old, he had apparently migrated to contiguous Johnson County, which is located to the southwest of Jefferson County. There, he was accused of sexual assault in September of that year, arrested, taken from the jailer's custody by a mob, and lynched on September 20. According to newspaper reports, at the time of his death in 1882, Gus was employed as a mill worker (*Atlanta Constitution*, September 21, 1882).

Jim Torney was also sixteen years old when he was lynched on Trout Creek Mountain, near Greensport, in St. Clair County, Alabama, on July 13, 1888. Greensport, in north-central Alabama, hugs the western bank of the Coosa River and is less than ten miles due east of Ashville, the county seat. Like Gus Knight, Jim Torney was accused of having an improper relationship with a young white woman, although in Torney's case, it is quite clear that the relationship was consensual. He and the young woman, Maude Broyles, also aged sixteen, attempted to elope. They were pursued by a mob of white men after their plans were discovered. A newspaper article appearing in the July 14, 1888, issue of the *Montgomery Advertiser* reported that the young Ms. Broyles "fought her captors with the fury of a tigress" in an effort to save her fiancé's life, although she was ultimately unsuccessful.

Unlike Gus Knight, Jim Torney was enumerated in the 1880 census living with his family—both parents and an older sister, whose name is unreadable in the census manuscripts. The Torney family was settled in Hayneville, in Lowndes County, Alabama, a crossroads town located just south of Alabama State Highway 8, about midway between Selma and Montgomery. Jim's father, Isral, was listed as literate and employed as a minister, while his mother, Jane, was illiterate and working as a house-keeper. Jim and his fifteen-year-old sister both were attending school, and although the siblings were reported to have been born in Alabama, their parents had been born out of state—Isral in South Carolina and Jane in Florida. At the time of his death in 1888, Jim was four counties away, some 140 miles northeast of Hayneville. The newspaper article detailing the circumstances of his murder indicated that he was working as a laborer for his fiancée's father, reported to be a wealthy white farmer.

Jim Torney and Gus Knight were black teenagers when they were killed, both actively involved in the labor market, and targeted for re-ported violations of the prevailing social code that placed constraints on interactions between black men and white women. Despite their apparent similarities, several factors differentiated Jim Torney and Gus Knight from each other and may have influenced the likelihood that they would be targets for mob violence. These young men each had charac-teristics that simultaneously marked them as both insiders *and* outsiders within the rural South. Gus was an "insider" in that he appears to have had family roots in Georgia, may have lived close to extended family members, and was lynched within just a few miles of the place where he had been enumerated. He would have been marked as an "outsider," however, because he was not employed in the agricultural sector, was not sharing a household with family members at the time of the census, and had moved to a new county just prior to his lynching. Jim Torney, on the other hand, would have been considered an insider thanks to his employment in agriculture and because at the time of the census he was enumerated as living with his family. However, he may well have been considered an outsider because it appears that his family had relocated to Alabama relatively recently and because he had migrated some distance—perhaps with his parents and sister, or perhaps without—in the years between the census enumeration and the time that he was killed.

Building on the preliminary descriptive evidence presented in chapter 3, which provided an initial comparison of the characteristics of victims with those of a sample of black men who were not lynched, we will now begin to systematically examine whether black and mixed-race men who were outsiders or marginal in the counties where they were killed in some way were at greater risk than other men in their communities for falling prey to mob violence. We root this examination largely in Roberta Senechal de la Roche's hypothesis about the sociogenesis of lynching, which we discussed in chapter 1. This theory posits that individuals with fewer social and economic ties to a community and who were accused of committing an offense against a white insider were at increased risk of victimization in part because they were able to marshal fewer friends and kin to come to their aid in times of crisis. Intervening in a conflict to protect someone targeted by a lynch mob entailed a high degree of risk. Indeed, newspaper accounts relate that many people ultimately killed by lynch mobs were not the initial intended targets but people who tried to provide safe harbor to the intended victim or to negotiate with the mob to spare the life of their friend or family member. For example, many of the victims in the infamous massacre that occurred in Rosewood, Florida, during the winter of 1922–23 were targeted because they collaborated to protect a young man accused of sexual assault from a pursuing lynch mob. Even some whites who sought to intervene in a lynching were seriously injured or killed by members of the mob.

Lynching provides just one example of intergroup violence in which the victim's membership in a particular group forms at least part of the motivation for the assault or governs its severity. Because lynching has become mainly a relic of American history, much of the research currently conducted on intergroup violence focuses on hate crimes, intimate partner violence, sexual assault, and forms of bullying. This literature provides some support for Senechal de la Roche's theory in that much of the work suggests that specific people might be targeted for victimization because they are newcomers or relatively friendless in the communities where they are attacked (Harlow 2005, Table 8; Lauritsen and Schaum 2004). Their lack of a protective web of strong social relationships makes these outsiders more vulnerable to an attack and their victimization likely to be more savage if there is no one willing to come to their assistance when they are in danger (Senechal de la Roche 1996, 1997, 2001). And, as noted in chapter 1, a greater vulnerability of socially marginal individuals to victimization is also predicted by the Routine Activities Theory of criminal behavior. If lynch mobs are viewed as potential criminal offenders and African American men as their possible victims, Routine Activities Theory predicts that an offense (for example, lynching) is more likely to occur in the absence of "capable guardians." Black men who were outsiders to, or who were more weakly integrated within, the local community presumably had access to fewer capable guardians who might be prepared to risk their own safety by intervening to prevent a lynching.

The case of Tommy Ray illustrates the benefits to black men of having a white benefactor. Ray stood accused of murdering DeWitt Faulkner, a wealthy farmer in Baldwin County, Georgia, in June 1920. On June 23 the *Macon Telegraph* reported, "According to information reaching Milledgeville early tonight it is feared the negro, if caught, will not be taken to jail. Open threats, it is said, have been made that Ray will not be jailed. . . . All trace of Ray was lost by the posse on the plantation of George Hollingshead after the negro had been followed for about five miles. The section in which the negro is believed to have taken refuge is very swampy and this makes the hunt all the harder."[1]

By October 1920, Tommy Ray was locked up in jail, for Faulkner's murder, in Detroit, Michigan, hundreds of miles north of Baldwin County, Georgia. A prolonged and spirited debate ensued between the governors of Georgia and Michigan over Ray's fate. Ultimately, Governor Alexander J. Groesbeck of Michigan denied a request to extradite the accused man to Georgia because he feared that a lynch mob would be waiting, despite the fact that Ray claimed that he had acted in self-defense in killing Faulkner.[2] But it is how Ray got to Detroit that interests us most. Interviews conducted by Mark Schultz for his book *The Rural Face of White Supremacy* suggest that Winton Edmund, Ray's white landowner, helped him hide in the swamp, supplied him with food, and deliberately decoyed the sheriff's posse away from Ray's hiding place. Eventually Edmund was able to secretly arrange for Ray's safe passage to Milledgeville, hidden under a wagonload of hay, and then ultimately to Atlanta, where he put Ray on a train headed to Detroit. That Ray ultimately gained his freedom when Governor Groesbeck released him from jail in August 1921 can be attributed directly to the effort by Winton Edmund to protect his sharecropper. Without Edmund's assistance, Ray most likely would have been captured and lynched.

Another dimension to social marginality is the strength of the "signal" that the characteristics of marginality sent to members of the larger community. The stronger that signal, the more salient was any individual-level quality that may have identified a particular black man as an outsider. For example, transients or drifters passing through town would have stood out quite clearly as strangers, particularly in smaller communities where residents were well known to one another, and their outsider status might have carried threatening connotations of danger to the established members of the community. Even residents with weak family and friendship connections within the community could have been considered somewhat marginal. However, the signal associated with those qualities was likely weaker than the signal associated with transients and drifters. Black men who stood out in a community because their personal profile marked them as outsiders or marginal men might have been more vulnerable to targeting by lynch mobs. Furthermore, the extent to which their personal profile raised their visibility likely varied by the concentration in the larger community of the specific characteristics that signaled their marginality. In short, a solitary marginal man stood out more prominently than an outsider among many other outsiders.

Our earlier research suggests that it was indeed black men who were socially and economically marginal in their communities who were at the greatest risk of lynching (Bailey et al. 2011). But that study was limited in the personal characteristics that it considered and did not explore the possible role of the local context in shaping the influence of individual-level characteristics on the likelihood of victimization. In this chapter, we examine the relationship between individual marginality and the risk of lynching, with a particular focus on whether qualities associated with marginal status mattered differently in communities where those traits were more or less common.

Victims as Possible Outsiders

One piece of evidence that might suggest the degree to which the people killed by mob violence were marginal members of their local communities is whether their names were included in media reports about their lynching. While meaningful as evidence, these reports correspond only to people who were lynched and do not lend themselves to comparisons with other black and "mulatto" men who were not lynched. One can imagine, however, that victims who were well-known members of their communities would have been specifically identified when their deaths were reported. For example, Pickens County, South Carolina, experienced two lynchings within the span of less than a year. The first, on December 3, 1890, was reported in the *Charleston News and Courier*. The article, which was prominently featured on the paper's front page, announced that a black man known both as Henry Wilsby and Henry Johnson had been accused of raping a white woman and was lynched four miles outside of the town of Central. It provided extensive detail about the assault Wilsby (or Johnson) was accused of perpetrating as well as about the slow and painful death inflicted on him by the mob. The article also alleged that he had an extensive history of sexual assault.

The second lynching occurred the following summer, on August 6, 1891, and also involved a black man accused of sexual assault, in this case on a "Mrs. Rowland, a respectable and crippled white woman." This incident was reported in a brief notice—barely receiving a column inch of space—on the front page of the August 7 edition of the *Atlanta Constitution*, but no identifying information was provided about the man who was killed, other than the fact that he was black, nor were specifics about his capture and murder detailed.

There are alternative explanations for why these two newspaper reports for such high-profile events include disparate levels of detail about the lynch victims. One possibility is that the man who was accused of assaulting Mrs. Rowland was not well known in Pickens County while Henry Wilsby (Johnson) was. That is the explanation that we pursue in the following pages. However, it is also possible that the name of the second victim was simply not known to the reporter who prepared the story but was familiar to local residents. And it is even possible that his name was reported in subsequent stories of the lynching that have escaped our notice. The level of detail available in newspaper reports was also influenced by whether the incident was reported in a local newspaper or by a regional or national paper. These alternative explanations for why the names of victims in the original Beck-Tolnay inventory (2010) may have been unknown should be kept in mind as we proceed to consider the absence of a name to indicate a lynch victim's social marginality.[3]

Two additional characteristics of lynch victims, which we discussed in chapter 3, might yield insights into whether they were socially marginal or embedded within their communities. First, we can distinguish those victims who were enumerated in their state of birth from those who had experienced interstate migration at some point between birth and the most recent census. Second, it is possible to determine whether a victim was lynched in the same county in which he was enumerated in the census. Victims who were more transient would have been less likely to have lived—and been recorded in the census manuscripts—in the communities where they were lynched and therefore would probably have been less well known to their attackers. Like being lynched outside of one's state of birth, being lynched in a county that was different from the county in which one was enumerated in the census might be considered to be associated with social marginality and outsider status.

Figure 4.1 displays two pieces of information for each of the five decades of our analysis. The vertical bars indicate the percentage of all victims who were living in the county where they were lynched at the time of the census, and this measure references the legend on the left-hand axis. The line depicts the percentage of black and "mulatto" male victims who were born out of state in each decade, with the percentages identified on the right-hand axis. These two metrics increase in tandem across the decades we are examining, suggesting that the two processes may have been operating simultaneously.

Over time, victims were increasingly likely to have been enumerated within the county in which they were ultimately killed, although the statistical significance of this trend is somewhat weak. This pattern *may* signify that, over time, the conflicts that led to lynching became more personal and the victims more known to their assailants. The growing percentage of victims who were born outside the state in which they were lynched also suggests that in the later decades of the lynching era, the choice of victim was more narrowly focused on individuals who were less embedded within their communities. Being from out of state probably made it less likely that these men enjoyed extended kinship networks within the communities in which they lived or the kinds of enduring, lifelong friendships that might motivate heroic efforts to intervene in an escalating conflict—such as Winton Edmund's efforts

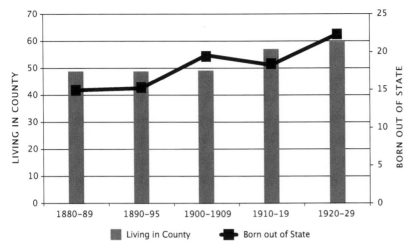

Figure 4.1 Black Male Lynch Victims Born out of State and Enumerated in County of Lynching, by Decade

to protect Tommy Ray from the manhunt that very likely would have ended in his death.

We have speculated that being unnamed in the newspaper accounts of his death suggests that a lynch victim was more likely to be an outsider or socially marginal in the local community. If that is true, then we can take advantage of the spatial and temporal variation in the proportion of unnamed victims to determine whether being born out of state or being lynched outside of one's county of census enumeration were reflections of social marginality. In order to do this, we have determined the following three pieces of information for fifty state-decade time periods:[4] (1) the percentage of all victims whose names are unknown to us, (2) the percentage of all victims who were killed outside of their state of birth, and (3) the percentage of all victims who were lynched in the same county where they were enumerated in the census.

The fifty unique state-decade observations represent the five decadal periods that are available for the ten southern states included in our study. To the extent that being from out of state is suggestive of social marginality or being an outsider, then it should be *positively* related to the percentage of unnamed victims—that is, larger percentages for one variable should be associated with larger percentages for the other variable. By the same token, men who were well known in their local communities

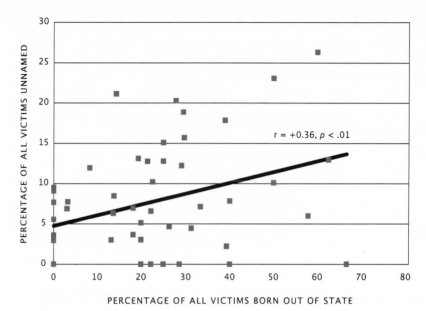

NOTE:
Observations are state–decade units, *N* = 50.

Figure 4.2 Scatterplot of Percentage of Lynch Victims Born out of State and
Percentage of Victims Unnamed, 1882–1929

(that is, lynched in the same county where they were enumerated) should
have been *more likely* to have had their names reported in the newspaper.
So we would expect higher percentages of unnamed victims to have a
negative relationship with the percentage of victims who were killed in
the same county where they were enumerated.

The scatterplot in Figure 4.2, which has the percentage of unnamed
victims on the vertical axis and the percentage of victims born out of
state on the horizontal axis, reveals the expected positive relationship between the two variables. The bivariate correlation coefficient,
frequently referred to as *r*, is +0.36. This represents a relationship of
moderate strength and is statistically significant at the *p* < .01 level, suggesting a very high likelihood (that is, 99 chances out of 100) that the
relationship portrayed in the scatterplot is not a "fluke" or simply due to
chance. This relationship is summarized by the solid line, which shows
a clear upward slope (0.134) and has an intercept of 4.74. This is valuable circumstantial support for the argument that interstate migration

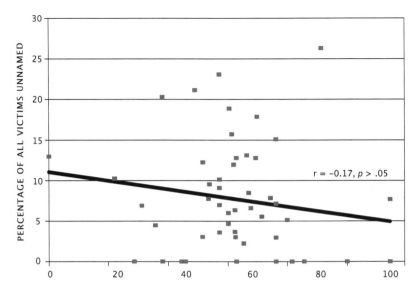

r = −0.17, p > .05

PERCENTAGE OF ALL VICTIMS LYNCHED IN COUNTY OF CENSUS ENUMERATION

NOTE:

Observations are state–decade units, $N = 50$.

Figure 4.3 Scatterplot of Percentage of Victims Lynched in County of Census Enumeration and Percentage of Victims Unnamed, 1882–1929

represents an appropriate measure of the degree to which black men were embedded within their communities.

In contrast, the extent to which victims were lynched outside of their counties of census enumeration is not strongly related to the proportion of victims whose names were unreported in the newspaper articles used to construct the original Beck-Tolnay inventory. The scatterplot shown in Figure 4.3 presents the percentage of unnamed victims on the vertical axis and the percentage of victims who were lynched in their residential county, as recorded in the census, on the horizontal axis. This scatterplot reveals little discernible pattern. Indeed, although the bivariate coefficient of correlation is negative, $r = −0.17$, it is not statistically significant $(p > .05)$. This relationship is summarized by the solid line, which has a slope of −0.061 and an intercept of 11.035. As a result, we have little statistical basis for concluding that intercounty migration represents a meaningful measure of social marginality for black men in these ten states during these five decades. Fortunately, that does not represent an important limitation for our purposes, because we are unable to measure intercounty migration for the sample of non-victims that we have extracted from the 1 percent PUMS files for the decennial censuses. In our data, we observe the lynch victims at two separate time points—the time of census enumeration and the time of their death—so we can identify intercounty geographic mobility by comparing these two measures. We observe men in the comparison sample only once and so have no additional information about their spatial movements after they were enumerated in the census. Therefore, it is impossible to compare victims and non-victims on that personal characteristic.

In the remainder of this chapter we consider whether black and "mulatto" men with weaker connections to, or who were less integrated within, their communities were at greater risk of being selected as the targets of mob violence. We also attempt to specify the degree to which social marginality affected the risk of victimization in places where relatively fewer—or relatively many—other community members and their families shared the same markers of marginality. That is, we attempt to identify whether being socially marginal predicted greater and lesser vulnerability within different contexts.

We are limited in our efforts to measure social marginality by the information available to us in the census enumerators' manuscripts. As indicated above, one useful indicator is based on the comparison between an individual's state of birth and the state in which the lynching occurred. In general, we assume that black men who were lynched outside of their state of birth had weaker connections to the local community than those men who had not moved across a state line. A limitation to this measure is that we do not know how old migrants were when they left their state of birth. Those who moved when they were young children might have enjoyed nearly the same level of local embeddedness as those who were born in the area.

We also have information on whether each individual was employed and, if so, whether he was working in the agricultural sector. We assume that black men who were not in the labor force were more weakly connected to the local community than those who were employed. Further, being employed in agriculture might signal greater embeddedness in the rural South's foundational economic driver and so possibly afforded additional protection by planters who sought to safeguard their workers (as occurred in the incident involving Tommy Ray). However, as the lynching of Jim Torney demonstrates, agricultural employment by itself was not sufficient to protect black men from mobs. Indeed, Tolnay and Beck (1995) have suggested that lynching was used as a mechanism for the control of labor, which might imply that agricultural workers were exposed to a *higher* risk of victimization than were those in the nonagricultural sector. In light of these conflicting possibilities and our *bivariate* finding that a higher proportion of black and mixed-race male victims were farm owners than was true of the comparison sample (see Figure 3.3), it is possible that the risk associated with working in the agricultural sector varied by type of community.

Finally, the census identifies how each member of the household was related to the person listed as its head, if they were related at all. Gus Knight, for example, was living in the home of his employer so would have been enumerated as unrelated to the head of the household. We assume that married black men who headed their own household were more strongly integrated within the local community than were those who were enumerated as unrelated to the head of the household or those who were listed as unmarried head of household, many of whom lived alone.

In addition to examining the relationship between the characteristics of individuals themselves and the relative likelihood of being lynched, we also examine how social marginality may have mattered differently in varied contexts. It is possible, for example, that the relationship between having been born out of state and the risk of being targeted for racial violence was affected by the percentage of other interstate migrants in a community. In a more established state like Mississippi, where the large majority of the black population had been born in the state, being from someplace else would have been an unusual trait, and perhaps a personal characteristic noteworthy enough to place a person in the category of outsider. In more rapidly developing states like Florida and Arkansas, conversely, a larger proportion of state residents had moved in from other states. Under those circumstances, having been born in another state would have been less noteworthy, and the level of embeddedness within the local community would have been more strongly influenced by other criteria.

A Note on Methodology

To assess the degree to which social marginality, or embeddedness within the local community, was related to the likelihood of being targeted by lynch mobs, we use a statistical technique called "logistic regression." In a nutshell, logistic regression allows us to determine whether the likelihood of an event with *only two possible outcomes* is related to other known factors. If the likelihood of one of these binary outcomes—in this study, being lynched—*is* associated with other factors, logistic regression also allows us to determine *whether the relationships are weak or strong*.

In our case, we are comparing the likelihood of being lynched to the likelihood of not being lynched. We use records for each victim we were able to successfully locate in the census manuscripts as well as the census records for a random sample of black and mixed-race men and adolescent boys who were enumerated in the counties where the victims we located were killed. This is the same sample of non-victims that was described in chapter 3. Logistic regression allows us to simultaneously include several factors that might predict our outcome and isolate the effects of each. That is, it identifies the effects of each factor on the likelihood of being lynched, net of the effects of all other factors we include that might also be expected to be important in determining the risk of becoming a lynch victim.

For example, we know that the likelihood of being lynched varied by age. When we compared the ages of victims and non-victims in chapter 3, we found that victims were more likely than non-victims to be older adolescents or younger adults and that there were notably fewer victims among men at the older ages. We also observed in chapter 3 that interstate migrants were more likely to be targeted by lynch mobs than were those African American men who had not migrated from one state to another during their lifetimes.

But let us also consider the possibility that African American adolescents and young adults were more likely than older men to have moved across a state line. This is a plausible speculation given the increasing volume of interstate migration for African American southerners during the late nineteenth and early twentieth centuries. In such a situation, without simultaneously considering both characteristics—migration history *and* age—we could draw misleading conclusions about the extent to which having been born out of state influenced the likelihood of

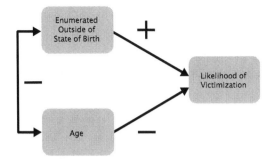

Figure 4.4 Heuristic Conceptual Map of Multivariate Logistic Regression Analysis

being lynched. Logistic regression allows us to compare the percentage of men who were interstate migrants within our group of victims and in the census records for the sample of non-victims while also making an allowance for possible differences in the age distributions for the two groups. A conceptual illustration of logistic regression, accounting for more than one predictive factor, is presented in Figure 4.4. The heuristic model represented in Figure 4.4 shows that interstate migration is *positively related* to the likelihood of victimization, while age evinces a *negative relationship*. Furthermore, interstate migration is negatively associated with age. The implication of this model is that any estimate of the effect of interstate migration on the risk of victimization will be positively inflated unless the role of age is also considered.[5]

For each measure of social marginality, we first present what we refer to as the "naive view." The naive view describes the relationship between a single dimension of marginality while also taking into consideration only the age of the victim,[6] the decade in which the lynching occurred, and the number of adult black and mixed-race men living in the county of lynching.[7] It does not adjust for the possible relationships among the alternative measures of social marginality. The naive view might be likened to the conclusions that we draw from our everyday observation of differences between individuals or groups, or to evidence that is reported by the news media. For example, we might see reported that life expectancy in the United States varies significantly by race—a newborn black male in 2013 can expect to live a total of seventy-one years, while a white male newborn is projected to live until age seventy-six. Based on this limited piece of information, we might decide that biological differences between black and white men are responsible for such a large disparity in life expectancy. However, we know quite well that there are compositional differences between black males and white males in terms of socioeconomic status and behavioral factors that help to determine longevity. But those compositional differences generally are not considered in the naive presentation of evidence, such as the difference between seventy-six years and seventy-one years of life expectancy mentioned above.

We next consider what we describe as the "refined" view in which the relationship between each measure of social marginality and the likelihood of being lynched is adjusted for the extent to which the various measures of marginality are themselves interrelated. To continue the demographic example, a refined view of racial differences in male life expectancy would compare black and white males who were nonsmoking college graduates—thereby accounting for racial differences in education and smoking behavior. It is rarely possible in our everyday observations of differences between groups to "hold constant" factors other than the ones we are directly observing. Therefore, the refined view is generally limited to studies that are able to apply relatively sophisticated statistical approaches—like multivariate logistic regression.

Finally, we consider the possibility that social marginality had greater or lesser influence on the likelihood of being targeted by lynch mobs depending on the average characteristics of people in victims' communities. As mentioned above, for example, being from out of state could matter differently depending on whether a large or small percentage of the local population had also been born out of state. We do this by testing for a statistical phenomenon known as "interaction effects," which simply means that the existence, or strength, of the relationship between two variables depends on the level of a third variable. Figure 4.5 identifies how this might work conceptually.

As Figure 4.5 demonstrates, whether an individual was born out of state directly affected the likelihood that he was lynched. This is illustrated by the solid arrow pointing from the box labeled "Individual Enumerated Outside of State of Birth" to the box labeled "Individual Likelihood of Victimization." The arrow represents a relationship between the two facts, and the direction in which the arrow head is pointed suggests causation.[8] Similarly, the solid arrow pointing from the box labeled "Percentage of Population Enumerated Outside of State of Birth"

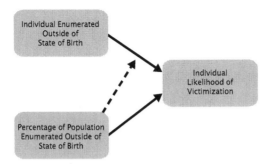

Figure 4.5 Heuristic Conceptual Map of a Statistical Interaction between an Individual-Level Characteristic and a Contextual Characteristic

and the box labeled "Individual Likelihood of Victimization" identifies our expectation that the risk of being targeted for lethal mob violence was directly affected by the concentration of interstate migrants in the local community. More important is the third, dotted, arrow pointing from the box labeled "Percentage of Population Enumerated Outside of State of Birth" to the *solid arrow* that connects the other two boxes. This suggests that the *relationship between* whether an individual was an interstate migrant and his risk of becoming a lynch victim was *modified* in some way by the percentage of the local male African American population that had been born in a different state. We can think of an interaction as something that either amplifies or dampens the strength of another relationship. If having migrated between states increased a person's risk for victimization, the statistical interaction portrayed in Figure 4.5 allows for the possibility that the size of the increased risk associated with interstate migration might be larger or smaller, depending on the context in which a person was living and the percentage of other African Americans in the community who had moved between states.

When discussing the evidence yielded by our logistic regression analyses of the likelihood of being lynched, we rely heavily on a measure referred to as an "Odds Ratio." The Odds Ratio—abbreviated in equations as OR—is a useful and relatively simple measure comparing two or more groups on a single outcome, such as the likelihood of being lynched. For instance, let us take a hypothetical case in which 2 percent of agricultural workers in our combined sample of victims and non-victims were lynched and that only 1 percent of nonagricultural workers were lynched. In this case, the "odds" for agricultural workers being lynched is determined by dividing their probability of being lynched by their probability of not being lynched. If we use Odds_{aw} to identify the odds of agricultural workers being lynched, then $\text{Odds}_{aw} = 0.02/.98 = 0.0204$. The odds for nonagricultural workers being lynched, which we represent using Odds_{naw}, is calculated in the same fashion so that $\text{Odds}_{naw} = 0.01/0.99 = 0.0101$. And the Odds Ratio describing the likelihood of agricultural workers being lynched relative to the likelihood of nonagricultural workers being lynched is represented using OR_{aw}. $\text{OR}_{aw} = \text{Odds}_{aw} / \text{Odds}_{naw} = 0.0204/0.0101 = 2.02$.

An Odds Ratio of 2.02 informs us that the odds of agricultural workers being lynched were slightly more than twice as great as the corresponding odds for nonagricultural workers. Note that the Odds Ratio describing the likelihood of being lynched for nonagricultural workers relative to agricultural workers, symbolized using OR_{naw}, would be $\text{OR}_{naw} = \text{Odds}_{naw} / \text{Odds}_{aw} = 0.0101/0.0204 = 0.49$. Not surprisingly, this Odds Ratio of 0.49 indicates that the likelihood of being lynched for nonagricultural workers was roughly one-half the corresponding odds for agricultural workers. Odds Ratios greater than +1.0 in value indicate a greater likelihood of being lynched for the focal group (in this case, agricultural workers) relative to the reference group (nonagricultural workers). Odds Ratios less than +1.0 in value suggest a lower likelihood of being lynched for the focal group than for the reference group. An Odds Ratio of exactly +1.0 tells us that the two groups being compared have equal likelihoods of being lynched. Unlike logistic regression coefficients, Odds Ratios always have positive values.

Our discussion also takes further advantage of the useful concept of "statistical significance," which was introduced in chapter 3. To recap that discussion, relationships that are "statistically significant" are strong enough that we can be highly confident (meaning that there is at least a 95 percent likelihood) that they are not due to sampling variation or other chance factors. In other words, we can state with great confidence that statistically significant relationships are "real." In contrast, relationships that do not clear the rigorous threshold of statistical significance are weak enough that they leave some doubt about their origin. Are they real? Or are they a fluke resulting from chance? Combining Odds Ratios and statistical significance allows us to draw original and important conclusions about the predictors of the vulnerability of black men to mob violence. In the following two figures, Figure 4.6 and Figure 4.7, Odds

Ratios that are statistically significant at the $p < .05$ level (meaning that there is a 95 percent likelihood that we are observing a real relationship and not a fluke) are accompanied by an asterisk.

Evidence of Individual-Level Risk Factors for Lynching

A "naive" consideration of the individual-level characteristics related to the likelihood of lynching suggests that victims were not selected randomly from the larger population of black males. We will focus this discussion on those Odds Ratios reported in Figure 4.6 that differ significantly from +1.0 (which indicates no difference between groups). This set of "naive" differences reveals a number of interesting patterns of differential risk. Somewhat surprisingly, black men who migrated between states at some point between birth and the year of census enumeration were exposed to a significantly *lower risk* of victimization than those who continued to reside in their birth state.[9] The odds of an interstate migrant being lynched were only three-quarters of the corresponding risk for non-interstate migrants (OR = 0.76).

An individual's role in the local economy, however, does not appear to have been related to his likelihood of being targeted by mobs—at least in the naive view. Neither gainful employment in the agricultural sector (compared with employment in the nonagricultural sector) nor being out of the labor force entirely was significantly related to the likelihood of lynching.

Men's status within their household of residence does appear to have had some bearing on their likelihood of being lynched. Compared to those men who were married heads of households, unmarried household heads were 67 percent *more likely* to be victimized (OR = 1.67). The odds of being lynched for relatives of the household head were *more than twice as large* as they were for married heads of households (OR = 2.12). Interestingly, men who were unrelated to the head of the household, and therefore presumably less embedded within the local community, were slightly *less likely* to be lynched than even married household heads (OR = .91). However, the latter difference falls short of traditional thresholds for statistical significance, meaning that the relationship is not strong enough for us to determine whether we observe it by chance or due to the existence of a real relationship, so it must be interpreted with caution.

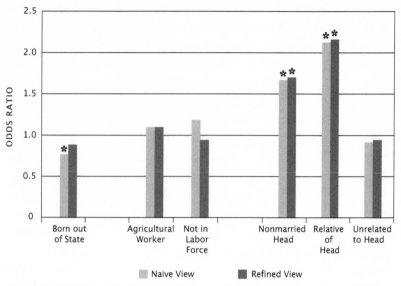

Figure 4.6 Naive and Refined Relationships between Individual-Level Characteristics of Social Marginality and the Likelihood of Being Lynched, 1882–1929

The *lower level of vulnerability* for married heads of households supports the hypothesis of a connection between social marginality and the likelihood of being lynched. In contrast, that interstate migrants were exposed to a *lower risk* of victimization runs counter to the social marginality perspective. Recall, however, that the naive view takes into account only an individual's age, the number of adult black and mixed-race men living in the county, and the decade of observation when estimating the independent role of the different potential risk factors.[10]

In addition to the controls considered by the naive view, the refined view simultaneously adjusts for all three measures of social marginality. By doing so, it recognizes that the separate indicators of marginality themselves might be correlated—for example, that someone who was born out of state might also be more likely to be a married head of household. When this additional adjustment is made to the Odds Ratios reported in Figure 4.6, the same basic pattern of results as those observed for the naive view persist. Specifically, black men who were married and the head of their household were *less likely* to be targeted by lynch mobs than men who were either unmarried heads of households (OR = 1.70) or those who were related to the household head (OR = 2.17)—even when we also take into account employment status and whether someone was born out of state. Likewise, employment status characteristics— both being out of the labor force entirely or being employed in the agricultural sector—remain unrelated to the likelihood of victimization (when compared to employment in the nonagricultural sector). The one notable difference between the naive and refined results is that being born out of state is *no longer significantly related* to the probability of being lynched, in the statistical sense, once the other measures of social marginality are taken into account (OR = .89).

In sum, the evidence regarding the possible individual-level risk factors for being lynched offers modest support for the hypothesis that socially marginal individuals were more vulnerable than those who were more firmly embedded within their local community. It appears that married men who were heading households enjoyed *some protection* from the violence of southern mobs when compared with unmarried heads of households and household members who were related to the head.

Evidence of the Contextual Conditioning of Individual-Level Risk Factors

The statistical evidence presented in Figure 4.6 regarding the role of individual-level indicators of social marginality in determining the risk of victimization is based on an important assumption. That is, it specifies that the relationship between social marginality and the likelihood of being lynched was uniform throughout the South. This is a bold and somewhat implausible assumption considering the substantial subregional variation that we know existed in the South during this era— in terms of both the prevalence of lynching and the concentration of characteristics that might signal marginal social status. We now explore the possibility that the importance of social marginality for the risk of being lynched was conditioned or moderated by the nature of the local context. For example, as mentioned earlier, it is possible that being born out of state sent a stronger signal of being an outsider in communities where most residents were born in the state than it did in areas with many migrants from out of state. Or, being unemployed could more effectively mark an individual as less embedded within the local community in those settings where unemployment was relatively uncommon. If this kind of spatial variation in the relationship between social marginality and the likelihood of lynching exists, then we would expect the Odds Ratios for the individual-level characteristics to vary across social contexts (as introduced conceptually earlier in the discussion of Figure 4.5). And it is even possible for a given indicator of social marginality to have a statistically significant effect on the risk of victimization in some types of locales but not in other types.

To explore this possibility, we constructed county-level equivalents to the individual-level indicators of social marginality that were reported in Figure 4.6 and discussed in the previous section, using the same 1 percent Public Use Microdata Samples for the historical censuses that we used to create the comparison sample of non-victims. For each county in which one of the victims was lynched, we calculated the percentage of adult black and mixed-race males with the different individual-level characteristics—born out of state, not in the labor force, unmarried head of household, and so on. These county-level variables, then, describe the prevalence of each individual-level characteristic within the broader local community, as defined by counties. We include in our predictive models here both the *individual* characteristic, the percent of black and mixed-race men in the county who share that characteristic, and what is known as a "multiplicative interaction term." Interaction terms allow us to specify how the relationship between individual characteristics and the likelihood of being lynched varies by local context.

By adding the county-level measures and "interaction terms"[11] to the logistic regression equations that were the source for the evidence presented in Figure 4.6, we are able to relax the assumption that the relationship between social marginality and the likelihood of an individual being lynched was invariant throughout the South. We use the results from this augmented logistic regression analysis to determine whether the relationship between each individual-level indicator of social marginality and the likelihood of being lynched varied across different levels of the prevalence of the relevant indicator within the county.

A simple summary of our findings when we relaxed the assumption of a uniform relationship between social marginality and victimization is

Table 4.1 Summary of Evidence of Contextual Variation in the Relationship between Individual-Level Characteristics of Social Marginality and the Likelihood of Being Lynched, 1882–1929

Individual-Level Characteristic	Evidence of Contextual Variation?	Direction of Contextual Variation
Born out of State	Yes	Odds Ratio declines with increasing concentration
Agricultural Worker	Yes	Odds Ratio declines with increasing concentration
Not in Labor Force	No	Not applicable
Nonmarried Household Head	Yes	Odds Ratio declines with increasing concentration
Relative of Household Head	No	Not applicable
Unrelated to Household Head	Yes	Odds Ratio declines with increasing concentration

provided in Table 4.1. Two of the individual-level characteristics *did not vary significantly* across the South in their relationship to the likelihood of being lynched—being out of the labor force and being a relative of the household head. All of the other individual-level risk factors had varying influences on the risk of lynching, depending on the frequency or rarity of their occurrence within the local area. And, importantly, in every case, the impact of these individual-level characteristics on the likelihood of being lynched declined in magnitude as their frequency within the local area increased. In other words, social marginality was more salient for determining *who* was selected to be victimized by lynch mobs in those settings where a particular "flavor" of marginality was less common.

To further illustrate the nature of contextual variation in the relationship between social marginality and the likelihood of lynching, we have estimated the Odds Ratios for each individual-level characteristic at three specific locations along the distribution of its contextual equivalent—the 25th, 50th, and 75th percentiles of the *county-level distribution*.[12] At a lower percentile (for example, the 25th) the relevant characteristic was less common within the county than it was at a higher percentile (for example, the 75th). These Odds Ratios are shown in Figure 4.7. When

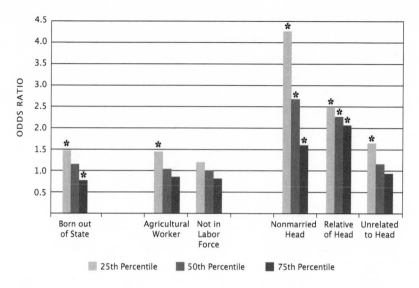

Figure 4.7 Variation in Relationship between Individual-Level Characteristics of Social Marginality and the Likelihood of Being Lynched, by County Context, 1882–1929

examining this evidence, it is important to keep in mind the reference groups for the characteristics that appear along the horizontal axis. These are identified in the note at the bottom of the figure.

Consistent with the summary contained in Table 4.1, there is little variation across context in the effect of being unrelated to the household head on the likelihood of being lynched or of being out of the labor force (compared to nonagricultural workers). For every other variable, the Odds Ratio declines, in some cases quite sharply, as the concentration of the characteristic in the population becomes more prevalent. For example, the Odds Ratio for being born out of state is estimated to be 1.47 at the 25th percentile, 1.15 at the 50th percentile, and .77 at the 75th percentile. The Odds Ratio for the 50th percentile does not attain statistical significance at *p* < .05. The other two Odds Ratios are statistically significant, indicating a considerable difference in the likelihood of being lynched for interstate migrants compared to men enumerated in their birth states at those percentiles. At one extreme, black men who were born out of state were nearly 50 percent *more likely* to be lynched in counties where out-of-state origin was relatively unusual (that is, the 25th percentile)—in other words, they were outsiders in a county where outsiders were uncommon. At the other extreme (that is, the 75th percentile), men who were born out of state were 23 percent *less likely* to be lynched in counties where out-of-state origin was the norm.[13]

While agricultural workers (OR = 1.45, $p < .05$) and men who were unrelated to the head of the household (OR = 1.65, $p < .05$) were more likely to be lynched than nonagricultural workers and married heads of households, respectively, at the 25th percentile, those differences fell to nonsignificance at the 50th and 75th percentiles. The finding that agricultural workers living in communities with a lower concentration of other workers in the agricultural sector experienced a high risk of lynching is somewhat contradictory to our expectations, a topic we return to later in the chapter. The most dramatic variation in the Odds Ratios across percentiles is observed for the difference between married and nonmarried household heads. At the 25th percentile, the odds of unmarried household heads being lynched are over four times greater (OR = 4.26, $p < .05$) than those for married household heads. At the 75th percentile, the Odds Ratio remains statistically significant but falls to only 1.60. In contrast, the difference between married heads of households and relatives of the head of household is quite stable, varying only from an Odds Ratio of 2.49 ($p < .01$) at the 25th percentile to an odds ratio of 2.07 ($p < .05$) at the 75th percentile.

Our final objective in the consideration of contextual variability in the importance of individual-level characteristics is to determine at what levels of concentration within the county-level adult black male population the relationship between the individual-level risk factors and the likelihood of being lynched was statistically significant. That is, how common, or how rare, did a given risk or protective factor need to be within the local community before its influence on the likelihood of victimization was strong enough for us to conclude that the relationship observed in our data was not simply due to chance? To do this, we extend the approach used in Figure 4.7 by estimating the relationships between the individual-level measures of social marginality and the likelihood of lynching at each decile[14] in the distribution of the associated county-level variable. Table 4.2 indicates simply whether the relationship is statistically significant at the $p < .05$ level and whether a given significant relationship is positive (+) or negative (−). In cells for which neither a "+" nor a "−" appears, the relationship is statistically nonsignificant. We also include information for the 25th and 75th percentiles for continuity with the evidence presented in Figure 4.7, as well as to enhance slightly our ability to identify transitions in the strength of the relationship. To some extent, this exercise can be interpreted as a type of simulation in which we consider the implications of our empirical evidence under a variety of different hypothetical circumstances.

The evidence contained in Table 4.2 is consistent with the conclusions that we drew from Figure 4.7, but it allows a finer-grained determination of the contextual circumstances under which social marginality posed the greatest risk of lynching for black men. Two types of individuals—unmarried heads of households and co-resident relatives of household heads—were exposed to a higher likelihood of victimization under nearly all contextual conditions, although their relatively higher risks shrank in communities where their statuses were more common within the general black adult male population.[15] In contrast, three individual-level characteristics—out-of-state birth, being an agricultural worker, and being unrelated to the household head—increased the likelihood of lynching only within areas where relatively few men shared those statuses. Being born out of state or working within the agricultural sector increased an individual's likelihood of being lynched only in counties at the 30th percentile or below for the county-level equivalent (that is, the percentage of adult black men who were born out of state or working in the agricultural sector).[16] Interestingly, it appears that being born out of state, which *increased* the likelihood of lynching at lower levels of concentration within the population, actually *reduced* the risk of victimization at the highest levels of concentration. However, given the scarcity of significant *negative* relationships shown in Table 4.2 (3 out of a total of 66) we are reluctant to overinterpret the contextual conditions under which social marginality might have *buffered* black men from the threat of mob violence.

The empirical evidence, then, suggests that social marginality did expose black men to a greater likelihood of being targeted by southern lynch mobs. Importantly, however, the extent to which these "outsider" characteristics operated as a risk factor for lynching depended heavily

Table 4.2 Relationship between Individual-Level Characteristics of Social Marginality and the Likelihood of Being Lynched, by Percentiles of Their County-Level Equivalents, 1882–1929

Individual-Level Characteristic	Percentile for County-Level Characteristics										
	10th	20th	25th	30th	40th	50th	60th	70th	75th	80th	90th
Born out of State (Ref. Born in State)	+	+	+	+					–	–	–
Agricultural Worker Not in Labor Force (Ref. Nonagricultural Worker)	+	+	+	+							
Nonmarried Head of Household	+	+	+	+	+	+	+	+	+		
Relative of Head of Household	+	+	+	+	+	+	+	+	+	+	+
Unrelated to Head of Household (Ref. Married Head of Household)	+	+	+	+							

Note:

+ denotes statistically significant positive relationship ($p < .05$) between individual-level characteristics and likelihood of lynching.

– denotes statistically significant negative relationship ($p < .05$) between individual-level characteristics and likelihood of lynching.

upon the nature of the community in which black and mixed-race men resided. The key findings can be summarized as follows:

- Married household heads enjoyed some measure of protection from mobs in most southern locales, although the strength of this protection grew weaker as the concentration of family/household embeddedness among black men within the community increased.
- Having been born out of state increased the vulnerability of black and mixed-race men to targeting by lynch mobs but only in settings where interstate migrants were less heavily concentrated.

- Contrary to our expectations, agricultural workers were exposed to significantly higher levels of victimization than were nonagricultural workers, but only in settings with lower concentrations of black male agricultural workers.

It appears, then, that the vulnerability associated with social marginality was most intense in settings where there were relatively fewer marginal black men. One might compare this phenomenon to the social stigma associated with tattoos. For the members of the "Greatest Generation," body art often reflected either a military background (typically a World War II veteran) or membership in a rebellious social group (for example, the Hell's Angels). But inferences drawn about those with tattoos during the 1960s would have been very much different from those drawn today, when body art has proliferated to a much larger segment of the American population and its association with specific group membership has atrophied. While this analogy should not be taken too far, we do believe that it serves to illustrate the potential for different signaling processes of individual-level characteristics under circumstances when those qualities are common versus when they are rare.

Concluding Comments

Having access to data on the individual-level characteristics for a large number of lynch victims and identical information for a corresponding comparison sample of non-victims has allowed us to assess empirically and rigorously the utility of the social marginality perspective of victimization. For the most part, our findings offer partial support for the contention that socially marginal adult black and mixed-race males were exposed to a higher likelihood of being lynched than were their more socially embedded neighbors. Being a married head of a household appears to have offered the greatest protection from lynching. Drawing from the theoretical propositions articulated in Roberta Senechal de la Roche's "sociogenesis of lynching," men who were married and headed households would have benefited from reduced relational and cultural distance from, and greater functional interdependence with, the broader community—black and white. On the one hand, mobs might have been reluctant to target them for lynching, even in the face of traditionally provocative circumstances, such as a suspected crime or violation of the southern racial code. On the other hand, it is possible that they would have enjoyed greater protection from the local community if threatened by a potential lynch mob. In the language of Routine Activities Theory, they would have been more likely than socially marginal men to benefit from the intervention of "capable guardians."

An alternative explanation for the lower vulnerability of black men who were married heads of households could emphasize a much different set of conditions. That is, perhaps it was not the social embeddedness of such men that offered some protection from lynch mobs. Rather, their risk of victimization could have been lower because they were less likely than men with other marital statuses or residential situations to commit the serious crimes that motivated mob activity. To explore this alternative explanation, we conducted supplementary analyses that considered the seriousness of the alleged offenses committed by the victims. The results of those analyses suggested a lower likelihood of being lynched for married heads of households, regardless of the seriousness of the offense of which they were accused.[17]

By incorporating information about the characteristics of the local area (that is, the county), we were also able to document substantial spatial variation in the degree to which social marginality placed adult black and mixed-race men at greater risk of victimization. Put simply, the status of being an outsider, or socially marginal, was more consequential in communities where those characteristics were less common. In some cases, an individual-level characteristic increased susceptibility to lynching *only in settings* where that characteristic was relatively uncommon—as we discovered for agricultural workers and those who were born out of state. The finding for agricultural workers is particularly instructive, as it illustrates the importance of the local environment in determining which individual-level traits put black and mixed-race men at risk. The use of terroristic violence as a means of controlling the black labor supply was most "necessary" in communities where employers faced a potential labor shortage, *and it was only in those communities that employment in the agricultural sector predicted victimization.*

In other cases, an individual-level characteristic increased the likelihood of victimization in most types of settings but was more salient in areas where the characteristic was more unusual—for example, being an unmarried head of household or the relative of a household head. As a result of this type of spatial variation in the risk factors for lynching, the potentially lethal consequences associated with a given individual-level characteristic would have been inconsistent across the South in a way that would not necessarily have been perceptible to adult black men.

In chapter 1 we posed the possibility that lynch victims were selected randomly from the general population of black men. We can now reject that possibility with considerable confidence. Furthermore, we can also state that some types of social marginality exposed individual black men to a higher probability of being targeted by a lynch mob. Finally, context mattered. The level of vulnerability that was associated with social marginality varied substantially across the South, placing socially marginal men at greater risk where their type of marginality was less common. It is likely that other individual-level characteristics were also related to the risk of victimization at the hands of southern mobs. We explore that possibility in chapter 5 by considering the role of status transgressions in the selection of lynch victims.

CHAPTER FIVE

Targeted Because of Their Success?

Sterling Thompson was a black man, born in Georgia in 1849. We do not know whether he was born to an enslaved woman, a fact that would have consigned him to being defined as another person's property in the eyes of the law, or into a free family. Regardless of his personal circumstance, Sterling Thompson certainly lived his childhood years in a society ruled by the "peculiar institution" of slavery, and his racial status would have sharply restricted the course his life was expected to take. But the possibilities available to black men, and to a lesser degree to black women, were altered when Sterling was a teenager. On January 1, 1863, President Lincoln proclaimed the emancipation of Americans held in bondage in the rebellious regions. For most enslaved people, Lincoln's proclamation was only symbolic and had little consequence for their day-to-day lives. It was not until the end of Civil War hostilities that the transition from slavery to freedom could truly be enjoyed by the large majority of former slaves. Upon their occupation of the former Confederacy, federal troops introduced the Freedmen's Bureau and brought northern schoolteachers to the South. Soon, the sheer size of the freed population became a transformative factor in southern politics as their support for the Republican Party eroded the traditional dominance of southern Democrats. Based on the evidence, Sterling Thompson must have thrived in this new environment. He learned to read and write, set up farming, married, and had at least one child, a son named Clifford, who was born when Sterling was in his late twenties. In 1883, while in his early thirties, Sterling Thompson married a second time, to a woman named Fannie, although they had no surviving children that we can identify.

In 1900 Sterling, Fannie, and Clifford Thompson were enumerated as living in the Rivertown District of Campbell County, Georgia, located about ten miles west of Fairburn, along the eastern bank of the Chattahoochee River. In late December of that year, when he would have been fifty-one years old, Sterling Thompson drew the attention of a group of white men who were interested in acquiring his farmland. The party posted letters near the Thompson home demanding that he leave the county. When he failed to comply, a group of masked men, described in journalistic accounts as both "whitecaps" and "regulators," went to visit Mr. Thompson, called him out of his home, and opened fire, killing him and wounding his son (*Atlanta Constitution*, January 5, 1901). In the 1900 census, the Thompson family was listed as living on a rented farm, so it is unclear whether the conflict involved the white men's wish to assume the lease of the land or if Sterling and his family had managed to purchase that farm or another parcel of land. Both Sterling and Clifford were listed as "farmers" rather than as lower-status farm laborers or day hands.

In addition to farming desirable land, Sterling Thompson apparently found a calling in public service and had become both economically prosperous and a prominent politician. By 1900, as the campaign to disenfranchise black men was sweeping southern states and the black vote in Georgia had been effectively suppressed (Kousser 1974; Woodward 1956), Mr. Thompson's influence surely would have been waning, although his position would have brought him to the attention of local whites, regardless of the conflict over land. Indeed, Georgia's governor Allen D. Candler offered an $800 reward for the capture of his killers. One of the local newspapers lauded him and expressed that they "deplored" the circumstances surrounding his death (despite also mildly criticizing him for having a "big head") (*Campbell News*, January 4, 1901; see also *Dawson News*, January 16, 1901). Certainly, the actions of the governor and the local media suggest that Sterling Thompson had a relationship with power brokers in the white community starkly different from that enjoyed by most blacks, and even by many disadvantaged whites.

Steve Jenkins also appears to have interacted with the local white power structure in a way that deviated from the patterns that were deemed to be acceptable for southern black men of the era. In Steve Jenkins's case, as well, that deviation may have led to his own murder. Mr. Jenkins was accused of stabbing a white planter to death after the two men quarreled over a farming contract—an act suggesting a direct challenge to the way that the South's race-based political and economic hierarchy affected relationships between individual black and white people. He was lynched on May 11, 1929, in Noxubee County, Mississippi (*Daily Clarion Ledger* [Jackson, MS], May 14, 1929). But much more than the nature of these men's supposed offenses distinguish the cases of Sterling Thompson and Steve Jenkins. Mr. Jenkins was enumerated in the

1920 census as living by himself in the town of Shuqualak. Shuqualak is located in Noxubee County, which is situated on the state line that Mississippi shares with Alabama, roughly equidistant between the northern border with Tennessee and the Gulf of Mexico. The 1920 census records Jenkins's age as fifty-one years, although newspaper articles reporting his lynching placed his age at sixty-five at the time of his death in 1929. By all accounts, he, like Sterling Thompson, was an older man and had also been born in the state where he was lynched. However, unlike Mr. Thompson, Steve Jenkins was illiterate, was an agricultural laborer working for wages, and had no neighboring blacks who shared his surname, suggesting that perhaps he had no nearby relatives (at least none were listed on the census page on which he was enumerated).

Roughly thirty years and 275 miles separate these two events. The victims share several commonalities and also vary concerning some striking individual characteristics. Both could be seen as challenging the prevailing racial hierarchy in important ways. Sterling Thompson clearly enjoyed material success, held political influence, and appeared to have been well regarded by leaders in Georgia's white community. Judging from his strong integration with the local community, it would not seem that Mr. Thompson was vulnerable to the risks of social marginality that were revealed in chapter 4. However, if theories suggesting that lynching was a response to racial competition are correct, then Sterling Thompson could have been singled out for victimization *because* he attained a level of success deemed unacceptable for African Americans by at least part of the white community. He clearly posed a threat to white supremacy on economic and political grounds, and perhaps in terms of social esteem as well, given the governor's willingness to intervene to help find his attackers and the local newspaper's lament at reporting his death. Certainly, not even all *whites* in the community could have expected such a response if they had been the ones unfortunate enough to have been murdered.

Both Sterling Thompson and Steve Jenkins also exhibited, in the very behavior that was used as justification for their killings, evidence of a willingness to challenge mistreatment and attempts at intimidation by whites, and perhaps even a rejection of the subordinate status blacks were expected to endure. Sterling Thompson refused to turn over his land to the white men who demanded it and similarly refused to vacate Campbell County when notice was publicly posted ordering him to do so. Steve Jenkins, likewise, directly challenged the white planter for whom he worked on the terms of a farm contract and, according to newspaper accounts, stabbed the man in the course of the altercation. Steve Jenkins and Sterling Thompson asserted their own rights and refused to capitulate in conflicts with members of the white community, in defiance of the Jim Crow–era expectations that blacks defer to whites in all matters. These individual-level narratives fit well with the evidence about the social, economic, and political climates in which lynching was most likely, discussed in chapter 1.

We know, from the results of prior research, that lynchings were more likely to occur when the economic, political, or social status of the white community was being threatened by blacks. In this chapter, we will explore whether the same logic governing the *volume* of lynching within a certain area or during a given time period also was systematically related to the *individual characteristics* of lynch victims. Put another way, we ask if the community-level factors that guided *when and where* lynchings occurred most frequently can be applied at the individual level to help determine *who* was most vulnerable to being targeted as a victim. From a theoretical perspective, if we extend the logic of prior aggregate-level analyses of the intensity of lynching to the selection of individual victims, we would hypothesize that black men who posed a challenge to the caste-based superior status of whites were more vulnerable to mob violence. In light of the nuanced support we found for the social marginality perspective in chapter 4, we now engage in an equally rigorous examination of the relationship between vulnerability and level of social and economic status.

Early observers and interpreters of the lynching era frequently asserted that successful blacks were disproportionately targeted by southern mobs. Walter F. White, leader of the NAACP from 1929 to 1955, claimed that "lynching is much more an expression of southern fear of Negro progress than of Negro crime" and went on to conclude that "one of the most active stimulants of race hatred is the advance—particularly economic—which the Negro has made during the years since the Civil War" (White [1929] 1969, 11). In *The Tragedy of Lynching*, Arthur Raper ([1933] 1969, 340) noted that resentment among poor whites of the economic success of some southern blacks contributed to interracial tensions: "The uncertainty of employment and the slump of farming had further embittered the propertyless whites who openly begrudged the

Negroes any evidence of accumulated savings or regular employment." A report prepared for the Commission on Interracial Cooperation by Jessie Daniel Ames (1942, 65) observed that "the records of Mrs. Ames' office in Atlanta show that in more than one instance Negroes were lynched on non-existent grounds at the instigation of white men who coveted the crops that Negroes had cultivated."[1] The lynching of Sterling Thompson in Georgia in 1900 would seem to be an illustration of the phenomenon revealed by Mrs. Ames's records.

Booker T. Washington offered a different point of view. According to Washington, poor blacks were more likely than successful blacks to be targeted by lynch mobs. Further, he argued that property accumulation and economic progress by southern blacks would serve to protect them from mob violence rather than increase their exposure to it (Grant 1975, 36–37). Even those who saw a connection between the socioeconomic success and progress of southern African Americans and their vulnerability to the action of lynch mobs would not have argued against such success and progress. However, as evidenced in the writing of Walter White, many black leaders disagreed with Washington's interpretation of the personal qualities that exposed blacks to a greater or lesser likelihood of victimization.

At this point, as we consider whether status transgressions (economic, political, or social) by southern black men increased their exposure to lynching, it is important to differentiate *microlevel* from *macrolevel* processes. These processes very well could have operated independently or even in opposing directions. For example, it is possible for either of the following two, seemingly contradictory, scenarios to prevail:

SCENARIO 1. Success by blacks at the macrolevel (for example, within specific geographic areas or time periods) increased the frequency of mob violence, but, at the microlevel, relatively successful black individuals were not disproportionately represented among lynch victims.

SCENARIO 2. Success by blacks at the macrolevel was unrelated to the frequency of mob violence within specific areas or time periods, but, at the microlevel, relatively successful black individuals were more likely than their less successful neighbors to be victimized by lynch mobs.

Most prior empirical research has focused on macrolevel processes and has demonstrated that lynching was more intense in areas where, and during time periods when, southern whites were socially and economically threatened by southern blacks, especially when the interests of poor and wealthy whites aligned. But most investigators who have inferred a positive association between macrolevel status threats from African Americans and the intensity of mob violence have been careful to avoid committing an "ecological fallacy" (Robinson 1950) by concluding that it necessarily was higher-status blacks who were disproportionately lynched. In contrast, no systematic research has been done at the microlevel to determine if more successful black men were disproportionately targeted by southern lynch mobs. That is our goal in the remainder of this chapter.

Victims Challenging the Southern Racial Hierarchy

To the extent that lynching was used as a means of threatening members of the southern black community who challenged the prevailing racial hierarchy, we might expect to find a systematic link between characteristics suggestive of higher social or economic status and vulnerability to lynching. As with our analyses in chapter 4, we are somewhat constrained in this effort by the limited number of characteristics recorded in the census manuscripts that we can marshal to help answer this question. Using census data, we cannot identify, for example, that Sterling Thompson held an influential political position and refused to turn over his land to the white men who wanted it. We similarly cannot determine that the assault of which Steve Jenkins was accused developed out of an argument over the terms of a labor contract, or discern whether Jenkins had a history of advocating for his own rights. We have gleaned this information about Mr. Jenkins and Mr. Thompson from newspaper articles. Not all journalistic reports included the same level of detail about victims or the circumstances surrounding their murder.

However, several pieces of information that are available in the census records should provide valuable insights into the relative positions of individual black men within the southern stratification system. These include measures linked to economic status, social standing, occupational status, human capital, and possible markers of upward mobility. Specifically, we use racial classification, home and farm ownership, occupational status, and literacy to help determine whether the similarities between the lynchings of Sterling Thompson and Steve Jenkins reflect broader patterns in susceptibility to racial violence. Replicating our work in chapter 4, we use logistic regression analyses to identify whether these factors predict the likelihood that an individual was victimized, how large of an effect each of the characteristics had on the probability of being lynched, and whether the size of that effect is variable across local contexts.

RACIAL CLASSIFICATION

We take advantage of the Census Bureau's distinction between "mulattos" and "blacks" or "Negros" in the 1880, 1910, and 1920 censuses to allow for the possibility of status differences between lynch victims and in the comparison sample of non-victims. Racial stratification regarding European-origin and African-origin Americans in the United States relied very heavily on the "one-drop rule" during the late nineteenth and early twentieth centuries. By this criterion, anyone with a hint of African heritage was considered black, "Negro," "colored," Afro-American, African American, or whatever pan-African label was in current usage in a given time period. And, on average, membership in the white racial category was associated with socioeconomic standing that was superior to that for members of the nonwhite racial category. The "one-drop rule" that defined the racial classification system in the United States during the lynching era can be contrasted with the less dichotomous approach that has prevailed in Brazil, for example, where multiple racial categories are used, based largely on skin tone (see, for example, Gullickson and Torche 2014; Marteleto 2014; Telles 2004). Even in Brazil, however, skin tone has been shown to be related to socioeconomic standing on a variety of indicators. Our distinction between "mulattos" and blacks/"Negroes" is based on the assumption that similar gradations of socioeconomic status existed by skin tone in the American South during the time period we examine. The availability of the "mulatto" racial category in 1880, 1910, and 1920 permits us to test that assumption.

As discussed in chapter 3, the "mulatto" classification was legally defined in biological terms, but there is evidence to suggest that it was also linked to social status. Mixed-race people were overrepresented in higher-status occupations, and, as discussed in chapter 3, Aliya Saperstein and Aaron Gullickson (2013) have found that the racial classification assigned to individuals during the time period we are interested in was somewhat fluid. Specifically, they demonstrate that men who were enumerated as "black/Negro" in one census were more likely to be enumerated as "mulatto" in the subsequent census if they experienced *upward* occupational mobility during the decade. Conversely, men who were enumerated as "mulatto" in one census were more likely to be enumerated as "black/Negro" in the next census if they experienced *downward* occupational mobility. Both Sterling Thompson and Steve Jenkins were recorded in the census records as being "black" rather than "mulatto." It should be noted, however, that in 1900 the Census Bureau racial categorization scheme considered all people with any African ancestry to be "black," so Mr. Thompson may well have been considered a "mulatto" within his community but just not recorded as such.

There was no such omission in the case of Weakly Ridly, a fifteen-year-old "mulatto" boy enumerated in the 1880 census living in Civil District No. 6 in Crockett County, Tennessee, with his widowed mother and three younger sisters. Crockett County lies in the far western section of Tennessee, about eighty miles northeast of Memphis. Weakly is recorded as being able to read and write and had attended school within the past year. His nine-year-old sister, Mosella, also attended school but apparently had not yet learned to read or write. In addition to Weakly, his mother, Rosalee; sister Mosella; and the one-year-old baby, Margaret, are listed as "mulatto," while the eldest daughter, thirteen-year-old Rebecca, is classified as "black." Rebecca was able to read but not to write and did not attend school during the year prior to the census enumeration. Both Rebecca and Weakly worked as farm laborers. On March 29, 1886, when he would have been just twenty-one years old, Weakly Ridly and a black man named Tobe Williams were accused of murdering a white man. While they were being held in jail in the town of Alamo, in Crockett County, a group estimated at 100 men overpowered the jailer and shot Weakly and Tobe to death in their jail cell (*Memphis Appeal*, March 30, 1886).

Mixed-race members of the black community, like Weakly Ridly, posed a particular challenge to the dualistic and hierarchical racial ideology prevailing among white southerners. On the one hand, the people who were enumerated in the census as "mulatto" had demonstrable familial and biological relationships with members of the white community, perhaps originating in the distant past. On the other hand, mixed-race people literally embodied the idea of racial equality—or at least their physical existence posed a challenge to the notion that people with their ancestral origins on the continents of Africa and Europe were destined by God to perform different social functions. Being of mixed racial heritage, then, might be expected to confer protection, or to increase the individual risk of victimization, depending on which of these ideologies prevailed in a particular time and place. We test whether being specifically identified as having mixed racial heritage served to increase an individual's likelihood for exposure to racial violence or served as a protective factor. If African American men classified as "mulatto" were considered by whites to have higher social standing than men classified as black or "Negro," and if social and economic success increased the likelihood of victimization, then we should expect to find a positive relationship between "mulatto" racial status and lynching.[2] However, if "mulatto" racial classification was a signal of stronger connections to the local community, especially the white community, then it is possible that "mulattos" were less likely to be lynched than were men who were enumerated as black or "Negro."[3]

LITERACY

Perhaps no issue provided greater evidence of the black community's efforts at upward mobility and broader social incorporation than the increasing levels of literacy among southern blacks in the late nineteenth and early twentieth centuries. The public provision of education within the states of the former Confederacy lagged far behind that occurring in northern and western states well into the twentieth century, for both blacks and whites. As a consequence, illiteracy was common among both blacks and economically disadvantaged whites in the South. Both Sterling Thompson and Weakly Ridly were able to read and write—and, given their ages and the years in which they were killed, they must have learned when reading was an uncommon skill among southern blacks. Perhaps in Mr. Thompson's case, a special effort was required to gain literacy in adulthood. Reading had been widely discouraged among enslaved blacks—and indeed, in nearly all southern states, teaching a slave to read was a criminal act (Elkins 1959). Literacy provided newly emancipated blacks with access to knowledge about the world outside the South, gave them the ability to more fully understand the labor contracts to which they were subject, and, at least in theory, qualified them for a broader array of occupations than the agricultural, domestic service, and menial labor positions typically reserved for blacks. Indeed, in the case of Steve Jenkins, his *inability* to read and write likely increased his level of disadvantage in the process of negotiating and settling his labor contract with the presumably literate white planter. Southern blacks connected the ability to read and write with upward mobility and attempted to tackle the issue head-on—both as individuals and as a community. Black churches offered literacy classes for children and adults, and local black communities pooled their meager resources to build schools and hire teachers (Anderson 1988; Frazier 1964; Montgomery 1992). As a result, as described in chapter 3, the literacy rate among southern African Americans increased sharply during the late nineteenth and early twentieth centuries, and their disadvantage relative to whites shrank substantially.

Passionate public debates regarding the appropriate level of education for black children and the relationship between education and blacks' place in society raged throughout the late nineteenth and early twentieth centuries. Perhaps the most prominent contributors to the discussion were W. E. B. Du Bois and Booker T. Washington. Du Bois, the first African American to earn a doctoral degree at Harvard and a founding member of the NAACP, argued that "uplifting the race" required heavy investment in classical education for the most promising among the black community. He termed these bright stars the "talented tenth," and he encouraged black parents to think beyond preparing their children for occupations in agriculture and personal service. Washington held an equally exalted place within American culture as president of the Tuskegee Institute. Unlike Du Bois, however, Washington focused on a more gradational approach for black assimilation and advancement. With the backing of many wealthy white philanthropists, Washington's educational proscription for the African American community focused on attaining the basic skills needed for industrial employment and implementing a more scientific approach to agriculture. In Washington's view, economic security could allow blacks to gain "arm's length" acceptance from whites—a status perhaps eventually approaching economic parity but not one that sought integration or social equality. Yet, while Du Bois and Washington may have differed in their assessment of the value of higher education for southern blacks, they certainly agreed on the importance of attaining basic literacy.[4]

The rapid pace at which the black community gained on southern whites, however, minimized the objective status differences between the two groups—particularly when blacks were compared to disadvantaged whites. Literacy, then, was likely to have been seen by some whites as a direct threat to white supremacy, and being able to read and write may have increased black men's vulnerability to racial violence. The temporal patterning in the percentage of lynch victims who were reported to have been literate and the literacy rate among the comparison sample of black men reflect broader trends in literacy throughout the South, as discussed in chapter 3. In the 1880 census, only one in four lynch victims, as well as an equivalent fraction of men in the comparison sample aged ten and older, was able to read and write. By the 1920 census, nearly 70 percent of both groups were literate. Differences in literacy between lynch victims and the comparison sample were quite small in each of the five decades that we investigated, and, indeed, when comparing the entire sample, we found that 45 percent of victims and 47 percent of non-victims were able to read and write. We used each man's reported ability to both read and write as a means of determining whether vulnerability to racial violence increased for those who challenged this dimension of the dominance of whites in southern society.

Literacy may have taken on different meanings for specific individuals, depending on whether being able to read and write was a relatively common or a relatively rare skill in their local community. It is possible that literacy for black men was of special concern to some elements within the white population when the overall level of black literacy was high. A highly literate black population would have seemed to contradict prevailing stereotypes of African Americans as ignorant and of limited intellect. It is equally plausible, however, that being one of only a few literate black men would have become a mark of distinction and perhaps raised suspicions of political activism or that one was encouraging local blacks to join the Great Migration's exodus to northern cities. We assess how the individual ability to read and write may have differentially affected vulnerability to racial violence in different local contexts based on overall levels of literacy.

OCCUPATIONAL STATUS

In chapter 4 we explored the relationship between employment in the agricultural sector and individual-level vulnerability to lynching. We found that agricultural workers were exposed to a significantly higher risk of lynching than were nonagricultural workers, but only in areas with lower concentrations of agricultural employment among black men. It is possible, however, that holding a higher- or lower-status occupation also had an important influence on who was targeted for racial violence. For example, a black man who owned and farmed his own land might have posed a much greater threat to white dominance than a black man who was employed as a farm laborer. Likewise, a black teacher or lawyer could have been viewed as having committed a more serious status transgression through his educational and occupational accomplishments than a black man who worked as a janitor in a local bank or as a servant in a white household.

To identify how occupational status might have been related to an individual's risk of lynching, we classified each of the occupations that were reported for both the lynch victims and for other black men living in the counties where they were lynched. Individuals were classified as having a lower-status job, a higher-status job, or not participating in the labor force, using the same taxonomy that we used in chapter 3. In light of the preliminary bivariate evidence presented in chapter 3, which indicated that victimization was greater for men with lower occupational status in both the agricultural and nonagricultural sectors,[5] we simplify the following analyses by focusing on occupational status regardless of employment sector. Finally, we continue to identify separately men who were not engaged in the labor force, even though they were not observed in chapter 4 to have a risk of victimization that was significantly different from either agricultural or nonagricultural workers.

HOME OWNERSHIP

At the end of the Civil War very few southern African Americans owned property. This was largely because the vast majority of them, over 4 million, had been enslaved and legally prohibited from owning land. However, the general poverty of the southern black population in the decades following the war also limited their ability to acquire property over subsequent decades. By the time the first U.S. Census recorded the ownership of residential dwellings in 1900, roughly 20 percent of southern blacks were homeowners. Considering the social, economic, and political circumstances that prevailed in the region between 1865 and 1900, the increase in property ownership by African Americans—from essentially zero to nearly one in every five households—is quite impressive, as was the parallel steep increase in their ability to read and write.

Because the southern African American population remained over-whelmingly rural throughout the late nineteenth and early twentieth centuries, most of the dwellings owned by blacks were located on farms. Although the levels of farm ownership among southern whites during this time period far surpassed those for southern blacks, nearly 40 percent of white farmers rented or sharecropped the land that they cultivated. In an agricultural economy in which status was significantly influenced by land ownership and in which society was sharply strati-fied by race, the 20 percent of black farmers who owned their property served as a powerful affront to the 40 percent of white farmers who did not. Based on their analysis of county-level data, Tolnay and Beck (1995, 149–60) conclude that the racial and economic threat represented by southern black farm ownership served as a catalyst for mob violence, es-pecially within areas where cotton production was dominant. However, no previous research, including the work by Tolnay and Beck, has been able to determine whether property ownership increased the probability of victimization for *individual* blacks—as opposed to inferring a con-nection between the macrolevel conditions of white farm tenancy and the intensity of lynching. That is, we do not yet know whether black property owners were more likely than their landless neighbors to be targeted by lynch mobs.

Inventories of southern black lynch victims include very few cases like that of Sterling Thompson, in which the surviving details of the incident suggest that the mob was directly motivated by an interest in obtaining the land (or property) of the victim or his family. That lack of evidence alone might lead us to believe that black property owners were not exposed to an elevated risk of mob violence. However, two considerations leave us unwilling to embrace that conclusion without additional empirical evidence. First, we know that the reported motiva-tions of southern mobs provide an incomplete and potentially unreliable account of what actually happened during a given episode of lynching or why it happened. Second, and more important, until now we have not known whether individual lynch victims owned or rented their property.

Local tensions arising from property ownership by blacks do seem to have been implicated in some well-known cases of southern mob vio-lence against African Americans. On September 9, 1912, for example, Rob Edwards was lynched in Cumming, Georgia, the county seat of Forsyth County, located due north of Atlanta.[6] After Mr. Edwards was shot and killed by the mob that stormed the Forsyth County jail, his body was dragged behind a wagon, mutilated, and hanged by members of the white mob from a telephone pole "as if mounting a trophy to celebrate their handiwork" (Jaspin 2007, 128). Mr. Edwards had been implicated by his friend Ernest Knox in the brutal beating and rape of Mae Crow, an eighteen-year-old white girl from Oscarville, Georgia. Ms. Crow later died of her injuries. In a subsequent trial, Ernest Knox and Oscar Daniel were convicted of being Edwards's accomplices during the attack on Mae Crow and were sentenced to death. It was this incident involving the rape and murder of Mae Crow that helped to precipitate an intense, and ultimately successful, effort by the whites in Forsyth County to drive all blacks out of the county.

To be sure, the lynching of Rob Edwards, and the death sentences handed down to Ernest Knox and Oscar Daniel, cannot be directly connected to white resentment over black land ownership in Forsyth County. What transpired in the years to follow, however, might have been directly connected. The threatening atmosphere that was created by whites in Forsyth County forced many black families to flee the area before they had a chance to sell their land. Careful archival research done by Elliot Jaspin (2007) reveals that, in many cases, the title to land that was abandoned by blacks was later obtained by whites in Forsyth County, in some cases by unknown or nefarious mechanisms. As a result, a substantial amount of wealth changed hands—from black families to white families—due to the racial "cleansing" of Forsyth County that ensued after the death of Mae Crow.

In *The Tragedy of Lynching*, Arthur Raper describes in some detail an episode of racial conflict that occurred in Sumter County, Alabama. Like the events that took place in Forsyth County, Georgia, it is possible that underlying resentment over the economic success of local blacks helped to fuel the crisis in Sumter County. During a two-day period in 1930, from July 4 to July 5, three black men, one black woman, and two white men died. The violence was the result of clashes that originated over the sale of a car battery by Clarence Boyd, a white man, to Esau Robinson, a black man. Mr. Boyd accused Mr. Robinson of failing to pay for the battery. After Clarence Boyd removed the battery from Esau Robinson's car, a confrontation between two groups of men resulted in the death of Grover Boyd, Clarence's uncle. Esau Robinson was detained and later shot to death by a mob composed of men from Sumter County and nearby communities in neighboring Mississippi. As described by Raper ([1933] 1969, 61), "a rope was then placed about the neck of the corpse and it was pulled into a half-suspended position by the roadside so that passing Negroes could see it. The grim warning remained in this position until Saturday noon, July 5. It is reported that when the sheriff ordered the body taken down several white men rushed forward for souvenirs and that one cut off an ear."

Following the lynching of Esau Robinson, two more black men and one black woman would be killed in Sumter County as local whites organized in unofficial posses and roamed throughout the area in search of the other men who were present during the confrontation that resulted in Grover Boyd's death. A second white man was also killed, most likely shot by another member of the white mob as he stormed the house of a local black family. After the events of July 4 and 5, a climate of extreme racial tension developed as groups of white men continued to terrorize local blacks.

Again, as in the incident that precipitated the racial cleansing of Forsyth County, Georgia, there is no conclusive evidence that Esau Robinson's lynching was directly motivated by resentment over the prospering of local blacks in Sumter County, Alabama, including their ownership of property. Despite the fact that Mr. Robinson came from a relatively well-to-do landowning family in Sumter County, it is difficult to connect the family's success directly to his death—or to Clarence Boyd's decision to remove the battery from Esau Robinson's car. However, also reminiscent of the aftermath of the lynching of Rob Edwards in Forsyth County, black landowners in Sumter County had good reason to be concerned about the atmosphere of terror and intimidation that followed the eruption of violence in the summer of 1930. Recognizing their vulnerability to the marauding white mobs, some sought the protection of prominent white families. Others left. But, even more broadly, as noted by Raper ([1933] 1969, 83–84), black property owners in the county were "far from being independent farmers. Their avenue into ownership, as well as their security in ownership, was and is contingent upon their being acceptable; and being acceptable in this black belt county means that they will be punctiliously servile to the whites and find no fault with existing educational, social, political and economic conditions."

To investigate more directly the possibility that property ownership by southern blacks increased their vulnerability to targeting by lynch mobs, we take advantage of information that was collected in the 1900, 1910, and 1920 U.S. Censuses. For each household that was enumerated, the census recorded whether the dwelling in which its members resided was "owned" or "rented." We further distinguish between nonfarm and farm residences to construct the following four-category measure of property ownership: (1) farm owner, (2) farm renter, (3) nonfarm owner, and (4) nonfarm renter. This follows the distinction that we introduced in chapter 3 and allows us to determine whether property ownership had different consequences for the likelihood of victimization for farm and nonfarm families.

Evidence of Individual-Level Risk Factors for Lynching

As in chapter 4, we begin with the "naive" analyses of individual-level indicators of social standing that may have affected the risk of lynching. Recall that this naive approach does not adjust our estimates for the fact that the status-linked predictors of victimization may themselves be correlated. For example, being of mixed-race status and having a higher-status occupation may each be independently predictive of whether a man of color was targeted for racial violence. It is also possible, however, that census enumerators were more likely to list higher-status blacks as having mixed racial origins, or that because of their stronger familial relationships with the white community, mixed-race blacks enjoyed advantages in the hiring and (to the extent that they existed) promotion processes. This could mean, then, that it is necessary to simultaneously consider both mixed-race status and employment classification in order to disentangle the effects of each on the likelihood of mob victimization. That is the objective of the "refined" approach to follow. Our naive approach separately examines the effects of mixed-race status, literacy, occupational status, and home ownership on the likelihood of being lynched while controlling only for the decade of lynching, the age of the victim, and the number of black and mixed-race men enumerated in the county in which the lynching took place. This is identical to the approach that we used in chapter 4 to assess the naive relationships between indicators of social marginality and the probability of being lynched.

The evidence derived from the naive approach presented in Figure 5.1 indicates, once again, that southern mobs did not select their victims at random from the general population of adult black men. However, we

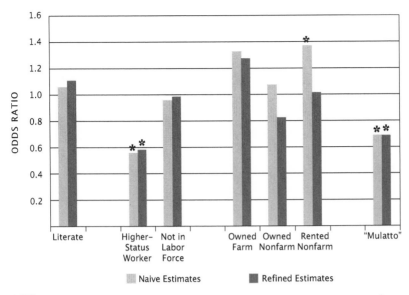

NOTE:
Odds Ratios that are statistically significant at *p* < .05 are denoted by an asterisk. Reference group for literate is illiterate. Reference group for higher–status worker and not in labor force is lower–status worker. Reference group for owned farm, owned nonfarm, and rented nonfarm is rented farm. Reference group for "mulatto" is black. These models also adjust for age, age squared, decade of lynching, and number of black men in the county of lynching.

Figure 5.1 Naive and Refined Relationships between Individual-Level Characteristics of Social Standing and the Likelihood of Being Lynched, 1882–1929

find no support for the hypothesis that successful black men were more likely to be victimized. Indeed, those relationships that are statistically significant suggest exactly the opposite—that higher socioeconomic status offered some *protection* from mob violence. In order to summarize the evidence we obtain from these logistic regression models, we continue to focus on Odds Ratios (which we abbreviate as OR). Again, an Odds Ratio of 1.0 (OR = 1.0) indicates that the individual-level characteristic is unrelated to the likelihood of being lynched. In other words, possessing the quality of interest (for example, literacy) is unrelated to the probability of victimization. Odds Ratios below 1.0 suggest a *reduced* vulnerability for black men with the focal characteristic, while Odds Ratios above 1.0 suggest an *elevated* risk.

According to the naive evidence, being able to read and write did not significantly affect black men's danger of victimization compared to those who were illiterate (OR = 1.06). Men with higher-status occupations, conversely, were less vulnerable than those with lower-status jobs (OR = 0.55) or those who were not gainfully employed (not reported in Figure 5.1). Home ownership, either of farm (OR = 1.32) or nonfarm residences (OR = 1.07), did not expose black men to a greater likelihood of being lynched than was experienced by those who rented farms. These Odds Ratios are greater than 1.0 (indicative of no relationship), but the differences from that value are not statistically significant at the $p < .05$ level (or a confidence level of 95 percent). "Mulatto" men were significantly less likely to be lynched than men who were enumerated as black or "Negro" (OR = 0.69).

Turning to the refined view, we find that simultaneously considering multiple measures of socioeconomic status has little influence on the evidence or the conclusions drawn from it.[7] Rather, the refined evidence continues to show that it was lower-status black men, rather than their more successful neighbors, who were more likely to be lynched. Higher-status workers were roughly one half (OR = 0.58) as likely as lower-status workers to be targeted by mobs. "Mulatto" men were exposed to only two-thirds (OR = 0.69) the level of risk that faced their similarly situated black/"Negro" counterparts. Neither home ownership nor literacy was useful for distinguishing lynch victims from non-victims, according to the refined view.

To sum up, the main conclusions that are suggested by our estimates of the refined relationships between the likelihood of being lynched and the measures of social standing of black men included in Figure 5.1 are as follows:

- In general, higher-status black men *were not* subjected to higher levels of mob violence than were lower-status black men.
- Men with higher-status occupations were significantly *less likely* to be lynched than men with lower-status occupations and those who were not in the labor force.
- African American men who were enumerated in the census as "mulattos" were significantly *less likely* to be lynched than men enumerated as "black" or "Negro."

When we combine the information contained in Figure 5.1 with the general conclusions drawn in chapter 4, a profile of the individual-level characteristics that placed southern black men at greater risk of mob violence begins to crystalize. That is, the empirical evidence strongly suggests that lower-status men who were weakly embedded within their local communities had the most to fear. However, we also observed in chapter 4 that the influence of social marginality on the likelihood of victimization varied markedly across the South—specifically, social marginality was a more powerful risk factor in communities where marginality was less common. Perhaps the conclusions that we have drawn thus far regarding the relationship between social standing and the risk of being lynched will also require elaboration after we relax the strong assumption that their importance was uniform throughout the South.

Evidence of the Contextual Conditioning of Individual-Level Risk Factors

The consequences of social standing, high or low, for the risk of victimization by southern mobs could have varied by the overall status of black men in the local community. For example, perhaps economically successful black men were more likely to stand out in areas where most black men struggled to feed and house their families. In contrast, in communities where higher social status was more common within the black population, such success might have been considered more routine. Furthermore, perhaps mobs feared potentially stronger negative responses, from both white and black residents, to their targeting of more successful blacks in locales where the black population held greater human and economic capital—for example, more education and property ownership. These possibilities are not allowed for by the naive and refined estimates of the relationship between *individual* socioeconomic status and the likelihood of being lynched presented in Figure 5.1.

We now relax the assumption that the same degree of association between social standing and the risk of victimization prevailed throughout the South. As described in greater detail in chapter 4, we do this by using the 1 percent PUMS files from the separate decennial censuses to construct county-level equivalents to the individual-level characteristics that were considered in Figure 5.1. For example, we calculate the percentage of adult black men in the county who were literate or classified in the census as "mulatto" rather than as "black" or "Negro." With those contextual measures in hand, we then augment the logistic regression model that was used to produce the refined estimates in Figure 5.1 by including "interaction terms" that are obtained through the simple multiplication of the individual-level characteristic (for example, literacy) by its county-level equivalent (for example, the percentage of adult black males who were literate). The results of this augmented logistic regression model, specifically the statistical significance of the estimated coefficient for the multiplicative interaction terms, tell us whether the relationship between an individual-level characteristic and the likelihood of being lynched was conditioned by the prevalence of the same characteristic within the county. In short, were there some subregional areas within the South where higher-status black men were exposed to a greater risk of mob violence than their lower-status neighbors and other subregional areas in which they were not?

The summary contained in Table 5.1 reveals strong evidence of community-level variability in the importance of social standing for the risk of victimization. Only the difference in the likelihood of being lynched between those residing on rented farms and rented nonfarms can be considered to have been invariant across the South (that is, the interaction is not statistically significant). For all other measures of social standing, a greater prevalence of a given characteristic within the local black population exerted downward pressure on the Odds Ratio. These findings echo those from chapter 4 in which we found that the consequences of social marginality for the risk of being lynched were weaker in counties where social marginality was more common. However, in order to appreciate the full importance of relaxing the assumption of a "uniform South," it is necessary to examine the appropriate Odds Ratio at varying levels of prevalence for each of the county-level characteristics. By doing so we can determine in what types of locations each measure of social standing (1) *increased* the likelihood of mob victimization, (2) *decreased* the likelihood of mob victimization, or (3) was *unrelated* to the risk of being lynched.

Figure 5.2 shows the relationship between each individual-level measure of social standing and the risk of victimization (as summarized by the Odds Ratio) at three separate locations along the distribution of the county-level equivalent—the 25th, 50th, and 75th percentiles. Recall that percentiles correspond to the percentage of all counties with a smaller value on that measure. So, for example, a county with a literacy rate at the 25th percentile has a *higher* rate of literacy than only one-quarter of the counties in our analysis. A county with a literacy rate at the 75th per-

Table 5.1 Summary of Evidence of Contextual Variation in the Relationship between Individual-Level Characteristics of Social Standing and the Likelihood of Being Lynched, 1882–1929

Individual-Level Characteristic	Evidence of Contextual Variation?	Direction of Contextual Variation
Literacy	Yes	Odds Ratio declines with increasing concentration
Higher-Status Worker	Yes	Odds Ratio declines with increasing concentration
Not in Labor Force	Yes	Odds Ratio declines with increasing concentration
"Mulatto"	Yes	Odds Ratio declines with increasing concentration
Owned Farm	Yes	Odds Ratio declines with increasing concentration
Owned Nonfarm	Yes	Odds Ratio declines with increasing concentration
Rented Nonfarm	No	Not applicable

centile has a higher literacy rate than do three-quarters of the counties, and so on.[8] A given personal characteristic, then, is more common within the local community at the 75th percentile than at the 25th percentile. This follows the identical approach that we used in chapter 4 to examine subregional variation in the association between social marginality and the likelihood of being lynched.

In a few cases, the Odds Ratios reported in Figure 5.2 change the story relatively little from the one told by the Odds Ratios in the refined view. For example, in all settings, higher-status workers enjoyed a significantly lower risk of lynching than did lower-status workers, although the degree of protection offered by higher-status jobs varied by local context (for example, men with higher-status jobs had more protection at the 75th percentile than at the 25th percentile). In other respects, however, important differences emerge, some of which alter the story considerably. Perhaps of greatest significance is the evidence that is suggestive of greater vulnerability for black men of higher social standing only *in certain kinds of locales*. Specifically, farm owners were significantly more

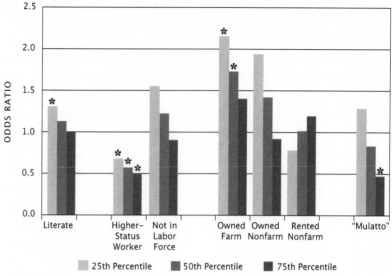

Figure 5.2 Variation in Relationship between Individual-Level Characteristics of Social Standing and the Likelihood of Being Lynched, by County Context, 1882–1929

likely to be lynched than were farm renters at both the 25th and 50th percentiles of black and mixed-race farm ownership within the county. In addition, although literacy failed to evince a significant relationship with the likelihood of being lynched according to either the naive or refined estimates in Figure 5.1, Figure 5.2 reveals that those men who could read and write were exposed to significantly higher risks of victimization in settings where literacy was less common (that is, at the 25th percentile and below). Finally, the protection offered by "mulatto" status that was evident in both the naive and refined estimates was apparently restricted to communities with larger concentrations of mixed-race populations (that is, at the 75th percentile and above).

    In light of the evidence of substantial areal variation in the relationship between social standing and the likelihood of being lynched contained in Figure 5.2, we once again attempt to identify more precisely the contextual conditions under which the separate indicators of individual-level socioeconomic status operated as either risk or protective factors for targeting by mobs. We do this by expanding the approach used in Figure 5.2 by estimating the respective Odds Ratios at each decile in the distribution of the appropriate county-level characteristic. We also include the 25th and 75th percentiles for continuity with Figure 5.2. Again, this approach is identical to the one we took in chapter 4 to more precisely determine the types of locations in which social marginality increased the risk of being lynched. We summarize this evidence in Table 5.2 by using a negative sign ($-$) to indicate a statistically significant *negative* relationship (at $p < .05$) between the individual-level characteristics and the likelihood of victimization; a positive sign ($+$) is used to represent a statistically significant *positive* relationship. Cells that contain neither a "$-$" nor a "$+$" correspond to places in the distribution of the county-level characteristic where the relationship between victimization and the individual-level indicator of social standing is statistically nonsignificant.

A fascinating general pattern of subregional variation in the relationship between the social standing of black men and their risk of mob violence is discernible in Table 5.2. The key patterns can be summarized as follows:

- More successful black men, at least as measured by higher-status occupations, were significantly less likely than their less successful neighbors to be lynched *in counties with a larger concentration of higher-status blacks.*
- *Where successful blacks were in shorter supply*, higher-status individuals, as represented by property ownership, literacy, and, to a lesser extent, "mulatto" racial classification, were actually exposed to a higher risk of mob violence than were their lower-status neighbors.
- Individual-level qualities that significantly increased the risk of victimization in some settings were quite benign in other locales (for example, literacy and farm ownership).
- "Mulatto" racial status served to reduce the likelihood of lynching in communities with higher percentages of mixed-race people but offered no protection in other areas.

By allowing for the strength of the relationship between the risk of being lynched and the individual-level indicators of social standing to vary by the relative concentration of those same characteristics within the local black population, a much richer, and also more accurate, story

Table 5.2 Relationships between Individual-Level Characteristics of Social Standing and the Likelihood of Being Lynched, by Percentiles of Their County-Level Equivalents, 1882–1929

Individual-Level Characteristic	Percentile for County-Level Characteristics										
	10th	20th	25th	30th	40th	50th	60th	70th	75th	80th	90th
Literate (Ref. Illiterate)	+	+	+	+							
Higher-status Worker		−	−	−	−	−	−	−	−	−	−
Not in Labor Force (Ref. Lower-Status Worker)	+										
Mulatto (Ref. Black/Negro)	+						−	−	−	−	−
Owned Farm	+	+	+	+	+	+	+				
Owned Nonfarm											
Rented Nonfarm											
(Ref. Rented Farm)											

Note:

+ denotes statistically significant positive relationship ($p < .05$) between individual-level characteristics and likelihood of lynching.

− denotes statistically significant negative relationship ($p < .05$) between individual-level characteristics and likelihood of lynching.

emerges from the statistical evidence. In short, the consequences of social standing for black men—in terms of their likelihood of being targeted by lynch mobs—were strongly conditioned by the nature of the local community and the average social standing of black men within it.

Putting Some Pieces Together

The evidence regarding the role of social standing in helping to determine the targeting of lynch victims by southern mobs shares a number of similarities with the parallel evidence regarding the importance of social marginality reported in chapter 4. For example, higher-status workers enjoyed lower levels of victimization across virtually all types of communities. This was also true of the protective influence of being a married household head that we observed in chapter 4. In contrast, the relationship between the probability of victimization and other measures of social standing—for instance, literacy, "mulatto" racial classification, and farm ownership—varied across different types of contexts. This was also found in chapter 4 for being born out of state and for employment in the agricultural sector. The emerging picture of the individual-level characteristics that determined southern black men's susceptibility to mob violence, then, is not a simple one. It now seems clear that the risk of victimization was significantly related to a variety of personal characteristics—those related both to social marginality and to social standing. We are comfortable, therefore, in soundly rejecting the notion that lynch victims were selected at random from among the general population of adult black males. Furthermore, the existence and strength of the relationships between victimization and individual-level characteristics—whether reflective of social marginality or social standing—were powerfully shaped by the nature of the local community.

At this point, it is reasonable to ask whether the principal conclusions that we have reached thus far would be altered substantially if we simultaneously considered indicators of social marginality and social standing within the same empirical analysis. For some personal characteristics, it would seem implausible to claim that their influence was the spurious result of measures from the other "domain." For example, one would be hard-pressed to argue that the heightened vulnerability of farm owners in some locales was really due to their greater social marginality. If anything, farm owners were more established in their communities than were those who did not own property. Likewise, it would require tortured logic to claim that the variable relationship between being born out of state and the likelihood of victimization—positive where interstate migrants were less common and negative where there were more of them—was actually a result of social standing (see Table 4.2). Nonetheless, we have conducted extensive supplemental analyses to investigate the possibility that the conclusions we have drawn from the empirical evidence in this chapter and in chapter 4 are actually due to the contamination of personal characteristics from the other domain.[9]

Our investigation of the robustness of our empirical evidence and the conclusions we have drawn from them consisted primarily of (1) including measures of social standing in those analyses that were designed to assess the association between social marginality and the risk of victimization (as we examined in chapter 4) and (2) including measures of social marginality in the analyses of the influence of social standing (in the analyses conducted for this chapter). For example, we reexamined the significantly lower level of vulnerability of married heads of households while simultaneously accounting for literacy and occupational status. Conversely, we considered whether the observed relationships for "mulatto" racial classification, literacy, and property ownership withstood the simultaneous consideration of out-of-state birth and the protective influence of being a married household head. Because of the complex nature of the evidence that constitutes the basis for our substantive conclusions (that is, drawn largely from statistical interactions), it is insufficient to simply add additional control variables to the refined models and then observe any changes in the Odds Ratios. Rather, we replicated the analyses represented in Table 4.2 and Table 5.2 that estimate each relationship between an individual-level characteristic and the likelihood of being lynched at various percentiles in the distribution of the county-level equivalent of the personal characteristic. We then compared the Odds Ratios and p-values that we originally obtained (that is, when only additional variables from the same domain—for example, social marginality—were included) with the new Odds Ratios and p-values from the supplementary analyses (that is, those that also included variables from the other domain).[10]

Given the very large number of Odds Ratios and p-values involved in the analysis of the robustness of our original analyses, it is implausible to present and discuss them all. Therefore, we provide an overview of the key findings. In the large majority of cases, the original evidence prevails when the analyses are expanded to simultaneously consider personal characteristics from both domains of predictors. That is, the Odds Ratios and p-values upon which Table 4.2 and Table 5.2 were based continue to tell the same story—with respect to both the direction (positive or negative) and the statistical significance (that is, whether significant at $p < .05$) of the relationships.

Three exceptions to the general pattern of similar results deserve mention. First, when literacy and occupational status are included in the analysis of the relationship between social marginality and the likelihood of being lynched, the positive and statistically significant effect of being an agricultural worker that was originally observed from the

10th through the 30th percentiles extends through the 50th percentile—meaning that the risk associated with being an agricultural worker was elevated for men living in counties with percentages of agricultural workers at or below the median. Second, the original relationship between being unrelated to the head of the household and the risk of victimization changes at several locations along the distribution of the county-level concentration of similar individuals. That is, the positive relationship originally observed at the 10th through 30th percentiles becomes nonsignificant, and the relationship becomes significantly negative at the 75th percentile. Recall that a negative relationship would indicate a lower likelihood of victimization than was experienced by married heads of households. Perhaps this reflects a "real" source of protection for unrelated household residents from mob violence. We cannot reject that possibility with the data at our disposal. However, we are more inclined to attribute the volatility in the nature of the relationship between our original evidence and the supplementary analysis to the very small number of such individuals in the data set—especially among the lynch victims. Third, when "mulatto" racial classification is included in the analysis of the relationship between an out-of-state birth and the likelihood of being lynched, the originally observed positive effect of interstate migration at the 10th through 30th percentiles becomes statistically nonsignificant. The relationship remains positive in direction but fails to attain significance at the $p < .05$ level. One possible reason for these differences from the original evidence might be the restricted sample that is required to include "mulatto" racial classification, which is not available in the 1900 census (see endnote 10).

In sum, despite the few departures from our original evidence, we take considerable reassurance from the overall similarity of the results from our supplementary investigation of the robustness of our findings and the conclusions that we have gleaned from them. In general, they increase our confidence that the relationships we have observed between the individual-level characteristics measuring social marginality and social standing and the likelihood of being targeted by southern mobs are "real" and not the result of the contaminating influence of variables from the other domain of predictors. That being said, the less robust nature of the effects of an out-of-state birth at the lowest concentrations of that personal characteristic when "mulatto" status is included in the model and any inferences regarding the relative vulnerability of individuals who were unrelated to the head of the household should be interpreted with caution.

Concluding Comments

Our primary objective in this chapter has been to determine whether black and mixed-race men with higher social standing were exposed to a greater probability of mob violence than were their lower-status neighbors. When we considered only the individual-level information available to us for the victims and a sample of non-victims, the answer appeared to be "no." Both the naive and refined relationships contained in Figure 5.1 suggest that "mulatto" men and those with higher-status occupations were actually significantly *less* likely to be lynched than their lower-status counterparts. That evidence offered little reason to conclude that more successful black men were disproportionately targeted by southern mobs.

Having learned in chapter 4 that the relationship between social marginality and the likelihood of victimization varied throughout the South, we allowed for the same intraregional variability in the relationship between social standing and susceptibility to mob action. The results from that more complex approach showed quite clearly that the preliminary answer of "no" was not entirely correct. Men with higher-status occupations remained significantly less likely to be lynched regardless of the local context—although the *degree* of protection offered by a higher-status job was not uniform throughout the region. However, we discovered that a "mulatto" racial classification, in contrast to being enumerated as "Negro" or "black," functioned as a protective factor for targeting by mobs *only in settings in which the concentration of "mulattos" within the African American population was relatively high* (60th percentile and above). Conversely, the risk of victimization was higher for men who could read and write *only within communities with the lowest concentration of literate black men* (30th percentile and below). Farm owners were more likely to be singled out by mobs, *except in communities with the highest levels of farm ownership* (70th percentile and above).

There is an intriguing similarity between the patterns of risk that we have observed with respect to both social marginality and social standing. Where social marginality increased the vulnerability of black men to mob violence, it did so more strongly in communities where marginality was less common within the black population. Where higher social standing exposed black men to an elevated risk of victimization, it did so more strongly in communities where proportionately fewer black men enjoyed higher social standing or success. This is not to say that all indicators of social marginality or social standing increased the likelihood of lynching in some kinds of settings. They did not. But when they did, the evidence suggests that standing out as an exception within the general African American population had an important influence on the targeting of lynch victims by southern mobs.

Based on the evidence presented in this chapter and in chapter 4, we can emphatically conclude that southern mobs did not select their victims at random from the general black male population. There were important differentials in the risk of victimization according to both social marginality and social standing. However, we cannot know what motivated mobs to exercise discretion in their targeting of victims. Were adult black men with one type of personal profile more likely to engage in behaviors that resulted in mob action? For example, were socially marginal men more likely to commit crimes or to violate the racial code? That would seem to be a questionable position to take, given the widespread and substantial contextual variation in the relationship between social marginality and the risk of victimization, as well as the elevated risk experienced by higher-status men in some settings. Did mobs respond to the specific statuses themselves, regardless of any triggering event such as a crime or violation of the racial code? For example, did mobs specifically target farm owners, either because they coveted their land or resented the success that was represented by their ownership of property? This interpretation would seem to be more likely for indicators of higher social standing than for indicators of social marginality—though it is possible that drifters, tramps, and transients were specifically targeted because of their statuses, just as visibly homeless people are often targeted for violent attack today.

Finally, to what extent did mobs consider the potential community response to a lynching when they differentially selected their targets from among the general black male population? The substantial contextual variation in the effects of several individual-level indicators of both social marginality and social standing on the likelihood of victimization would seem to be consistent with the notion that mobs *did* consider potential community reaction in their selection of victims. However, until we have access to better information about the decision-making calculus of southern mobs—information that we are unlikely ever to have—the precise explanation for the patterns of differential risk for black men that we have documented in this chapter and in chapter 4 must remain open for debate.

In the following chapter, we further explore the relationship between the vulnerability associated with individual-level indicators of social marginality or social standing and contextual factors. Specifically, we ask whether county-level economic, political, and religious measures, which prior research has linked to greater incidence of lynching, served to moderate the risk associated with specific characteristics for black and mixed-race men.

CHAPTER SIX

Vulnerability in Economic, Political, and Religious Context

Today, only a few thousand people live in Montgomery County, Georgia. The county is home to a small Baptist college and garnered international notoriety for continuing to host racially segregated proms for its high school students well into the twenty-first century. Its county seat, Mount Vernon, lies roughly midway between Macon and Savannah, a few miles south of today's Interstate 16. In the first few decades of the twentieth century, Montgomery County delivered a reliably Democratic voting bloc. No Republican presidential candidate garnered more than 15 percent of the vote between 1900 and 1924. In 1928, however, Montgomery County became a hotly contested political battleground by Jim Crow–era southern standards. In that year's presidential election, the Democratic candidate Al Smith won just under 60 percent of the vote, meaning that more than 40 percent of Montgomery County voters broke ranks with the "Solid South." In only about one-third of other southern counties did the vote swing more heavily in favor of Republican candidate Herbert Hoover. This level of political competition in Montgomery County was a new phenomenon and may have been amplified in part by the fact that Smith, the Democratic candidate, was Catholic.

Two years after the presidential election, Montgomery County experienced its first documented lynching in two decades.[1] Shelton S. Mincey, the slain man, was extraordinarily successful, particularly given that he was black and living in rural Georgia in the early twentieth century. Mincey was born just as the Civil War was drawing to a close and married his wife, Adena, around 1890, when he was twenty-six years old and she just sixteen. The Minceys were farmers and wise enough stewards of both their crops and their money that they were able to purchase a plot of roughly forty acres near Ailey, in Montgomery County, in addition to a home they owned in nearby Vidalia.[2]

Mr. Mincey apparently was able to parlay his economic status into advantageous positions in a variety of institutions. He held an appointment as the local postmaster and in the late 1920s was elected to a leadership position in an African American Masonic lodge. Like many blacks prior to the middle of the twentieth century, Shelton Mincey supported the Republican Party. His leadership skills and social connections enabled him to rise through the ranks of the party's infrastructure. He held office at the county, district, and state level and was elected on multiple occasions to serve as a delegate to the Republican National Convention. The part that Mr. Mincey played in facilitating Montgomery County's shift in political allegiances, from overwhelmingly and reliably Democratic to an encroaching Republican vote, is unclear to us today, but the prominent roles that he held in so many key social institutions must have made him quite visible within the local community. Did Montgomery County's rapid transition to contested electoral territory make successful and politically engaged black men like Shelton Mincey more vulnerable to lynching?

Because we have only recently been able to determine the identities of large numbers of lynch victims, much of the existing research on lynching focuses on the community-level factors that increased the volume of deadly racial violence. From that research, we have learned quite a lot about when and where we would expect to witness lynchings, based on constellations of economic and agricultural factors, the relative strength of political parties, and the local religious "marketplace." We discussed the findings of some of this earlier research in chapter 1. In chapters 4 and 5 we demonstrated that individual-level characteristics linked to social marginality or higher-status differentially affected black and mixed-race men's vulnerability to mob violence based on the local context. In this chapter we attempt to integrate these two sets of findings. We do this by examining the relationship between these individual-level indicators and the key sets of community-level factors that prior research on lynching has found to predict the overall level of racial violence. As in chapters 4 and 5, we attempt to determine if the relative risk associated with specific types of *individual* characteristics was stronger or weaker depending on the local community context. Our focus here remains on comparing black and mixed-race male lynch victims with other similar men and adolescent boys living in their communities, paralleling our work in earlier chapters.

The earlier chapters in this book have identified that the effects of individual characteristics varied by factors that had not been previously identified as shaping overall risk. We now turn our attention to questions of whether aggregated measures that *have* been documented by prior investigators as shaping the overall climate of danger also interacted with these measurable personal traits. We ask whether the same personal traits identified in chapters 4 and 5 also elevated or suppressed the level of victims' vulnerability across communities with different economic, political, and religious contexts. These include a variety of contextual measures that earlier investigators found to be important predictors of the *occurrence* and *intensity* of lethal racial violence. We are particularly interested in these factors because they represent larger community-level power dynamics that may have underlain the logic of the selection of lynch victims. We also retain our focus on the individual characteristics that predicted vulnerability to mob violence—in particular, whether the differences between victims and non-victims would lend support to Senechal de la Roche's marginalization hypothesis or to a perspective that predicts elevated vulnerability for men who posed a threat to the prevailing racial hierarchy through their success.

The Importance of Local Context

The historical experience of racial violence during the lynching era was not uniform throughout the South. Some areas lynched more black men than did other areas—for example, mobs were more active in Mississippi and Georgia than they were in North Carolina or Tennessee. The per capita likelihood of being lynched was greater for black men in the northern counties of Florida than for those living in the Mississippi Delta. We know, further, that the spatial distribution of lynchings throughout the South was correlated with the social, economic, demographic, political, and religious environments that helped to define different locales. And the evidence presented in chapters 4 and 5 demonstrated that even the impact of individual-level risk factors for victimization was shaped strongly by the relative concentration of those characteristics within the local area. For example, literate men were more vulnerable in communities where literacy was less common among black men.

Clearly, local context mattered in determining both the volume of mob violence and the extent to which certain personal traits exposed individual black men to higher or lower likelihoods of victimization. In this chapter we assess the benefits of blending the knowledge gained through aggregate studies of the intensity of lynching with the knowledge that individual-level risk factors for lynching also differed according to the characteristics of the local community. More specifically, we test the hypothesis that the importance of distinguishing personal risk factors varied by the *level of danger for black men* within the local area, as defined by the economic, political, and religious profiles of southern counties.

By "level of danger," we are referring to the general social atmosphere that prevailed within a community regarding the conditions of life faced by the African American population—particularly black and mixed-race men. By its very nature, this is a slippery concept. Perhaps it is best conceived as a continuum running from "less dangerous" to "more dangerous" and as linked to the degree to which local whites felt the need—and importantly, had the ability—to reinforce the racial hierarchy and publicly uphold white supremacy. We might expect that the personal qualities that affected the risk of victimization for black men would be magnified in communities with higher levels of danger. Communities that were more dangerous, for example, would be less accepting of socioeconomic success or progress by blacks, especially if it coexisted with overall low levels of success for local whites. The white community in "more dangerous" counties might be less tolerant of minor violations of the racial code of white supremacy, which demanded that all blacks give deference to all whites, regardless of their relative social standing. And in more dangerous communities it would have been deemed more necessary and acceptable to use lethal violence to control the black workforce but not the white workforce.

In the absence of a valid and reliable "barometer of danger" with which to locate southern communities on this hypothetical continuum of white supremacy, we have opted for a multidimensional measurement strategy. In order to measure the level of danger to which African American males were exposed within local areas throughout the South, we have drawn from the empirical research that has documented the aggregate patterns of the intensity of mob violence. Much of this work, which we discussed in chapter 1, has identified the community factors associated with elevated levels of black victimization. Many of these contextual features seem to have been linked with maintaining the racial hierarchy and supporting the system of white supremacy. Within that large and growing literature, we focus on the economic, political, and religious dimensions of the local context, acknowledging that many of these factors are braided together in complex ways (Hahn 1983).

We also recognize that this is not an exhaustive set of environmental conditions that might have determined the intensity of lynching or that perhaps shaped the relative influence of the personal risk factors for victimization. However, we consider this to be primarily an exploratory extension of our investigation of the possible interplay between the aggregate and individual-level determinants of lynching. Indeed, we recognize the potential for more dangerous local environments to either *increase* or *decrease* the extent to which specific individual qualities exposed black men to the risk of victimization. It is also possible that the operation of traits associated with individual-level vulnerability to violence was *unrelated* to the overall level of danger for black men that prevailed in the local community. Our investigation is designed to assess the empirical support for these alternative possibilities.

Economic Danger

Scholars have devoted considerable energy to examining the connection between the intensity of lynching in a community and the nature of the local economy (see the discussion in chapter 1). The organization of southern agriculture has received most of this attention because the southern economy was primarily rural and agricultural during the lynching era, and wide variation existed within local communities in terms of patterns of land ownership, crop production, and the racial composition of the available labor force (Hahn 1983). One influential body of work focuses on the role that lynching served as a means of controlling black agricultural labor. The practice of lynching was tightly bound to the cotton economy and the system of farm tenancy or sharecropping. Earlier research by Stewart Tolnay and E. M. Beck (1995) identifies that lynching was more common in counties with a higher percentage of agricultural land devoted to the cultivation of cotton, as well as in those places where lower percentages of farmers—and particularly white farmers—owned their land. Thus, *we consider communities that depended more heavily on cotton production to drive their economies, and counties in which a larger proportion of farmers were tenants rather than farm owners, to be more dangerous environments for black men,* net of other county characteristics.

The southern cotton economy during the era of "King Cotton" was organized around a plantation system in which large landowners relied on the labor of landless sharecroppers, tenants, and laborers (Daniel 1985; Mandle 1978; Tolnay 1999). The demand of the cotton crop is highly seasonal, with intensive work required during planting, "chopping" (that is, clearing out weeds), and picking. Less work is required during the summer "lay by" period. Tolnay and Beck (1995, chapter 5) found that the intensity of lynching increased during the spring cotton chopping season and then declined during the summer lay by, suggesting the use of mob violence to exercise control over the black labor force in periods of peak labor demand. They observed no comparable spike in lynching during the harvest period and speculated that the use of violence earlier in the crop season could have been sufficient to accomplish the control of labor desired by white planters. Areas in which cotton cultivation represented a larger percentage of agricultural production would have been more inclined to invoke strategies for controlling a labor force whose work was seasonally variable.

The plantation system of cotton production relied on the semiautonomous efforts of sharecropping families who exchanged their labor for a percentage of the crop they produced. The pecuniary arrangements of the sharecropping system were unfavorable for the landless families that made up its backbone, and it was common for sharecroppers to end the growing season owing money to the landowner and/or local merchant. While credit was generally available, the interest rates charged to sharecroppers were usurious. The resulting trap of debt peonage locked many sharecropping families into contracts with the same landowner, year after year. Resistance to this oppressive agricultural system, as well as the migration of sharecropping families in search of better conditions, often was met with violence (Mandle 1978; Tolnay and Beck 1995).

Many landless white families shared essentially the same disadvantaged position as landless black families in the cotton economy. The financial arrangements with landowners for the two groups were generally similar. Perennial debt was common for both groups. The opportunities for upward economic mobility for both groups were grim, though somewhat more favorable for white families (Tolnay 1999). Yet white landless farmers held claim to a superior position in the southern racial caste system that was granted to them by virtue of the color of their skin. Some scholars have hypothesized that this contradiction between economic standing and racial status created an environment favorable for mob activity. This may have been perceived acutely as large landowners expanded their holdings and concentrated the ownership of wealth in many areas of the South, relegating many whites to tenant status for the first time and providing tangible evidence of downward mobility (Hahn 1983).

Tolnay and Beck (1995, chapter 5) find support for this claim for racial violence that occurred during the late nineteenth century, with lynchings happening more frequently in counties with larger concentrations of landless white farmers. Further, they conclude that the most dangerous economic environments for southern blacks were those in which the interests of poor whites and elite whites aligned. Those conditions prevailed, for example, when the labor control concerns of white landowners coexisted with economic competition between white and black tenant farmers and with the racial hostility generated by the juxtaposition of the distressed economic standing of white landless farmers and their alleged racial superiority to equally distressed black landless farmers. Our work here will examine whether the presence of these dangerous local conditions imposed different levels of risk on black and mixed-race men who were more and less marginal, or held greater or lesser social status, within the community.

Political Danger

A second body of work has linked the degree of political domination exerted by the Democratic Party to local variation in lynching patterns. Because the Civil War had been waged by a Republican federal administration, and because the aspects of Reconstruction perceived by white southerners to have been most injurious to their "way of life" and well-being were imposed by a Republican coalition, the states of the former Confederacy grew increasingly allied with the Democratic Party for the span of a century, lasting from the Civil War until the Civil Rights Era. Because of this link, earlier researchers have considered the possibility that the level of local support for the Democratic Party, or for various political challengers to the party, might be related to a community's level of racial violence.[3]

Arthur Raper proposed a link between the strength of the Democratic Party and the racial climate within local areas of the South in *The Tragedy of Lynching*. In his overview of lynching incidents from 1930, Raper included a brief profile of selected sociodemographic characteristics for the county where each lynching occurred. The proportionate vote cast for the Democratic candidate in recent elections was one of the characteristics considered by Raper. For example, in his description of Irwin County, Georgia, where James Irwin was lynched in February 1930, Raper ([1933] 1969, 169–70) wrote, "The rank and file of white people in Irwin and adjoining counties are descended from non-slaveholders and are ardent supporters of the doctrine of 'white supremacy,' always most virulent among the less privileged whites, who cling to the Democratic Party for protection from 'nigger-lovin' administrations in Washington and for a guarantee of 'pure white' rule at home."

The relationship between political climate or political competition and racial violence, however, has been less consistently identified than the link between lynching and other social structures, particularly in statistical analyses. Different researchers, using different data and with different political foci, have identified a variety of relationships with varying degrees of confidence. In general, the theoretical framing used to predict the kinds of political environments that would be expected to increase the likelihood of a lynching has focused on political threat— either a "boundary crisis" posed by a challenge to dominance of the Democratic Party and the white supremacist dogma it represented, as James Inverarity (1976) argues, or political competition itself, which could lead to higher levels of violence, as is hypothesized by both Sarah Soule (1992) and Tolnay and Beck (1995). These earlier research efforts have yielded inconsistent findings.

In contrast to the deployment of lynching as a means to suppress *economic* competition, blacks seem to have been at greater risk when the political dominance of the Democratic Party was more certain. As Tolnay and Beck note, this relationship is *opposite* of what would be predicted by the political threat model (1995, 199).[4] Rather, it suggests that blacks were actually safer in areas where a stronger Republican Party served as a more viable counterweight to the Democratic Party, which is typically considered to be the party of white supremacy during this era. Despite reasonable theoretical predictions to the contrary, there is little empirical evidence that the strength of the Populist Party was related to the volume of mob violence during those relatively brief periods when Populists offered a political alternative to the southern Democratic Party (Soule 1992; Tolnay and Beck 1995). In the analyses to follow, we consider communities with a more dominant Democratic Party to have been more dangerous environments for black men during the lynching era, in line with Raper's observation regarding Irwin County, Georgia, and other communities where the Democratic Party was strong. Our question, then, is whether and in what ways the overall level of danger inherent in specific local political environments might have been amplified or suppressed based on personal attributes.

Religious Danger

Religion and religious culture and imagery were suffused through all facets of southern life, including race relations broadly conceptualized and the practice of lynching more specifically. Social and racial divisions, however, were reflected in varying perspectives on faith and community and on the link between race, violence, and the sacred. Blacks, for example, believed that emancipation provided evidence of God's favor, while whites fervently believed that segregation and white supremacy were willed by God (Remillard 2011, 46–48). Journalistic reporting on acts of lynching were frequently cast with religious overtones in the white press, justifying mob actions as "a terrifying retribution, ordained and consecrated by God, against the black man's transgressions" (Wood 2009, 48). Black writers and the larger black community, conversely, viewed the practice of lynching as ritual sacrifice and its victims as martyrs for the race. As Donald G. Mathews succinctly puts it, blacks "understood that Christ, too, had been lynched" (2000).

Other sociological research has focused on the role that racial violence played in reinforcing the moral solidarity of the southern white community. Viewing the relative power of different kinds of religious organizations as indicating the degree to which these key social institutions undergirded or resisted traditional southern power dynamics, Bailey and Snedker (2011) tested whether challenges to a monolithic religious structure affected the incidence of lynching. They found that communities with more diverse religious options, and where larger percentages of the local black population belonged to denominations controlled by blacks, experienced a higher level of racial violence than did counties where just a few denominations competed for membership or where religious options for black believers were under greater white control. They also found that places where a higher percentage of church members belonged to groups that admitted both blacks and whites to membership had fewer incidents of lynching. These findings appear to support contradictory interpretations related to the effects of religious culture on mob violence. Challenges to a dominant, white supremacist power structure, evidenced by strong black-controlled denominations and a broader array of options,[5] are associated with a more dangerous environment for blacks, while communities where interracial organizations were strongest appear to have been safer.

These details about organizational history are particularly important for understanding whether a specific religious group posed an ideological threat to southern racial hegemony. From the times of slavery, whites had retained a stranglehold on black religious organizations, insisting on controlling both theological content and administrative structure. Virtually all of these organizations practiced varieties of Christianity, and one might imagine how important whites would have considered it to control the packaging and conveyance of religious messages to blacks. The story of Moses leading the Israelites out of slavery in Egypt and into the Promised Land, for example, provided inspiration and hope to generations of enslaved people whose families had been unwillingly brought to the New World. White religious leaders, conversely, attempted to emphasize scriptures that focused on obedience and the slave's obligations to his or her master. Similarly, whites had suppressed black efforts to participate fully in many aspects of civil society, and religious organizations were one more venue from which whites attempted to exclude blacks. We can only imagine how the powerlessness of the southern black community was magnified when its most prominent and capable members were denied the opportunity to accrue significant experience in administrative tasks and organizational leadership. This lack of direct institutional experience probably served to diminish the likelihood that southern blacks would be able to mount a successful defense of their own rights or a meaningful challenge to prevailing power hierarchies.

Once the legal obstacles to black religious autonomy had been removed, southern blacks acted decisively on their interest in controlling their own social institutions and spiritual futures. The decades following the Civil War witnessed, for the first time, a documented explosion in the formation of indigenous faith sects among southern blacks. Some of this "church building" involved the establishment of new organizations altogether, such as the Church of God in Christ. In other cases, blacks merely disassociated from white-controlled organizations and established their own administrative structures. For example, the Southern Baptist Convention had included both black and white congregations during the decades immediately following the Civil War, although the black wing of the denomination was forced into an auxiliary status. Blacks were relegated to a subordinate role within the church, and black congregations fell under the supervision of a white-dominated power structure. While some smaller racially defined schisms had occurred earlier, in the 1890s black Baptist churches resigned from the Southern Baptist Convention en masse and formed a new administrative structure, the National Baptist Convention.

Drawing directly from the work done by Bailey and Snedker, then, we consider the local religious environment to have been more dangerous for African American men where (1) there were more religious options, (2) blacks exercised greater control over their spiritual organizations, and (3) racially integrated denominations were less common. The task to which we now turn seeks to identify whether black and mixed-race men whose own characteristics appeared to challenge the dominant social arrangements, or who were only weakly tethered to the local community, faced different levels of risk in more and less dangerous counties.

Local Contexts of Danger and Individual-Level Risk Factors

Chapters 4 and 5 clearly demonstrated that variation existed in the relationship between personal traits and the likelihood of being lynched across the South. In those chapters we found strong evidence that the consequences of both social marginality and social standing depended upon the relative concentration of other black men in the local community who shared the same attribute. In the analyses that follow, we extend that line of inquiry by considering whether the consequences of social marginality and social standing also varied by the local level of economic, political, and religious danger, as we have defined and measured them.

As was mentioned earlier, we are agnostic regarding the exact form that any environmental conditioning effects on individual-level risk factors might have taken. That is, for example, for black men living in areas with a high level of danger, greater social marginality and higher social standing could have either *amplified* or *attenuated* their risk of victimization. It is also possible that the influence of individual-level risk factors was *independent* of the local context of danger. Let us briefly consider these three possibilities, using as examples literacy as the individual-level risk factor and strength of the Democratic Party as the contextual measure of danger.

In settings where the political danger for black men was high, the ability to read and write could have increased opportunities for attracting the attention of local whites and running afoul of the local codes of acceptable behavior or appropriate social standing. The perception of being "uppity" in an area of Democratic Party dominance, with an atmosphere strongly supportive of the regime of white supremacy, could have marked black men as possible lynch victims—either for their own specific behaviors or as the targets of mobs that were motivated to action by the behavior of other black men or by the more general conditions of racial tension and conflict in the area. Literate black men could have been especially vulnerable if they used their ability to read and write to actively oppose the social and political philosophy espoused by the Democratic Party, for example by attempting to register to vote or to mobilize the local black population—behaviors that might have contributed to the victimization of Shelton Mincey in Montgomery County, Georgia, in 1930.

Applying a different logic, exactly the same personal profile (that is, literacy) and potentially provocative behavior (that is, political activism) described in the previous paragraph might have exposed black men to a higher likelihood of victimization in areas where the Democratic Party was struggling for dominance against relatively strong competing parties. To the extent that the Democratic Party was identified with a philosophy of white supremacy, as suggested in the earlier quotation from Arthur Raper, anything short of political domination by the party might have been perceived as unacceptable. In communities like these, the fate of white supremacy may have been conceived to have been conjoined with the local power of the southern Democratic Party. According to this perspective, literate black men, and possibly even their political activity, posed little threat and therefore could be tolerated where the Democratic Party enjoyed total, or near total, dominance. In such settings, erudite black men might have been viewed by the white elite as a minor annoyance and not as a serious threat to the political status quo. In contrast, where the Democratic Party's control was contested, the same well-educated black men could have been perceived to be political threats and therefore more vulnerable to the deadly work of southern lynch mobs.

Finally, we acknowledge the possibility that the relationships between individual-level characteristics (both social marginality and social standing) and the risk of victimization were insensitive to the environmental conditions that prevailed within local communities. That is, being literate or a married head of household or a higher-status worker or a farm owner could have evinced the same relationship with the likelihood of being lynched regardless of the level of economic, political, or religious danger for black men. Extending our example of the variation in risk that could have been attached to literacy based on the local alignment of the political parties, it is possible that the relationship between victimization and being literate or illiterate for the risk of mob victimization was invariant, regardless of the local political climate. This does not mean that literacy lost its power to influence vulnerability, nor that the risk associated with being literate did not change across communities in which black men collectively shared different *literacy "profiles."* Finding no relationship between the degree of danger attached to a specific *political climate* and the level of personal vulnerability associated with literacy merely tells us that the relationship between literacy and victimization was relatively uniform across southern political environments.

This "null finding" conclusion would offer perhaps the most intriguing possible outcome. That is, it would suggest that the levels of risk associated with individual profiles of social marginality or elevated status *were not moderated* by the local level of political, economic, and religious danger. Given the multiple ways in which these environmental features overlap—for example, the race- and class-based cleavages that shape religious membership (Hahn 1983, 17), or the assorted patterns of land ownership and their effect on the web of political allegiances (52)—finding no link in light of the evidence we have marshaled so far would be surprising. To be clear, it *would not* suggest that victims were randomly selected from the local population. However, finding "no effect" of the local contexts of danger would tell us that it was likely other factors, which are unmeasured in our data, and in fact in any other large-scale data we are aware of, that governed the selection of victims across communities that harbored different background levels of danger.

Analytic Strategy

In this chapter, we again rely on the statistical tool of logistic regression to determine whether black men's personal characteristics were variably related to their vulnerability to mob violence across different local contexts of danger. In statistical terms, we consider the possibility of interactions between the personal attributes related to the risk of being lynched and the intensity of danger faced by African American men in the community, as measured by the economic, political, and religious county-level characteristics mentioned above. This analytic strategy is identical to the one that we used in chapters 4 and 5, where we demonstrated contextual variation in the importance of several indicators of social marginality and social standing according to their frequency of occurrence in the local area. The arrow with the dotted line shown in Figure 6.1 represents the conditioning effect of local context on the relationship between individual-level risk and protective factors and the individual risk of lynching. That is our focus in the following analysis. It informs us whether the relationship between a given personal characteristic and the risk of victimization is strengthened or weakened by the relevant measure of local danger.

The lens through which we view economic, political, and religious local cultures is clearly sociological. We strive to understand patterns of social behavior by observing variation in the characteristics of population aggregates (that is, southern counties) rather than by approaching the endeavor as a historian might, attempting to elicit fine contextual detail and a deep understanding of lived experience. Certainly, historians are also students of patterns and coincidence—it was historian Donald G. Mathews (2000), for example, who pointed out that southern church membership swelled in tandem with the rise of lynching. We acknowledge, however, the limitations of the disciplinary perspective we bring to bear on these questions and encourage the reader to assess the evidence that we present in light of our disciplinary approach. And

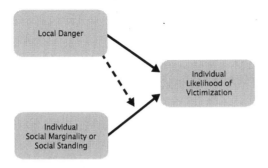

Figure 6.1 Heuristic Map of Conditional Influence of Local Danger on the Effect of Individual Risk Factors on the Likelihood of Victimization

we definitely encourage scholars of different disciplinary persuasions to seek answers to the questions that motivate this chapter using different evidentiary styles and decision rules.

For this investigation we once again compare the characteristics of lynch victims to those of black male non-victims that were drawn from the 1 percent PUMS samples for the same counties and decades in which we located victims. Victim and non-victim differences are determined by estimating the likelihood of being lynched, measured as a binary outcome that is coded "1" for victims and "0" for non-victims. We have slightly redefined some of the individual-level measures of social marginality and social standing for this investigation in order to take advantage of the most salient patterns that emerged in chapters 4 and 5 and to simplify the statistical analyses that consider multiple measures of local context and several individual-level characteristics. These small changes should not compromise our ability to detect the kinds of first-order interactions between individual-level and county-level traits that were mentioned in the previous paragraph. We describe the personal qualities considered in these analyses, and any changes from the measurement strategies we used in chapters 4 and 5, in Table 6.1. As a reminder and point of clarification, we consider those who were born out of state and were not married heads of households to have been more marginal or less embedded within their local communities.[6] In our estimation, higher social standing was associated with literacy, higher-status occupations, "mulatto" racial status, and farm ownership.

Table 6.1 Summary Measures of Social Marginality and Social Standing Used in the Analysis of Variation in the Relationship between Individual-Level Risk Factors and the Level of "Danger" in the Local Community

Individual-Level Characteristic	*Definition*
SOCIAL MARGINALITY	
Born out of State	Unchanged from chapter 4
Agricultural Worker	Agricultural workers versus all other workers (as well as not in labor force)
Married Household Head	Married heads of households versus all other marriage/relationship to head of household combinations
SOCIAL STANDING	
Literacy	Unchanged from chapter 5
Higher-Status Worker	Higher-status workers versus all other workers (as well as not in labor force)
"Mulatto"	Unchanged from chapter 5
Owned Farm	Residence on an owned farm versus all other dwelling/ownership combinations

Measuring Local Danger

In chapters 4 and 5, our focus on contextual factors was drawn from information that was readily available in the population census. We calculated the percentages of black and mixed-race men who were, for example, literate or homeowners based on the characteristics of those men included in the 1 percent sample from the appropriate census. Our interest in the attributes of the local agricultural economy, political organizations, and religious marketplace created the need to incorporate data on contextual factors that were not recorded in the population census. In order to accomplish this, we have utilized information from other sources of historical information that were collected by the federal government. We now turn to a brief discussion of these information sources and the ways we have incorporated them into this component of our investigation.

THE LOCAL AGRICULTURAL ECONOMY

The Census Bureau canvassed farmers every decade, gathering details about a wide array of information regarding each farmer's economic health and agricultural productivity in an agricultural census, collected at the same time as the decennial census of the population. These measures reflect agricultural factors for the prior year, so, for example, the 1900 agricultural census captures information on farmers' production and economic standing in 1899 (Inter-university Consortium for Political and Social Research 2001). The metrics included the number of acres that were available to farm operators as farmland (either the acres that they owned or the number they were under contract to use via a tenancy agreement); the number of those acres that had been improved (meaning cleared and plowed—essentially made ready for use in planting or as pasture); what crops they had planted in the previous year; how many acres were allocated to each crop; whether they owned their land, rented it for cash, or exchanged use of the land for a percentage of the annual harvest; and so on. This information was then combined for all farmers in each county and released in aggregated numbers.[7]

We used these raw numbers to calculate two community-level indicators of economic danger. First, we determined the percentage of a county's total agricultural lands that were devoted to cotton production by dividing the number of acres planted in cotton by the total number of improved acres of farmland. This metric helped to identify the degree to which the economic fortunes of each county were bound to King Cotton. Second, we identified the level of economic insecurity among a county's farm population by dividing the number of tenant farmers—those paying cash rents or sharecropping—by the total number of farmers in a county. In some decades, the numbers for farm tenancy are available separately for black and white farmers, and in others, only overall numbers have been compiled by the Census Bureau.[8]

LOCAL DEMOCRATIC PARTY DOMINANCE

As the late Speaker of the House Thomas (Tip) O'Neill famously opined, "All politics is local." Electoral politics, and particularly the level of dominance enjoyed by the Democratic Party, are hypothesized to have been related to the structures that guided the local incidence of racial violence. While the Census Bureau did not directly collect individual-level information on voting behavior, election data, including the percentage of votes cast for the candidate representing each political party, are available at the county level for all presidential elections (Clubb, Flanigan, and Zingale 2006).[9] Although evidence is far from conclusive, as discussed earlier, prior work suggests that places where the hegemony of the Democratic Party was most entrenched may also have been places that witnessed the highest levels of predatory racial violence.

In the following analyses, we include the percentage of the vote cast in each county for the most recent presidential election that supported the Democratic Party's candidate as a measure of local political danger. So, for example, for lynch victims who were killed between 1884 and 1887, we incorporate the percentage of all votes that were cast in the county for Grover Cleveland, the Democratic candidate, in the 1884 presidential election. For lynch victims who were killed between 1888 and 1891, our analyses include the percentage of the county vote that (again) supported Cleveland in 1888 in his unsuccessful bid for a second presidential term.[10]

LOCAL RELIGIOUS ENVIRONMENT

To measure the nature of the local religious environment, we relied on the Census of Religious Bodies, or CRB, which was collected intermittently between 1890 and 1936 (U.S. Bureau of the Census 1894, 1906, 1916, 1926). The CRB amassed a wide array of data from local religious organizations like churches, temples, and synagogues but did not gather information directly from individuals. Rather, each congregation reported membership information to the Census Bureau, and the Census Bureau issued reports with data aggregated to the county level. So, for example, using the 1906 CRB, we know that in Warren County, Mississippi, where Vicksburg is located, there were 1,428 members of the congregations affiliated with the African Methodist Episcopal Church and 207 members of Jewish synagogues.

In addition to numerical tables listing the number of members for each organization by county, the Census Bureau also published historical reports on each religious group that might be considered a denomination or sect. That is, additional information was captured for all groups that were of sufficient size and complexity to encompass multiple local congregations and to operate under the guidance of some sort of organizing congress or administrative body. Among this material were brief narrative histories of each denomination and indicators of whether the denomination included any (segregated) black congregations or had a membership that was entirely black. These often contained information on the location of the church headquarters and specifics about the circumstances surrounding the founding and administrative structure of each organization. The historical accounts also summarize major conflicts within the organization or decisions to subdivide into constituent groups.[11]

Bailey and Snedker (2011) used the narrative information provided in the CRB about each denomination to create three specific metrics that we have incorporated in our analyses. They combined information on specific organizational membership with data about the total number of church members and the total size of the black population in the county to calculate two of these indicators. First, they categorized denominations as being monoracial, or as having membership policies that allowed both blacks and whites to join, and added up the total number of members in *all* religious groups that admitted both blacks and whites.[12] They then calculated the relative strength of these "mixed-race" churches by calculating the percentage of *all church members* in a county who belonged to denominations with both black and white members.[13]

Second, they identified predominantly African American religious groups based on whether they were controlled and organized by whites or were controlled and organized by blacks. As with the measure of mixed-race religious denominations, they next summed up the *total number of members* in all organizations that were controlled and organized by blacks. They then used this information to calculate the percentage of black residents in each county who belonged to religious groups that were organized and led by blacks themselves, dividing the number of members in black-controlled denominations in each county by its *total black population*.[14]

Third, Bailey and Snedker calculated a measure of the degree of competition for members among organizations within the local religious "marketplace" by examining the extent to which the church landscape was dominated by one or just a few organizations or included a variety of options for county residents. This "pluralism index" accounts for both the *number* of different denominations competing for members and their *relative sizes*. So, for example, a county that housed only two denominations, with both having roughly equal numbers of members, would be considered more religiously diverse and competitive than another county that also had only two denominations but where 80 percent of church members belonged to one group and only 20 percent of church members belonged to the second group. Similarly, a county where all church members were divided roughly equally among eight different sects would be considered more competitive than the county where just two organizations had equal numbers of members. Mathematically speaking, the pluralism index is calculated as $1-\sum p^2$, where p is the proportion of all church members who belong to each specific denomination.[15] The range of possible values is a function of the number of groups, with a minimum value of 0 and a maximum value that approaches 1. Larger values (values that are closer to 1) indicate a greater amount of local religious pluralism, and smaller values (values that are closer to 0) indicate a community with less religious pluralism.

TECHNICAL CONSIDERATIONS FOR THE COUNTY-LEVEL DATA

The county-level data for all three contextual analyses require a bit of additional technical explanation. The county-level religious measures are not available for the 1880 decade, so we conducted the religious analyses only for the period 1890 through 1929. The Census of Religious Bodies was collected simultaneously with the population census only in 1890. Subsequent CRBs were fielded in 1906, 1916, and 1926. This temporal disjuncture between the recording of individual characteristics and the submission of statistics on religious organizations complicates the analyses somewhat, due to the rapid economic development and population growth that occurred in the South during this period and the resulting increase in political-administrative complexity. In many southern states, the number of counties increased markedly between the late nineteenth century and the middle of the twentieth century.

Seminole County, Florida, for example, was created in 1913 from a section of the northern part of Orange County. Seminole County is about thirty miles inland, on Florida's Atlantic Coast, roughly midway between Daytona Beach and Cape Canaveral. The county has a long and troubled history of race relations and also illustrates the challenges of using county-level data and our efforts to compensate somewhat for those shortcomings. Seminole County most recently catapulted into the spotlight of international public focus in 2012, when Trayvon Martin, an unarmed black teenager, was shot and killed by Neighborhood Watch captain George Zimmerman in Sanford, the county seat. That was not the first time, however, that Seminole County captured headlines for its local racial dynamics. In 1947, Seminole County residents forced the Montreal Royals, a Triple-A minor league affiliate of the Brooklyn Dodgers, to relocate their spring training camp from Sanford to Daytona Beach rather than tolerate the presence of a team that was racially integrated by Jackie Robinson (Lamb 2004). Earlier in the county's history, on February 24, 1915, a black man named Will Reed was accused of attempting to rape a white woman and was lynched in Forest City, about twenty miles southwest of Sanford.

Our efforts to locate this victim identified two men named Will Reed enumerated in the 1910 census manuscripts. We believe these men to be equally likely to have been the Will Reed who was lynched in Seminole County in 1915. In 1910, a literate, twenty-three-year-old unmarried black man named Will Reed was enumerated as living in the Sixth Election Precinct of Seville, Florida, about fifty miles north of Forest City in Volusia County. Reed is listed as a lodger and seems to have been unrelated to the other four men with whom he shared a home. Every person on Will Reed's census page for whom an occupation was recorded is listed as working in the turpentine industry, and of the eleven households listed on the census page, all but one were boardinghouses or collections of seemingly unrelated workers sharing living quarters. Reed worked as a teamster, and although he and both of his parents were born in Florida, many of the other men listed on his census page appear to have been relatively recent transplants to the state—perhaps labor migrants seeking work in the rapidly expanding agricultural industry. Our best guess, based on the evidence, is that this "Will Reed" lived in a labor camp that was linked to a turpentine distillery.

The second man we located as possibly having been the Will Reed who was lynched in Forest City, Florida, in 1915 was a literate, forty-two-year-old black man named William M. Reed. This Reed, who had never been married, was enumerated as living by himself in Paisley, Florida, a small town in Lake County about thirty-five miles south of Forest City. William M. Reed had been born in South Carolina, as had both of his parents. He was a laborer in a work camp that made railroad ties. William M. Reed's neighbors were quite diverse, with geographic origins in Florida and several other southern states, and worked in agriculture, a naval stores outfit, and the work camp that also employed Mr. Reed.

The fourteen households listed on the same page with William M. Reed included a mix of unmarried men living alone, married couples living both with and without co-resident children, including a few who took in boarders, and households composed of employers and employees sharing living quarters. Four households had all white members, and ten were composed exclusively of black or mixed-race people.

Our attempts to identify the economic, political, and religious characteristics of Seminole County, and the ways in which they might be related to Will Reed's individual traits, became complicated because of the year in which he was lynched. Because his death occurred in 1915, logic would dictate that we use data about Seminole County from the 1910 population census, the 1912 presidential election, and the 1916 Census of Religious Bodies. Seminole County, however, was not created until 1913, meaning that no data exist for Seminole County in either 1910 or 1912. In order to determine, for example, the degree to which the county's economy was rooted in cotton production or the intensity of support for the Democratic Party and how these may have been linked to Will Reed's own characteristics in shaping his vulnerability to mob violence, we needed to rely on information for Orange County, the county that was partitioned to create Seminole County.

When we considered how the characteristics that increased personal vulnerability to lynching may have been affected by economic, political, and religious contexts, then, we used the smallest geographic unit that remained consistent during the time period we were interested in. In the vast majority of cases, of course, this was a single county. In instances where county boundaries changed, however, we bundled more than one county together to form a cluster for the time period when the boundary change occurred, and the economic, political, and religious measures reflect the aggregate of this geographic area.[16]

EVIDENCE OF THE CONTEXTUAL CONDITIONING OF INDIVIDUAL-LEVEL RISK FACTORS

The findings from our logistic regression analyses, summarized in Table 6.2, offer powerful evidence that, in the large majority of cases, social marginality and social standing had uniform effects on the risk of victimization across local contexts. That is, for the most part the level of environmental danger, as represented by the economic, political, and religious characteristics of communities, neither elevated nor reduced

Table 6.2 Evidence of Conditional Influence of Local Context of Danger on the Effect of Individual-Level Characteristics on the Likelihood of Being Lynched, 1882–1929

Individual-Level Characteristics	Democratic Party Strength	Cotton Dominance	Percentage Tenant Farmers	Mixed-Race Denominations	Religious Diversity	Percentage Black Churches
SOCIAL MARGINALITY						
Born out of State	0	0	0	0	0	0
Agricultural Worker	0	0	0	0	0	0
Married Household Head	0	0	0	0	0	0
SOCIAL STANDING						
Literate	0	0	0	0	0	0
Higher-status Worker	0	0	0	0	0	0
Mulatto Status	0	+	0	0	0	0
Owned Farm	+	0	0	0	0	0

Note:
"o" indicates statistically nonsignificant interaction ($p > .05$) between individual-level and
county-level measures.
"+" indicates a positive and statistically significant interaction ($p < .05$) between individual-level
and county-level measures.

the consequences of individual-level risk factors. The zeroes shown in Table 6.2 indicate that the referenced interaction between the corresponding county-level measure and the indicator of social marginality or social standing is statistically nonsignificant (meaning that $p > .05$). In only two cases was the interaction found to be significant, as indicated by a "+" rather than by a zero, in Table 6.2. Those results suggest that the protective influence of "mulatto" status on the likelihood of victimization grew weaker[17] in counties where cotton was a more important component of the local agricultural economy. In contrast, the greater risk of victimization associated with farm ownership appears to have intensified in settings where the Democratic Party was more dominant. Interestingly, both of these significant interactions suggest a toxic effect of more dangerous environmental circumstances—either by attenuating the influence of a protective characteristic (that is, "mulatto" status) or by amplifying the effect of a risk factor (that is, farm ownership).

Before fully embracing these minority findings, however, it should be acknowledged that there are two alternative, and considerably different, interpretations for the statistically significant interactions between these two measures of social standing and the prevailing level of danger in the local community. We shall consider both. On the one hand, it might be claimed that the two cases of significant interactions are a statistical fluke. In fact, there is a total of forty-two possible cross-level interactions represented in Table 6.2—the combination of six indicators of local context and seven individual-level measures. The two statistically significant interactions that we found represent 4.8 percent of the possible forty-two interactions—almost exactly the number we should expect to observe by chance, alone, when using a level of statistical significance of $p < .05$. Therefore, rather than representing actual situations in which the effects of personal attributes on the risk of victimization are conditioned by the local context of danger, the two significant interactions contained in Table 6.2 could simply be the result of chance or probability. If this is the case—if we are observing relationships that are actually the result merely of chance—then concluding that the association between "mulatto" status or farm ownership and the risk of victimization *is actually conditioned* by cotton dominance or the strength of the Democratic Party, respectively, would involve committing a Type I inferential error—rejecting a null hypothesis (that is, no cross-level interaction) that is actually true.

On the other hand, perhaps the two significant interactions reported in Table 6.2 reveal a true moderating influence of the local context of danger on the relationship between social standing and the likelihood of victimization. This possibility motivates us to explore these two significant interactions just a bit further. Toward that end, we have repeated the analytic strategy used in chapters 4 and 5 by estimating the effects of "mulatto" status and farm ownership at various percentiles for county-level cotton dominance and Democratic Party strength, respectively. The lines shown in Figure 6.2 display the Odds Ratios at each percentile considered, with the darker line representing "mulatto" status and the paler line representing farm ownership. Recall that an Odds Ratio larger than 1.0 indicates that the characteristic of interest (that is, "mulatto" status or farm ownership) is associated with a *greater* likelihood of being

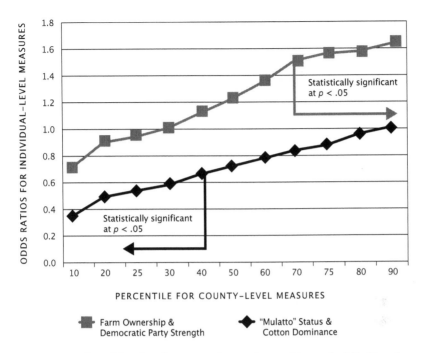

Figure 6.2 Effect of "Mulatto" Status and Farm Ownership on the Likelihood of Being Lynched, by Level of Cotton Dominance and Democratic Party Strength, Respectively, 1882–1929

lynched than experienced by the reference group (that is, blacks and nonfarm owners). In contrast, an Odds Ratio of less than 1.0 suggests that the characteristic of interest is associated with a *lower* likelihood of victimization than that experienced by the reference group. The corresponding darker and lighter arrows shown in Figure 6.2 indicate the range in which the reported Odds Ratios for "mulatto" status and farm ownership are statistically significant at $p < .05$.

The evidence summarized in Figure 6.2 is consistent and intriguing. Mixed-race men were considerably less vulnerable to mob activity than were men enumerated as "black" *in areas where cotton production was a less important component of the agricultural economy.* In contrast, where cotton was king, "mulatto" status offered no protection for African American males. The Odds Ratio for the effect of "mulatto" status on the likelihood of being lynched is 0.72 and statistically significant (at $p < .05$) at the 40th percentile of cotton dominance. This means that the risk of lynching was

28 percent smaller for men who were recorded as "mulatto" in counties with this level of concentration of cotton dominance. Where cotton was less dominant (that is, below the 40th percentile), the protective influence of "mulatto" status was even stronger. In contrast, in counties where cotton production represented a larger share of the agricultural economy (that is, above the 40th percentile), "mulatto" status offered no protection from mob violence for African American men.

A substantively similar pattern is found for the conditioning effect of Democratic Party dominance on the relationship between farm ownership and the probability of victimization. Where the Democratic Party was relatively weaker, farm ownership was essentially a benign status— unrelated to the likelihood of being lynched. However, in counties that were Democratic Party strongholds, farm ownership significantly increased the vulnerability of African American men. The Odds Ratio for the effect of farm ownership on the likelihood of being lynched is +1.51 and statistically significant (at $p < .05$) at the 70th percentile of the percentage voting for the Democratic candidate in the most recent presidential election. This means that, at this level of Democratic Party strength, the risk of victimization was 51 percent greater for black farm owners than it was for African American men who were renters or who did not live on farms. Where Democrats garnered a greater share of votes (that is, above the 70th percentile), farm owners were exposed to an even higher risk of mob violence. In contrast, in counties where the Democratic Party was less dominant (that is, below the 70th percentile), farm owners were not more vulnerable than others to mob violence.

Given the paucity of findings that suggest a significant conditioning influence of the local context of danger (see Table 6.2), we are reluctant to emphasize too strongly these two pieces of contrary evidence contained in Figure 6.2. Rather, we will simply point to them as a tantalizing suggestion of the possibility that the influence of some individual-level correlates of victimization was shaped by the extent to which cotton production and the Democratic Party reigned supreme in the local community.

Concluding Comments

Previous research has shown that lynch mob activity varied considerably throughout the American South and that this heterogeneity was correlated with a range of social, economic, and demographic characteristics of local areas. The earlier chapters of this book have demonstrated that a variety of individual-level traits were also related to the likelihood of being lynched. We showed, further, that the risk associated with those attributes varied based on the concentration of those same markers of marginality and social status among other African American men in the community. In this chapter, we sought to merge these two established "facts" about the lynching era to determine whether the influence of individual-level factors on the exposure of black men to victimization was itself shaped by the nature of the local context of danger, as measured by economic, political, and religious variables.

Our initial posture was agnostic regarding the predicted direction of the many possible cross-level interactions considered by our analytic undertaking. That is, we recognized that the influence of individual-level risk and protective factors for lynching could be intensified, attenuated, or perhaps even unaffected by the level of local danger. For the most part, we discovered that the operation of individual-level determinants of victimization was essentially uniform throughout the South—at least with respect to the economic, political, and religious environmental conditions considered in our analyses. This large-scale insensitivity of individual-level predictors of lynching to the local context of danger contrasts sharply with the evidence presented in chapters 4 and 5, which suggested that, in general, social marginality and elevated social standing increased the vulnerability of black and mixed-race men in circumstances where those statuses were less common in the community.[18]

Two intriguing possible exceptions to the general pattern of null findings emerged from our analyses. The protective influence of "mulatto" status on the likelihood of victimization was significantly degraded in areas where cotton production dominated the local agricultural economy (that is, above the 40th percentile for percentage of cultivated land devoted to cotton). In a similar fashion, although farm ownership was unrelated to the likelihood of being lynched in communities where the Democratic candidate claimed a smaller percentage of votes (that is, below the 70th percentile) in the most recent presidential election, it represented a significant risk factor where the Democratic Party was stronger (that is, at the 70th percentile and above). Both examples suggest a conditioning effect of the local context of danger on the relationship between individual-level characteristics and vulnerability to mob activity—either by weakening the influence of a protective factor (that is, "mulatto" status) or by bolstering the effect of a risk factor (that is, farm ownership). In light of the small proportion of all cross-level interactions that attained statistical significance in our analyses (= 5 percent), however, these exceptional cases must be interpreted with caution. Nevertheless, we believe that they are at least provocative suggestions of additional ways in which the local context helped to determine the relationship between personal markers of social status or marginality and the vulnerability of African American men to mob violence.

It is worthy of mention that the analyses presented in chapters 4 and 5 identified differences in risk accruing to personal characteristics based on the prevalence of the same specific qualities within the community. In this chapter, we explored the possibility that the social marginality or elevated status of African American men mattered differently based on the level of overall danger associated with configurations of the county's economic, political, and religious institutions. Note that we do not have individual-level measures of political involvement or religious adherence and only the roughest outlines of economic standing. Our findings in this chapter are somewhat tenuous not only because they tend to be weak statistically but also because we lack the means to measure the interplay between individual behavior and the quotidian character of that behavior within the local community. It is certainly possible that, for example, politically active black men faced harsher mob retribution for small social transgressions in counties where many blacks were active in political life and members of the white community felt threatened. It is equally plausible that where the black community was highly engaged with the local political structures, a black man's activism would be normative and insufficiently noteworthy to bring him to the attention of a bloodthirsty mob. We simply do not have the information to allow us to make those claims. Future research could possibly exploit the information available in local church rolls, voter registration data, and the agricultural census and various tax records. With this additional information, it might be possible to more fully replicate our analyses from chapters 4 and 5. For now, our findings remain largely speculative.

It is, however, equally intriguing to consider the possibility that, as the bulk of our evidence suggests, the risk associated with particular individual-level measures of status or marginality were completely unaffected by the character of local power arrangements as reflected in economic, political, and religious indicators. The results from chapters 4 and 5 suggest that individuals who were more normative within their local communities enjoyed some degree of protection—perhaps a level of anonymity granted by being unremarkable. The converse of this, of course, is that being unusual could seal a man with the mark of vulnerability that increased his likelihood of being targeted. The evidence from this chapter suggests that these processes operated in a more or less similar manner throughout the South, in communities dominated by King Cotton and heavily integrated into global markets by virtue of this fact, as well as in those communities composed mainly of yeoman farmers who produced primarily for their own consumption. Despite overwhelming evidence that unusual levels of social status or marginality made some men targets and provided others with relative immunity, we find no evidence here that these factors were linked to the local institutional structures *most imbued* with power—the economic foundations, the political arena, and the religious alignments. That in itself is somewhat surprising.

To this point in the book, we have restricted our attention to the individual-level characteristics of southern black men—considering how those characteristics were related to the risk of being targeted by lynch mobs and how their influence on the likelihood of victimization varied by the nature of the local context. This restricted focus can be justified by the fact that southern lynch victims were overwhelmingly African American males. However, some lynch victims were not black, and a small number were females.[19] In the next chapter we consider in some depth these atypical victims of southern mob violence.

CHAPTER SEVEN

Atypical Victims: Females and White Males

Bob Sims

In the late nineteenth century, Bob Sims was a white man living in Choctaw County, Alabama, an accident of fate that in itself set him apart from the vast majority of lynch victims. Choctaw County is situated on the western edge of the state's midline. Its county seat, Butler, is roughly thirty-five miles south and east of Meridian, Mississippi, the nearest city of note. Mr. Sims was reported to be a self-proclaimed religious prophet and the leader of a notorious band of outlaws. The Sims Gang—or Simsites, the appellation given by some newspaper reports—operated an illegal still and terrorized the area around the county. In December 1891, they were said to have murdered three people and burned their victims' house to the ground, their most heinous crime yet. A group of local residents banded together to form a posse and bring Bob Sims and the rest of his outlaw gang to justice. On Christmas Day, Choctaw County's sheriff was able to negotiate a surrender involving Mr. Sims and either two or three of his fellow outlaws—the newspaper reports were unclear on the number of people involved. While the men—Bob Sims, Tom Savage, Savage's nineteen-year-old son, and possibly another member of the Savage family—were being transported to Butler, the county seat, they were overtaken by a mob, and Bob Sims and both (or possibly all three) men from the Savage family were lynched (*Chillicothe [MO] Constitution*, December 28, 1891; *Frederick [MD] News*, December 28, 1891). Over the course of the next three weeks, in a sustained frenzy of violence, a total of seven members of Bob Sims's gang—which apparently included both black and white members—were captured and killed by mobs of local citizens.

We located a forty-year-old white man named Robert Sims, enumerated in the 1880 census, living in Choctaw County, Alabama, with his wife, Eliza, six of their children, and two of Eliza's adult brothers. Living in a household that included extended family members was not unusual for black lynch victims, and if Bob Sims is indicative, the practice may have been common among white victims as well. The next household recorded by the census enumerator following that of Robert and Eliza Sims was headed by a thirty-year-old man named James Sims (perhaps a brother of Bob Sims?) who was living with his sister, a widow named Harriet Moseley. One of the other lynch victims killed during Choctaw County's rampage of violence was a white man named Moseley Sims, who may have been related to both Harriet Moseley and Robert Sims and his family. A confluence of factors gives us considerable confidence that the white man we located in the 1880 census is the man who was killed by a lynch mob in December 1891, including the coincidence of the names "Moseley" and "Sims" and the fact that we also found Tom Savage and his two sons enumerated in the same rural precinct as Bob Sims. The appearance of the Savage and Sims families on consecutive pages of the enumerators' manuscripts suggests that the two families lived in close geographic proximity to each other. That there was only one other white man named Bob or Robert Sims enumerated in Choctaw County or any of its contiguous counties also increases our confidence that the white man we located in the 1880 census is the man who was killed by a lynch mob in December 1891.

Bob Sims was a farmer but something of an outsider in his adopted home of Alabama. He and both of his parents had been born in North Carolina. His wife, Eliza, and her mother had been born in South Carolina, while her father had been born in New York—not only out of state but outside of Dixie altogether. One of Eliza's brothers, who was nineteen years old when the census was conducted in 1880, had been born in Alabama, probably around 1861. This suggests that as the secession of the southern states became more likely, Eliza's family had relocated firmly within the Deep South. Both Bob and Eliza Sims were literate, as was the younger of Eliza's brothers. The three oldest Sims children were reported as having been enrolled in school during the prior academic term. Unlike the "average" profile of black and mixed-race men who were lynched, however, Bob Sims, a white man, had characteristics that suggest a relatively high level of social status. He was married, literate, and recorded as the head of his household. We do not know whether Mr. Sims owned his farm or was a tenant farmer.[1] He would have been a relatively old man compared to the profile of black and mixed-race men who were lynched, and the profile we gain from his census records—a middle-aged man living with his wife and children—hardly sounds like the leader of a gang of outlaws, although perhaps an older family man would be a likely candidate for a religious leader. Did a different logic affect white men's vulnerability to mob violence, relative to that for black men?

Ella Mays Wiggins

In 1929 Ella Mays Wiggins was a twenty-eight-year-old white woman who lived in Gaston County, North Carolina. Gaston County lies in the state's western Piedmont region, about ninety miles east and a bit south of Asheville. Ms. Wiggins had been deserted by her husband and was working in the local textile mills when, according to newspaper reports, she joined the union and attended a public organizing meeting held in the county seat of Gastonia. A mob shot and killed her, although the details surrounding the incident are unclear (*Raleigh News and Observer*, September 15 and September 16, 1929). We were unable to locate Ella Wiggins—or anyone enumerated under her unmarried name, Ella Mays—in the 1920 census records. We did locate her death certificate, however, and from this document we learned her age, the name of her husband, Jake Wiggins, and that Ms. Wiggins, née Mays, and both of her parents, Jonas and Katherine, had been born in Tennessee. Ms. Wiggins's death certificate confirms that she worked in the textile industry and had been killed by a "gunshot wound from [an] unidentified person in [a] mob attack."[2]

Ella Mays Wiggins's actions posed a threat to numerous tropes about southern white womanhood. She was apparently no longer sharing a household with her husband and engaged in paid labor outside of her home, challenging the cultural perception of white women as economically dependent. Ms. Wiggin's union activity was even more unusual and distinctive and suggests she at least partially embraced her identity as a worker. Her willingness to engage in high-risk unionization efforts in order to secure her rights as a laborer further signals that Ms. Wiggins saw paid employment as a likely part of her future. Participating in the labor movement within the southern textile industry also threatened the economic dominance of the South's elite entrepreneurial class. In what may have been a veiled attempt at questioning her virtue, the article that appeared in the *Raleigh News and Observer* documenting her lynching specified not only that she had been abandoned by her husband but that she had reverted back to using her "maiden" name (September 16, 1929). Was it perhaps the multiple ways in which Ella Mays Wiggins failed to conform to dominant expectations of white women's behavior and challenged the prevailing social arrangements that caused her to be singled out for mob violence?

Mary Dennis and Stella Young

Alachua County, which includes the city of Gainesville, sits at the intersection of Florida's panhandle and its peninsula. In August 1916, six African Americans—four men and two women—were lynched there over the course of two days. The trouble started when a man named Boisy Long shot two men, including a deputy sheriff, as they attempted to arrest him. The deputy was killed. Mr. Long was reputed to belong to a ring of hog thieves, and others in the gang supposedly assisted him in making an escape (*Jacksonville Sunday Times-Union*, August 20, 1916; *Atlanta Constitution*, August 20 and August 21, 1916). Mary Dennis, one of the black women who was lynched, seems an unlikely hog thief. In the 1910 census, we find her listed as a twenty-five-year-old widow living in a rented house with her father, his second wife, and Mary's four surviving children, ranging in age from nine to one. The household also included one of Mary Dennis's adult sisters, along with her three children, and two additional teenaged relatives. Ms. Dennis's father and his wife of three years were both born in Georgia, although each of the other family members was born in Florida. All members of the household who were older than nine years of age were actively employed and listed as working for wages as farm laborers. All of the adult and teenaged members of Mary Dennis's household were also literate, and the teenagers and school-aged children reported having been enrolled in school during the previous year.

Mary Dennis's death certificate provides more limited information, estimating her age at "about 35," although she likely would have been thirty-one or thirty-two years old, based on her age as recorded in the census. She is also listed as having been a married housewife. Both her birthplace and that of each of her parents is listed as unknown. Ms. Dennis's death certificate is clear and direct, however, in stating the cause of her death: "by neck being broken hanging from limb by ¾ inch Grass rope by Party or Parties unknown." However improbable it may seem that a widow (or perhaps a married woman, if her death certificate was correct) with several young children, who was rapidly approaching middle age, would be part of a gang of hog thieves, the southern newspapers reported it as such without question.

Believing that Stella Young, the other black woman lynched in Alachua County in August 1916, belonged to this same criminal enterprise may also seem somewhat untenable, if for no other reason than her apparent economic and social advantage. We were not able to locate Stella Young's death certificate, but we did find her listed in the 1910 census enumerator's manuscripts. In 1910 she was nineteen years old, unmarried, and living on a farm with her mother, stepfather, and ten siblings ranging in age from twenty to two years old. Determining that we had located the person who had been lynched required a bit of thought, since Stella Young was enumerated in the 1910 census as Estella McHenry. However, her stepfather's surname was Young, and Andrew McHenry, another of the lynch victims, is the eldest among her siblings recorded living in the household. Given the historic social expectation that young marriageable women would have a father figure as a "sponsor" when they entered the marriage market, we think it is probable that "Estella McHenry" was known socially by her stepfather's last name, or even that he had formally or informally adopted her.

The McHenry/Young family owned its farm free and clear, no small feat for African Americans in the early decades of the twentieth century. Stella's stepfather, William Redd Young, is listed as a farmer, and Stella, her mother, and the four oldest of her siblings are listed as working as farm laborers. All of the teenagers and adults in the household were literate, and every child over the age of five was enrolled in school. The matriarch and her husband had both been born in Georgia, as had Stella's biological father, but Stella and all of her siblings had been born in Florida.

In addition to having been accused of aiding a fugitive and lynched for this supposed transgression, Mary Dennis and Stella Young appear to have much in common. They were relatively close in age, both adult daughters from large farm families, and both living with parents who were in their second marriages. The parents in both families had migrated to Florida from Georgia. Both the Dennis and McHenry/Young families appeared to value literacy and education. And while Mary Dennis's family seems to have been somewhat less economically prosperous—evidenced by their status as renters and by the assortment of relatives comingled within the household—both families were able to provide formal education for their school-aged children. Was there something in these biographical commonalities that might suggest characteristics that increased black women's vulnerability to mob violence?

Our focus so far in the book has been on black male victims, like Gus Knight, the teenager from Jefferson County, Georgia, we introduced in chapter 4, and Steve Jenkins, the older man accused of stabbing a planter following a dispute over a contract in Noxubee County, Mississippi, whose case we discussed in chapter 5. This emphasis is not without reason: six out of every seven lynch victims were black or mixed-race men and adolescent boys. However, as the examples we have just provided illustrate, both black and white women, as well as white men,[3] also fell victim to mob violence. How much did the characteristics of white and black men who were lynched parallel each other? Who were the women unlucky enough to suffer and die at the hands of Judge Lynch?

Profiling the Atypical Victims

Because the number of female and white male lynch victims is so much smaller than the number of black male victims, we are constrained in our ability to empirically analyze their personal characteristics. There were only 79 women and 282 white men in the Beck-Tolnay inventory (2010). Among these, we were not able to search for people who had been killed between 1896 and 1899, whose names were not recorded in the newspaper articles reporting their deaths, or for whom we lacked complete enough names to allow us to conduct a search. This left us with just 63 women—only four of whom were white—and 218 white men among the more than 2,100 victims that we searched for, distributed across ten states and nearly five decades.

Because our inventory includes relatively few victims who were women or white men, we are unable to conduct meaningful statistical comparisons between these atypical victims and the other people living in their home communities, as we have done with black and mixed-race male victims in earlier chapters. We can, however, draw from the original Beck-Tolnay inventory of all lynch victims, as well as from the information obtained for those female and white male victims who *were* successfully linked to their census records,[4] to expand our understanding of who these atypical victims were and how their victimization compared to that of the far more vulnerable group—African American males. In this chapter, we examine some of the same characteristics that we did among black male victims, such as literacy, family structure, age, and occupation. We also present additional information on the types of crimes that women and white men were accused of committing, the temporal and geographic patterns associated with these "nontraditional" victims, and other, more narrative aspects of their stories.

White Male Victims

How common was it for lynch mobs to target white men? The share of lynchings that targeted white men varied substantially across both time and place. Figure 7.1 graphically depicts the percentage of all victims who were white men in each of the years between 1882 and 1930. In the early years of the lynching era, it is perhaps surprising to note that roughly one in five victims was a white man.[5] Many of these men, however, were easily identified as outsiders. These were victims like the eleven Italian immigrants rousted out of jail in New Orleans on March 14, 1891, and hanged for suspicion of conspiring to assassinate the local police commissioner (*Daily Picayune* [New Orleans], March 16, 1891). As the incidence of lynching increased rapidly during the "Bloody 1890s" and the practice became welded more firmly to other efforts to suppress and terrorize the southern black population, the percentage of victims who were white men declined rapidly and remained quite low until the years immediately following World War I. Not only did the concentration of white men among the population of lynch victims increase in the later part of the lynching era, but the characteristics of white male victims became distinct and again appeared to reflect an outsider status. White men who were targeted during the interwar years were often identified in local news reports as white ethnics and, like the eleven unlucky Italian souls killed in New Orleans in 1891, were frequently immigrants.

These were victims like John Pobin, an immigrant from Poland who settled in Bibb County, Alabama, where he lived in a rented house with his wife, Mary, and their six children. Pobin supported his family by

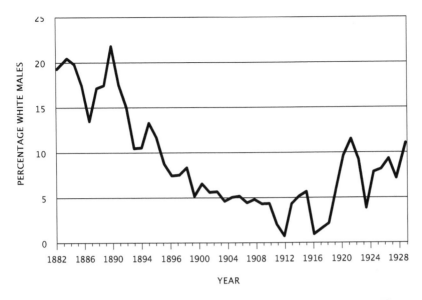

Figure 7.1 Percentage of Lynch Victims Who Were White Males, 1882–1930 (Smoothed Three-Year Averages)

working in the coal mines. In the summer of 1923, when he would have been forty-eight years old, John Pobin was attacked and killed for reasons that are unknown to us today (*Montgomery Advertiser*, July 14, 1923). More is known about the accusations against Nola Romey,[6] an immigrant from Syria who was enumerated as living in Valdosta, in Lowndes County, Georgia, in the 1920 census. In 1920 Nola Romey was thirty-five years old and lived with his Syrian-born wife, Fannie, and their two children, ten-year-old Icer and three-year-old Emmaline. By 1929 Nola and Fannie had relocated to Columbia County, Florida, roughly sixty-five miles south and west of Valdosta, and opened a store. In Columbia County they had an altercation with the chief of police, a Mr. Baker, over a sign the couple was displaying in front of their store. Baker was injured in the altercation, and Mrs. Romey was also shot and killed. Perhaps out of grief, Mr. Romey made threats against Chief Baker. A mob subsequently broke into the jail where he was being held and lynched him in retaliation (*Gainesville Daily Sun*, May 18, 1929). A more sensational case involving a white man who was an outsider was the lynching of Leo M. Frank. Mr. Frank was a Jew from New York who managed a pencil factory in Cobb County, Georgia. In 1915 this thirty-one-year-old son of German immigrants was

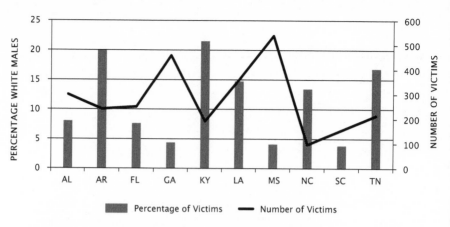

Figure 7.2 Percentage of Lynch Victims Who Were White Males and Total Number of Lynch Victims, by State, 1882–1930

accused of murdering Mary Phagan, a child laborer in his factory, taken from custody in the local jail, and hanged (Dinnerstein 1968).

We present in Figure 7.2 the share of victims who were white men in each of the ten states covered by our analyses. The vertical bars correspond to the left-hand axis, indicating the percentage of all people lynched in each state who were white men. The pattern that emerges here seems to demonstrate that white men were largely immune from the risk of lynching in some states, particularly those in the Deep South, while they constituted a substantial portion of those targeted by mob violence in other states. The degree to which white men were represented among a state's population of lynch victims has different implications, however, when viewed in conjunction with the overall level of mob violence in each state. The jagged horizontal line identifies the total number of known victims in each state (which includes men and women of all races) and corresponds to the axis on the right. Combining this information tells us that Louisiana, which appears to have a moderate *share* of victims who were white men, actually had the largest *number* of white male victims, at 53, because of the large number of people who were lynched in that state overall (N = 360). Despite having a relatively small number of lynchings (N = 191), Kentucky had one of the largest numbers of victims who were white men (N = 41) because white men comprised a high percentage of victims in the Bluegrass State.

Female Victims

Compared even to white men, far fewer southern women (either black or white) were lynched. The percentage of victims who were women remained relatively constant across space and over time, never climbing above 5 percent in any state or during any time period. One such female victim was named Mary Turner, a black woman living in or near Valdosta, Georgia, the seat of Lowndes County, in 1918. As World War I raged in Europe, her husband, Hayes Turner, was accused of participating in the murder of a white farmer. Mr. Turner was being transported by local police when a mob wrested him from the authorities and lynched him on May 18, 1918 (*Quitment Free Press*, May 24, 1918). Following her husband's brutal death, Ms. Turner—whom some news reports list as "Hattie" rather than Mary—made what were perceived by local whites to have been "unwise remarks" about the circumstances under which her husband had been killed. The day after her husband's lynching, she was taken by a mob to a spot sixteen miles north of Valdosta, near the town of Barney. The group set Mary Turner on fire, burning her clothes off. They then mutilated her with knives while she was still alive and finally hanged her and riddled her body with bullets (*Atlanta Constitution*, May 20, May 21, and May 23, 1918; *Macon News*, May 20, 1918; *Quitman Free Press*, May 24, 1918). Ms. Turner's alleged offense—having the audacity to question the actions of the mob that lynched her husband—involved a challenge to the prerogatives to which local whites assumed they were entitled. This fact is not surprising, in light of research by historian Crystal Feimster (2009), which suggests that black women who were lynched were frequently targeted because they challenged the practices of white supremacy and stood up for their family members. Mary Turner's case appears to confirm this assessment.

As discussed in chapter 2, however, our effort to locate the census records of female victims was made more difficult by the cultural convention of women adopting the family name of their husbands when they married. Searching for common names like Mary and Hattie (which may have been a nickname for "Harriet") Turner yielded too many matches for us to say with any degree of certainty whether any of them was the woman who was tortured and lynched in May 1918. We did identify two men who could have been Mary Turner's husband, although neither was married at the time that the census was taken in 1910. The first, named Hazel B. Turner, was enumerated at age seventeen as living with his parents and siblings on a farm family in Brooks County, Georgia, the adjacent county that lies directly west of Lowndes County. Seven years later, on June 5, 1917, Hazel B. Turner registered for the draft in Colquitt County, Georgia, about forty miles northwest of Valdosta. On his draft registration card, Turner listed his age as twenty-five and noted that he had a wife and four children. It is possible that this man was the person lynched near Valdosta, Georgia, and that the wife he identified on his draft registration form was Mary Turner, who, as a grieving widow, was brutalized and murdered the day after her husband's death. Because her name was not recorded in the draft document, however, we have no way of being certain.

The other possible match for Hayes Turner was a fourteen-year-old boy in 1910, living about fifty miles southwest of Valdosta, across the state line in the Drifton Precinct of Jefferson County, Florida. This young man also belonged to a farm family and was living with both of his parents and three brothers at the time the census was taken. "Hays" Turner from Jefferson County, Florida, would have been roughly twenty-two at the time that he—and his wife, Mary—were lynched, if he was indeed the victim. Regardless of whether either of the men we have identified as possible matches was the Hayes Turner who was married to Mary Turner in 1918, the fact remains that the process of finding female lynch victims is somewhat problematized by the practice that many women assume their husband's surname when they marry. In light of that, it is worth revisiting the fact that our efforts to search for female victims were even more successful than were our efforts to identify male victims. Overall, we located thirty-five of the sixty-three women who were included in the original inventory of victims, for a successful match rate of 55.6 percent. This number is significantly higher—in the statistical sense—than the 42.6 percent rate at which we successfully located black men in the census.

White women were particularly unlikely to have been victimized. Of the 2,805 victims in the Beck-Tolnay inventory (2010), only 5 (or 0.18 percent) were white women. The idea that mob violence would be visited upon white women is perhaps a bit unexpected—particularly because the protection of white womanhood was often given as an excuse for lynching black men. Indeed, the white women who were killed often exhibited characteristics, as did Ella Mays Wiggins, discussed earlier, that challenged southern patriarchal notions of appropriate femininity.

The case of Jane Wade, a white woman who was lynched along with a white man named J. R. Dorsey in 1884, provides a good illustration. Jane Wade and J. R. Dorsey were lynched in Centre, a small town in Cherokee County, Alabama. Centre sits in the northeastern corner of Alabama, nestled in a bend in the Coosa River a few miles west of the Georgia state line. The pair was accused of murdering Dorsey's niece, a Mrs. Mary Davis of Alpine, Georgia, a town situated a little more than twenty miles east of Centre. We located Jane Wade in the 1880 census living next door to James R. Dorsey, who was recorded in the census at age sixty-nine years. Mr. Dorsey lived with his wife, Elvira; their granddaughter, Emma Atkins; Emma's husband, William; and the Atkinses' young son, Joseph. Ms. Wade was listed as an illiterate thirty-five-year-old widow living with an eleven-year-old daughter, Arminda, and a thirteen-year-old son, John. Both of the Wade children attended school, and it appears that John worked on the Dorsey farm. Jane Wade and both of her children were born in Georgia. In a journalistic step akin to the language used to justify the lynchings of black men, the *Atlanta Constitution* reported that Wade was "a woman of bad character" and that she and Dorsey had "taken up with" each other several years earlier (October 22, 1884).

Two white woman lynched in Kentucky in 1895 similarly had their sexual morals questioned in the aftermath of their deaths. Both cases also present examples of women being victimized primarily because of the actions of the men with whom they were romantically entangled. During the height of the 1895 summer, on the evening of June 28, a man named Abitahl Colston reportedly murdered two men in Trigg County, Kentucky. Trigg County is in the southwestern corner of Kentucky, on the state line with Tennessee, about sixty miles southeast of Paducah and eighty miles northwest of Nashville. The *Louisville Courier-Journal* (July 2, 1895) relates that Colston sought refuge in "the cabin of his mistress," Mollie Smith, and that sometime overnight the two were attacked and killed by a vengeful mob. Six months after the deaths of Mr. Colston and Ms. Smith, a woman identified only by her husband's name—Mrs. T. J. West—was hunted down by a mob and burned to death in a cabin about four miles outside the town of Lebanon, in Marion County (*Louisville Courier-Journal*, December 30, 1895). Lebanon is small and isolated, with no major geographic landmarks nearby, but forms a triangle with two of Kentucky's leading cities, about sixty-five miles southeast of Louisville and sixty-five miles southwest of Lexington. Mrs. West's crime was that she had been living "in open adultery" with a man named William Dever.

The narrative evidence from the incidents in which white women were lynched is scant, consistent with the fact that the lynching of white women was an extraordinarily unusual phenomenon. The information we do have, however, suggests that if *actual* violation of the strict sexual codes of comportment imposed on southern white women was not a factor that enhanced these women's vulnerability to mob violence, the southern media did call white women's virtue into question once they had come to the attention of a mob. Indeed, this evidence is similar to historian Helen McClure's findings (2013) that postmortem discussions of white female mob victims in the press characterized the women as masculine, sexually permissive, engaged in the occult, or some combination of these. While black female victims were certainly cast as deviant once they had been killed, the public discourse appears to have been less likely to focus on their sexual behavior than was true for white women who were lynched.

The Alleged Offenses of Atypical Victims

The logic of lynching can also be better understood by examining group-level variation in the offenses that women, black men, and white men were accused of having committed. For example, because black men were often characterized in journalistic accounts of lynching and other white cultural discourse as sexual *predators*—a characterization that was not systematically applied to women or to white men—we might expect that black male victims would be more likely than either women or white men to have been accused of crimes of a sexual nature. Similarly, because white men's social transgressions would not be interpreted by other white community members through the lens of racial hierarchy, we might anticipate that white men would be less likely to have been lynched for acts construed to challenge the prevailing power dynamics. To explore these ideas, we categorized the offenses that were used to justify the lynching of women, black and mixed-race men, and white men in the Beck-Tolnay inventory (2010).[7] As a first step in identifying whether and in what ways the atypical victims were different from black and mixed-race men who were lynched, we first compared the offenses or crimes that were used to justify each lynching by group membership.

Note that because we have this information for all victims, regardless of whether we were able to search for or successfully locate their census records, we are able to include all documented victims.

In order to do this, we classified each case according to what the person who was lynched was accused of doing and established a set of categories to create a typology of supposed infractions. Recall that while some victims were, in fact, accused of very serious crimes, others were accused of what seem to us to be trivial violations of the social conventions that predominated in the Jim Crow–era South. The first category we established was whether someone committed a violent act or made threats of violence. This was, by far, the most common type of offense used to justify the lynching of black men. We also established a category of offenses that had sexual overtones. This included accusations of *actual* sex crimes like rape but also events in which it was somewhat unclear whether physical contact had occurred—consensual or otherwise. In these instances where the occurrence of physical contact was unclear, some sort of violation of the norms of appropriate sexual behavior could have been inferred from the circumstances or might have been their logical conclusion. For example, this category includes incidents where a man was found hiding in a woman's room or made flirtatious or romantic gestures toward a specific woman.

People who were lynched because of their relationship to another person, such as attempting to protect *someone else* who was being targeted by a mob, were identified as having been attacked because of a "connection" and were categorized as such. Victims accused of such acts as burglary or larceny were classified as having committed "property" offenses. For still other victims, the public discourse surrounding their death made generic accusations of their having a generally bad character—often expressed as being a "desperado" or an "outlaw"—without any specific accusations of a particular offense. These people are identified as having been accused of a "character" violation. A theoretically rich category of "challenger" offenses includes actions that seemed to defy the prevailing racial and economic hierarchies, such as attempting to vote, attempting to incite a race riot, or joining a union. We also included in this grouping actions whose purposes were often overtly rebellious, such as barn burning or other acts of arson.[8] Our final category includes people like John Pobin, the coal miner who emigrated from Poland and was lynched in Bibb County, Alabama, in 1923, for an unknown reason. For these cases,

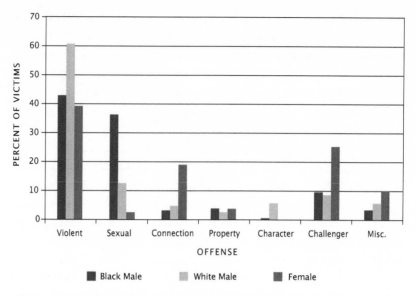

Figure 7.3 Percentage of Lynch Victims Accused of Different Types of Offenses, by Victim Demographic Characteristics, 1882–1930

the "offense" was either unrecorded or simply defied easy classification. These victims are grouped in a "miscellaneous" category.[9]

Figure 7.3 depicts the percentage of victims in each demographic category—black men, white men, and women—who were accused of each class of offense. As this bar graph clearly depicts, the type of behavior that was used to justify lynchings varied sharply according to the victim's demographic profile. Compared to black and mixed-race male lynch victims, white men were significantly *more likely* to have been accused of violent offenses or generic accusations of having a bad character. White men were much *less likely* to have been accused of offenses with sexual overtones than were black men. The proportions of black or mixed-race men and white men who were accused of other types of offenses was relatively similar, although it would be a gross mischaracterization to interpret that fact as suggesting that black and white men accused of, for example, property crimes were equally vulnerable to lynching. Only seven white men were recorded as having been lynched for property crimes across the ten states and nearly five decades covered in our analyses, compared to ninety-two black and mixed-race men.

There are simply too few white female victims to allow for meaningful exploration of whether black and white women were accused of similar offenses. We therefore compare the distribution of the types of offenses that *all female victims* were accused of to the accusations of transgressions that were levied against black and mixed-race men. We see that virtually identical proportions of women and black and mixed-race men were accused of violent offenses. Women were much less likely than men of either race to have been accused of sexual offenses. Indeed, for only two of the seventy-nine female victims (or 2.53 percent of all female victims) was the violation of sexual norms used as justification for their killing. As we discussed earlier in this chapter, however, white women experienced near-universal questioning of their sexual morality postmortem. Regardless, the percentage of women whose victimization was justified *at the time* with reference to sexual norm violations was significantly lower than the 33.68 percent of all men, or 36.53 percent of black and mixed-race men, who were accused of sexual offenses. Compared to both black and white men, women were significantly more likely to have been lynched for behaviors that challenged the prevailing racial and economic hierarchy—for example, Ella Mays Wiggins's lynching in apparent retaliation for union activity.

Women were also more likely than men to have been what we might think of as secondary or proxy victims. That is, nearly one in five female victims was lynched because of their *connection* to someone who was perceived to have committed some sort of offense. An example would be the lynchings of Mary Dennis and Stella Young, who were killed because they were suspected of having harbored a fugitive. In an even starker example of a lynching that fell in this category, in Mitchell County, Georgia, in 1906, a black man named Jett Hicks was accused of murdering a prominent white farmer. While he eluded capture for several days, his wife, Meta Hicks, was shot to death by unknown assailants while she worked in the fields of the farm where the couple was employed. We have identified no newspaper reports that allege that Ms. Hicks was involved in the crime of which her husband was accused. *After* his wife's murder, Jett Hicks was also captured by a mob and lynched (*Atlanta Journal*, November 9, 1906; *Daily Picayune* [New Orleans], November 9, 1906).

The Personal Characteristics of Atypical Victims

In chapters 3, 4, 5, and 6, we explored the basic demographic characteristics of black and mixed-race men who were victimized by lynch

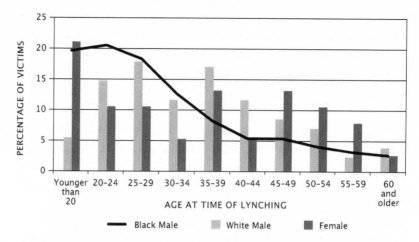

Figure 7.4 Age at Time of Lynching for Black Male, White Male, and Female
Victims, 1882–1929

mobs, with a particular focus on those characteristics that might have
identified victims as having marginal social status or characteristics that
challenged the prevailing racial hierarchy. We now ask whether those
same individual-level traits that suggest outsider or marginal status applied to the female and white male lynch victims we were able to locate
in the census manuscripts. It is worth repeating that the small number
of female and white male lynch victims prevents us from conducting
the same type of intensive statistical comparisons that were so important for obtaining the evidence described and interpreted in previous
chapters.

Earlier in this book (see Figure 3.1) we identified that black and mixed-
race male lynch victims were disproportionately concentrated in the
young adult years. Figure 7.4 presents the age distribution of female and
white male victims, identified by the vertical bars, and allows comparison
to the age distribution for black and mixed-race men who were killed by
mobs, presented graphically with a trend line.[10] From visual examination
of the graph, we can discern two key pieces of information. First, both
female victims and white male victims appear to have been older, on
average, compared with black and mixed-race male victims. Second, the
age distribution of white men appears to be more heavily concentrated
in young adulthood and middle age, while female victims are more likely
to be teenagers or older women, concentrated at the upper and lower

ends of the age distribution. This evidence suggests that important differences may exist between these groups of unlikely victims, as well as between women, white men, and black and mixed-race male victims.

These apparent differences in the age composition of the victim population by gender and race also yield statistically significant group-level differences if we examine the mean and median ages for each group at the time of their lynching. The mean age for black male victims at their time of death was roughly thirty-two years, and the median was twenty-nine years. On average, female and white male victims appear to have been somewhat older, with both groups having a mean and a median age of thirty-five years at the time of their deaths.

The number of female and white male victims is sufficiently small—particularly because we successfully matched only a fraction of them—to preclude our being able to make claims about whether statistically significant differences exist in the age distributions across categories of victims who committed specific kinds of offenses. In general, however, the limited evidence at our disposal suggests that for both female victims and white male victims, those who were accused of violent offenses were younger and those who were accused of challenging the prevailing racial and class hierarchies were older than was true of the victim population overall. Alternative interpretations of these age patterns are possible. First, challenging southern social hierarchies was likely more common among older individuals, particularly non-teens. The difference in the age distribution of victims by demographic category, then, may be reflective of the types of offenses used to justify the lynching of women, black men, and white men. Second, these differences indicate that individual traits may have affected vulnerability differently for people with different demographic profiles. Lacking the ability to conduct more sophisticated statistical analyses, such as multivariate logistic regression, we are unable to disentangle the relationship between age, "offense," and vulnerability for women and white men.

Atypical Victims and Social Embeddedness

We now turn our attention to assessing the degree to which the women and white men who were killed by lynch mobs appear to have been embedded within their local communities. As we did in chapter 4, when we focused exclusively on black and mixed-race male victims, we will examine measures of geographic mobility, employment status or sector, and the relational "location" of each victim within his or her household. We use these factors to compare the proportion of female and white male victims who appear to have been more and less central to the social and economic fabric of their families and local communities with the degree of embeddedness we found among black male victims.

We first classified female and white male victims by their role within the local agricultural economy, identifying those who were not labor force participants, those who were agricultural workers, and those who were employed outside of the agricultural sector. We found occupational patterns that are quite unsurprising based on normative gender roles and the economic underpinning of the American South during the lynching era. The majority of female victims are recorded as having no paid occupation, while just over one in ten male victims was not reported as engaged in the paid labor force, regardless of race. Among all three categories of victims, labor force participants were heavily concentrated in agricultural employment. Nearly three in four—roughly identical proportions—of female, white male, and black and mixed-race male labor force participants worked in the agricultural sector.

Comparing two additional metrics of social embeddedness—whether victims were likely to have been born out of state and whether victims were enumerated in the same county where they were lynched—we observed interesting differences and similarities between groups of victims. While there is only a modest difference in the proportion of female and black male victims who were born out of state (11.2 percent compared to 16.1 percent), white male victims were significantly more likely (28.7 percent) to have been born someplace other than the state in which they were lynched. This evidence suggests that for white men, this particular kind of outsider status might have entailed a certain level of risk not experienced by women or black and mixed-race men. The concentration of immigrants among white male victims undoubtedly contributes to this difference.

In contrast, no meaningful differences emerged between female victims, white male victims, and black male victims in the proportion that was lynched outside of their county of enumeration. The coincidence of higher levels of white male victims who were born out of state and a lack of group-level differences in the percentage of victims who were lynched outside of the county where they were enumerated hint

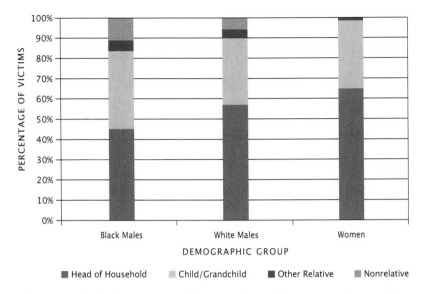

Figure 7.5 Relationship to Household Head for Black Male, White Male, and Female Lynch Victims, 1882–1930

at the possibility of underlying differences among these groups in the relationship between migration (interstate and intercounty) and the risk of victimization. However, the small number of atypical victims prevents us from exploring that possibility. Had we a larger number of white male victims, we could conduct meaningful comparisons between their geographic mobility and that of other white men living in their communities. However, we lack a sufficient number to make such a comparison, so this remains speculative.

We also examined the position of victims within their households—that is, whether they were the householder,[11] the child or grandchild of the household head, related to the head of household in some other way, or not related. We estimated these general percentages for all victims and also identified the percentage who were householders for a subsample of victims restricted to those aged sixteen years and older. We found that female victims were most likely to have been household heads and black male victims were least likely. Given the age distributions of our different categories of victims—with female and white male victims being somewhat older, on average, than black male victims—this difference might not be surprising. However, the disparity between groups is statistically significant and obtains when we use the entire sample of victims, as well as when we restrict the sample to include only those who were at least sixteen years old when the census was taken. Significant differences also emerged when we compared the proportions of victims who were unrelated to the head of household. While we located no female victims who were unrelated to the head of their household, one in twenty-five white male victims (4.22 percent) and one in nine black male victims (11.23 percent) were not related to the head of their household. These results, which suggest substantially different average social locations for victims based on racial and gender categories, are graphically depicted in Figure 7.5.[12]

Atypical Victims and Social Status

We also explored whether the demographic characteristics of atypical lynch victims were linked with their general levels of social and economic status. For this set of comparisons, we incorporated measures similar to those we used in chapter 5—literacy, occupational status, labor force participation, and home ownership. We compared these status-linked characteristics for atypical victims with those of black and mixed-race men who were lynched.

We first assessed whether, among active labor force participants, each worker was employed in a higher-status or a lower-status occupation, to determine the degree to which each victim may have enjoyed a modicum of protection afforded by higher social and economic standing. Similar to the way in which the concentration of victims across industrial categories reflected the South's economic reliance on cotton and other forms of agricultural production, the occupational distribution of victims reflects the racial and gender hierarchy that predominated within the United States during the late nineteenth and early twentieth centuries. As we mentioned earlier, the majority of female victims reported no paid employment outside of the household. Those women who did work for pay were almost exclusively concentrated in the lowest rungs of the occupational ladder.[13] The sole woman who was classified as having a higher-status job was Jennie Steer, a young black woman who was widowed, living in Caddo Parish, Louisiana, and listed in the 1900 census enumerator's manuscripts as both head of her own household and as a farmer. This designation appears to have bestowed higher rank than a farm laborer or someone "keeping house," as was often the convention for married women in farm families, and undoubtedly resulted from the absence of a male head of household. However, among male victims, white men were more than twice as likely as black men to have higher-status occupations[14]—57 percent of white men worked in occupations that were professional, skilled, semiskilled, or entailed some degree of autonomy and self-determination, compared with just 26 percent among black males—and about half as likely to be working lower-status jobs, 32 percent compared to 63 percent.

We also see the South's prevailing racial hierarchy reflected in disparities in the relatively high percentage of white male victims who were recorded as being literate. While female victims[15] and black male victims had nearly identical rates of literacy—hovering right around 45 percent—the rate of literacy for white male victims was nearly 80 percent higher. Three out of every four white male victims was able to both read and write. While the small number of female and white male victims precludes our conducting statistical comparisons between these groups and similar individuals from the counties where they were lynched, it seems that the racial literacy gap among these atypical victims may have reflected rather typical racial and gender educational inequalities prevailing in the southern states.

We identified in chapter 5 that owning a farm—reflective of both an individual's degree of embeddedness within the local agricultural economy and his economic success—affected black and mixed-race men's vulnerability. Similar proportions of female and black male victims were recorded as living on farms (53 percent and 56 percent, respectively), while again, the percentage of white male victims who were farm residents was much higher, at 69 percent. A surprising difference emerges, however, when we compare the home ownership levels for the three groups. Restricting our sample to only those victims who were either head of household or a relative of the householder, we see that black male victims were significantly less likely than were female or white male victims to live in a home that was owned by one of its occupants. Because home ownership was only recorded beginning in 1900, we lack a large enough number of observations in each group to determine whether *farm ownership* appeared to be particularly common among either group of unlikely victims. For example, we are able to identify only nine of the female victims and sixteen of the white male victims as living in an owned residence, regardless of farm status.

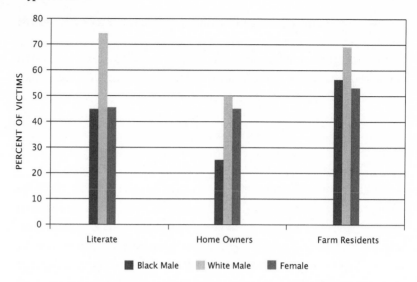

Figure 7.6 Indicators of Social Standing for Black Male, White Male, and Female Lynch Victims, 1882–1929

The percentage of victims in each demographic category who were recorded as being literate, living in a home owned by themselves or by one of their relatives, or living on a farm is graphically presented in Figure 7.6.[16] Because we restricted our comparisons to those victims who were at least ten years old at the time of the census for the only one of these characteristics that was plausibly linked to age—literacy—it is unlikely that the older average age of female and white male victims was driving the difference in home ownership rates between these groups and black and mixed-race men. Farm residence and home ownership include victims who were heads of their own households, or who were *related to* the householder—a measure that includes children and grandchildren as well as more distant relatives.

Concluding Comments

In this chapter, we have focused on the characteristics of atypical lynch victims—women and white men—and the circumstances surrounding their murders. We examined trends over time and between states in the percentage of victims who belonged to one of these groups and also compared the types of offenses that women and white men were accused of with the violations that led to the lynching of black and mixed-race men. We also compared the individual-level characteristics of each of these groups that were identified in chapters 4 and 5 as suggesting a level of social marginalization or relatively elevated social status. We compared these characteristics for women and white men to each other as well as to those of black and mixed-race male victims. We identified several expected differences, based on the racial hierarchy and gender norms prevailing during this era. For example, patterns of literacy and occupational status reflect the subordinate position held by both blacks and women in the post-Reconstruction and Jim Crow South.

We also identified some substantial differences, however, which suggest that lynch mobs targeted different *types* of people within each of these broad racial and gender categories and that certain types of offenses were more likely to have been used as justification for meting out mob violence on people with different demographic characteristics. For example, while African American male victims were most likely to have been adolescents or young adult men, the average age for female and white male victims was somewhat older, and the percentage of victims in each of these groups falling into older age categories was markedly larger than was true for black male victims. Women were more likely than either black or white men to have been lynched as "secondary" victims or because of the perceived threat they posed to the social and economic hierarchy, while white men were most likely to have been accused of violent offenses or being of "bad character."

It is, of course, possible that systematic differences existed between the female victims we were able to identify in the census manuscripts and those we were not. We may have been more likely to have successfully linked older female victims to their census records. Younger women were probably more likely to have been recently married and, therefore, to have changed their surnames between the time of the census enumeration and the time that they were lynched. It is also plausible that the female victims we located were both older and more economically secure than the female victims we did not successfully match. We did, however, successfully locate a higher percentage of female victims than we did male victims—particularly black male victims. So, absent a strong relationship between social marginalization or higher status that operated for only one category of victim, the bias should be relatively equivalent for all three groups and, therefore, not strongly affect intergroup comparisons.

While the number of lynch victims who were women or white men was relatively small—indeed, too small to allow us to conduct the same kinds of rigorous statistical analyses we were able to execute for black and mixed-race male victims—we believe that the variation between these key demographic groups that we *have* been able to highlight points to important ways in which the threat of lynching was differentially wielded against different groups of people. We can say with considerable confidence that these atypical victims differed in some important ways from each other and from black men who fell victim to mob violence.

Because we have focused our attention on the ten southern states that were included in the original Beck-Tolnay inventory of lynch victims, other groups of "atypical" victims are not represented in adequate numbers to have been considered in this chapter. Three significant groups are missing—Mexicans in the Southwest, Native Americans throughout the West, and Chinese on the West Coast and the interior West. Indeed, in some circumscribed geographic areas outside of the southeastern United States, these groups may have represented the "typical" lynch victim, with black males being a minority of victims. Perhaps, at some point in the future, an effort will be made to provide identities to those victims who were lynched outside of the ten southern states encompassed by our study.

CHAPTER EIGHT

The Victims of Southern Mob Violence

It has been more than eight decades since the original publication of *The Tragedy of Lynching*, Arthur Raper's classic treatment of the lynching era. This foundational book continues to establish the very high standard to which all subsequent studies of lynching can hope and strive to attain. Raper, the Commission on Interracial Cooperation's "Research and Field Secretary," had both a scientific and a political motivation for writing *The Tragedy of Lynching*. Appendix C of his book, while comprising only five pages, provides a statistical profile of the annual distribution of lynching between 1889 and 1932 by the race and alleged offense of the victims. It also offers a simple but informative analysis of the variation in lynching rates[1] for fourteen southern states according to the racial composition of the counties in which the lynching took place. And, as mentioned in chapter 1, Raper used these data to execute a basic time series analysis that revealed a negative relationship between the price of cotton and the annual number of lynchings (Raper [1933] 1969, 30–31). Although rudimentary, when compared with more recent empirical investigations of the lynching era, the appendix to Raper's book represented the most sophisticated statistical analysis of mob violence at that time.

The political importance of Raper's study is presaged in the very first paragraph of the book's introduction, written by George F. Milton, the chairman of the Southern Commission on the Study of Lynching: "The lynching problem is of high national importance. Until America can discover and apply means to end these relapses to the law of the jungle, we have no assurance that ordered society will not at any moment be overthrown by the blind passion of a potentially ever-present mob" (Raper [1933] 1969, v).

Through achieving his scientific objectives, Raper also strengthened his political message, which he hoped, as noted by Milton, would facilitate the end of mob violence. In his preface to the reprinted edition of *The Tragedy of Lynching*, published in 1969, Raper judged his work, which had been conducted in collaboration with the Southern Commission on the Study of Lynching, to have been a success. And he called for the further combination of scientific and political efforts to combat America's continuing struggle to come to grips with its "race problem." Raper wrote, "Racial exploitation in many other forms continues to plague us. May not the overall situation improve *as one segment after another of the problem is delineated, fully researched, and programmed for corrective action by appropriate leaders?*" ([1933] 1969, n.p.; emphasis added).

The chapters in *The Tragedy of Lynching* consist primarily of brief case studies for several lynching incidents that occurred in the South during 1930. Like the social scientist that he was, Raper approached these case studies in a systematic fashion. He first described the incident in some detail. Next, he reported how the local community reacted to the lynching. Finally, he turned to a discussion, titled "Facts about the Community," in which he highlighted the economic, political, and religious atmosphere that prevailed within the counties where the lynchings occurred. Implicit in Raper's treatment of these lynchings from 1930 is a conceptual framework that includes both the characteristics of the individual victims and the influence of the local environments within which the victims and the mobs were embedded.[2] That is the same conceptual framework that has guided our investigation.

We are not immodest enough to claim that this book will ever attain the status of a classic in the field, as has *The Tragedy of Lynching*. However, we do believe that we have been able to implement Raper's basic conceptual framework in a way that he could not have because of obstacles that were imposed on him by the limited data at his disposal and by the rather basic quantitative methodological capabilities of his time. Our investigation has benefited from access to data that simply were not available to Raper and his contemporaries—the personal characteristics for hundreds of lynch victims as well as for random samples of non-victims drawn from the general southern black male population for several decades throughout the lynching era. Some of the county-level data that we have used in our study *were* available at the time that Raper wrote *The Tragedy of Lynching*.[3] However, advances in computing technology and the methods of quantitative analysis have allowed us to combine the extensive individual-level and county-level data at our disposal and to analyze complex statistical models within mere seconds.[4] The results of those analyses have permitted us to answer questions that scholars of Raper's era could only pose and speculate about.

Let us revisit the central issues at the heart of our study. The overriding objective of our research has been to make progress toward filling a gaping hole in the scholarship on southern lynching by establishing the personal profiles of the victims of mob violence. Like Raper's effort that produced *The Tragedy of Lynching*, our motivation for pursuing this objective was twofold. First, we were driven by an interest in pure scientific discovery. That is, we sought to locate information that would allow us to construct a profile of a large number of lynch victims and to compare their personal characteristics to those of non-victims residing in the same communities. Second, we were also motivated by a sense of the social justice to be achieved by giving identities to hundreds of lynch victims who, for decades, had remained only brief entries in various inventories or, as is the case with the postmortem photograph of James Clark that we include in chapter 2, gruesome images that rob those who were brutalized by mob violence of all the vibrancy and complexity of their lives.

The first objective reflects our training as social scientists. As nature abhors a vacuum, so too do social scientists despise "gaping holes" in our knowledge. The second objective springs from our desire to right a historical wrong. Although the lynching era ended long ago, throughout the ensuing decades the individual men, women, and children who became unfortunate victims of southern mob violence have, for the most part, remained mysteries. Resurrecting their identities does not erase the tragedy of their extralegal executions, of course, but it does restore some small degree of their humanity, if not for them personally then for posterity. In a general sense, developing a fuller understanding of who these victims of mob violence were *as people* can help us come to terms with the historical roots of our nation's continuing difficulty in dealing fairly and constructively with the challenging issues of race and ethnicity in an increasingly diverse society. On a more personal level, tens of thousands of people who are alive today are the descendants of the people whose individual and collective stories we have shared in these pages. Included among them are many who can count at least one victim of mob violence among their direct ancestors. We hope that our efforts might be of some use for those who seek information about their family histories. We also hope that they might share their family's past and help us to paint a more accurate picture of the people who lost their lives to mob violence. We invite them to visit our website at csde.washington.edu/lynching for more information.

We organized our journey of scientific discovery by pitting two alternative theoretical perspectives against each other—a sort of contest, the outcome of which was to be determined by the relative weight of the empirical evidence. We then used these competing theoretical perspectives to make contrasting predictions about the selection process that was employed by southern lynch mobs when they targeted their victims. Drawing heavily from the theoretical work of Roberta Senechal de la Roche, we hypothesized that lynch victims were drawn disproportionately from the lower-status, socially marginal elements of the local black population. Without human capital of their own or social capital within the broader community that they could draw upon, these individuals were more likely to violate societal norms, and the mobs that lynched them were less likely to encounter strong negative reactions from the local population. Certainly, Senechal de la Roche's theoretical proposals are consistent with those contemporary observers and commentators who argued that some degree of immunity from mob violence was provided by higher social status in the form of land ownership and the protection of a local white benefactor or patron (see, for example, Raper 1936).

A much different set of hypotheses was drawn from the aggregate evidence suggesting the operation of racial threat or competition processes in shaping the intensity of southern mob violence over time and across space, as well as from the conclusions reached by contemporary observers of the lynching era. This theoretical perspective predicts that lynch victims were disproportionately selected from among the more successful members of the black population. It is possible that their success itself motivated the mobs to conduct their lethal business. In these instances, mob violence would have had the direct intention of punishing a specific person for posing a challenge to the prevailing racial hierarchy and would have communicated to the black population more broadly the risks involved in attaining "too much" success. In an alternative form of logic, but with similar outcomes, more successful black men made convenient targets for potential mobs whose original motivations had nothing to do with the social standing of the victim. Because of the relatively small number of women and white men who were lynched, we are only able to compare the characteristics of African American men to similar men in their communities—and our discussion here is primarily restricted to this comparison.

If this logic governed the behavior of lynch mobs, these groups of angry whites, aggrieved by general social and economic conditions or experiencing some other kind of motivation, may have selected more successful black men as their victims—not because those men were the specific targets of the mob's anger but because of the expressive power of warning local blacks not to "step out of line" and reminding them of the potential consequences if they did. While these predictions are gleaned from prior research that has focused on patterns and correlations among aggregated data, for example, across counties or over decades, it would be inappropriate to draw conclusions about the behavior of individual mobs and/or the characteristics of individual victims from such data. Doing so would be a classic example of the "ecological fallacy" (Robinson 1950).

Pitting these two perspectives against each other would seem to lead to a neat and clean outcome, with the empirical evidence supporting one or the other. If lynch victims were not selected randomly from among the larger black population within a community, then, when compared with non-victims from the same community, (1) they were either less socially embedded or they were not, and (2) they either enjoyed higher social standing or they did not. But, like Robert Burns's mouse, our "best laid schemes" went a bit astray. In short, the empirical evidence was more complicated than we originally anticipated, and the resulting story about the targeting of victims by southern lynch mobs is therefore more complex and nuanced. So, where does that evidence lead us?

One general conclusion that we can draw from our study, and one that conforms to Arthur Raper's observations from 1930, is that lynch victims were a heterogeneous group. Therefore, we must be cautious about considering a portrait of African American male victims based solely on their average characteristics. Yes, the average black male victim was twenty-nine or thirty-two years of age, depending on whether we use the median or mean, respectively, as our measure of central tendency. But some victims were old men and others were young boys. A majority of victims were illiterate, but 45 percent could read and write. Most victims held unskilled occupations and lived on rented farms. But some victims were skilled workers who owned their nonfarm dwelling. This heterogeneity is made quite clear by the profile of lynch victims that was presented in chapter 3.

When we move from the presentation of a simple descriptive portrait of victims to the comparison of their characteristics with those for a sample of non-victims, the heterogeneity necessarily fades into the background. In order to determine whether victims were selected randomly from the general population and, if not, which of the theoretical perspectives was supported by systematic patterns in the evidence, our attention was focused intensively on *average differences* between the two groups—with or without taking into account other potential sources for any differences we might have observed. That was our objective in chapters 4, 5, and 6. So, to what conclusions do these group comparisons direct us?

A second general conclusion to which the empirical evidence leads us is that context mattered. At first, this conclusion might appear to be "old news." After all, comparative studies of southern lynching have documented clearly that spatial variation in the intensity of lynching is correlated with spatial variation in a variety of other characteristics of local areas, including racial composition, agricultural specialty, political orientation, and religious organization. That Mississippi lynched nearly twice as many victims as did Alabama, despite the fact that these two states are adjacent to each other, demonstrates that context mattered. That the per-capita risk of being lynched for black men was highest in Florida—higher even than in Mississippi—also demonstrates that context mattered. Even Raper's consideration of the "facts about the community" was an implicit acknowledgment that the occurrence of mob violence was shaped by local environmental conditions.

But the empirical evidence presented in the previous chapters shows that context also mattered in a different way—by conditioning or moderating the relationship between individual-level characteristics and the likelihood of victimization by mobs. Put differently, the ways in which the personal characteristics of individual African American men influenced their vulnerability to being targeted by lynch mobs—for example, by being able to read and write or having been born out of state—depended upon the nature of the local environment. The character of the local community held the potential to magnify the importance of risk factors or to nullify the influence of protective factors. This is the finding that complicates our ability to offer simple, unqualified answers to the questions that guided our study: Were lynch victims socially marginal outsiders? Did victims have higher social standing than the general black population?

Overall, our comparison of the personal characteristics of victims and non-victims offers support for Roberta Senechal de la Roche's theoretical perspective that emphasizes the social marginality of victims. Black men who were married and the head of their household enjoyed a lower likelihood of victimization when compared to men who were not married and/or household heads. And that advantage prevailed in most settings throughout the South. We contend that married heads of households were more embedded within their local communities. Also supporting Senechal de la Roche's theoretical framework is our finding that men who experienced lifetime interstate migration suffered from a significantly greater likelihood of victimization than did men who had not moved across a state line, at least in some contexts. We argue that, on average, interstate migrants were less firmly embedded in their local communities than were nonmigrants. The positive relationship between the percentage of victims born out of state and the percentage of victims with unknown names, described in chapter 4 (see Figure 4.2), supports this position. However, the greater vulnerability of interstate migrants prevailed only in settings in which a higher proportion of the black male population (that is, above the 60th percentile) was born in their state of residence. Similarly, contrary to our prediction, agricultural workers were exposed to a higher likelihood of victimization, but only in communities that were home to smaller concentrations of agricultural workers among the black male population. In sum, then, the empirical evidence suggests that social marginality *did* make African American men *more susceptible* to targeting by southern mobs and that it was an especially powerful risk factor in communities where social marginality was less common. Clearly, the nature of the local context mattered for the relative vulnerability of outsiders and others who were socially marginal.

Context was particularly important for determining the relative risk of victimization for African American men with higher social standing. On the one hand, our findings show that, *without considering local context*, higher-status men were less likely to be targeted by southern mobs, contradicting the implications of aggregate-level racial threat models of lynching and claims by a number of contemporary observers of the lynching era. However, this protection was dependent upon how unusual specific individual-level characteristics were among the local black population. Higher social standing was found to *increase* the risk of lynching primarily in those communities where fewer higher-status black men resided. This was true with regard to literacy, farm ownership, and "mulatto" status. On the other hand, black men with higher-status occupations were significantly *less likely* to be lynched than their counterparts with lower-status jobs. The protective influence of holding a more skilled occupation existed in virtually all locales but was particularly powerful in communities with higher concentrations of skilled workers among the African American male labor force. Men enumerated as "mulatto" were exposed to significantly lower levels of victimization than their neighbors enumerated as "black" or "Negro," but only in areas with relatively more mixed-race men. In sum, higher social standing could be either a risk or a protective factor in determining the likelihood of mob victimization for African American men. Which of these situations prevailed, however, depended upon the degree of concentration of higher-status men in the local community.

Combining the evidence regarding the importance of social marginality and social standing leads us to conclude that, in general, African American men were exposed to the greatest risk of mob violence when their personal characteristics marked them as different from the larger black population. Furthermore, the risk associated with standing out among the local black community intensified as the indicator of social marginality or higher social standing became increasingly rare. This moderating or conditioning influence of the local context requires that our conclusions regarding the influence of social marginality and social standing on the likelihood of victimization be nuanced rather than simple. Furthermore, this complexity, introduced by the interaction between individual-level characteristics and the nature of the local context, can help us to better understand the conflicting conclusions that were drawn by contemporary observers and commentators about the relative risks of mob victimization. Their assessments associated the risk of lynching with both social marginality and privileged social standing among African American men. Our evidence suggests that both perspectives were correct. That is, it was literally the case that an individual-level risk or protective factor in one locale was unrelated to the likelihood of being lynched in another locale.

What we cannot discern from our evidence is *exactly why* those black men who stood out from the general population because of their personal characteristics were particularly vulnerable. To answer that question, we would need more information about the characteristics of southern mobs and the motivations for their actions. Short of an answer, we can propose hypotheses that may be useful for guiding future research on this issue. First, it is possible that the victims were targeted specifically because of their personal characteristics. That is, socially marginal men were targeted *because* they were outsiders in their community, and higher-status men were selected *because* they were successful. When there were proportionately fewer black men like them in the community, they could not rely on as many compatriots in the general black population for protection from the mob, and the members of the mob could be less concerned about possible negative reactions from the community.

Second, those who stood out from the general black population because of their social marginality or higher social standing could have been more vulnerable to targeting by mobs that were motivated by factors other than the victim's personal characteristics. During the era of lynching, any racially tinged conflict or perceived grievance had the potential to mobilize groups of men that could congeal into a lynch mob. One purpose of such mobs was to send a message to the local black population about the potential costs of unacceptable or caste-violating behavior. If the offending individual was available, then he was likely to be targeted. But if there was no specific offending individual, or if the offending individual was not available to the mob, an alternative victim would be selected in a process of "victim displacement." Perhaps, as the mob members searched for an alternative victim(s), their attention was drawn to black and mixed-race men who stood out from the general population because they were outsiders or due to their success.

Third, it is possible that the contextual conditioning that we have observed reflects a phenomenon that is connected to the signaling process more generally. That is, perhaps distinctive characteristics of the members of a group are more salient when those qualities are in relatively short supply. This could be the result of simple habituation through which the community at large grows less sensitized to the relevant distinctive traits because of their frequent occurrence in the social environment. Therefore, for example, the signals to the white population that resulted from an African American male being from out of state or having the ability to read and write would grow weaker, and the habituation process more powerful, in communities with more interstate migrants and literates.

Whether it was through specific targeting, victim displacement, habituation, or some combination of the three, it is clear that the personal characteristics that influenced the likelihood of being lynched for black and mixed-race men during the lynching era were not uniform throughout the South. Rather, at least with respect to the variable local concentration of the personal characteristics themselves, the profile of victimization was strongly influenced by the community context within which black men resided.

The findings regarding the fundamental importance of the local context, and the conclusions that can be drawn from them, led us to consider whether the relationship between the personal characteristics of African American men and their risk of victimization also varied by the degree of danger that prevailed within the local area. To measure the intensity of local danger for black men, which we equate with the strength of an ethos of white supremacy in the community, we relied on selected county-level indicators of the economic, political, and religious environments. That was our purpose in chapter 6. In contrast to our findings regarding the conditioning influence of the local concentration of individual markers of social marginality and social standing, the degree of local danger was not found to be especially important.

We found that the local religious environment had no influence on the relationship between individual-level characteristics and the risk of victimization. And in only two specific cases did the local political and economic contexts moderate the effect of social standing on the likelihood of being lynched: (1) the protective influence of "mulatto" racial status eroded sharply in counties in which cotton production was a more dominant component of the agricultural economy, and (2) farm ownership grew to be a significant risk factor in those counties where the Democratic Party enjoyed large majority support. Although they represent intriguing suggestions of a conditioning effect of the local context of danger on the relationship between personal attributes and the risk of victimization, we are reluctant to draw strong substantive inferences based on these two departures from the more general pattern of null findings for the conditional influence of local danger. Rather, we recommend these provocative, but minority, findings as a potentially fruitful direction for future research, possibly using alternative measures of individual distinctiveness, different indicators of local danger, and more complex modeling approaches than those used in our exploratory foray into the issue. Alternatively, in light of serious data challenges, perhaps this question could be more profitably investigated with an entirely different methodological approach, such as in-depth archival research.

Note also that we lack information on victims' (and non-victims') political affiliation or religious membership. We were unable to specify, then, whether black and mixed-race men who were politically active, who attempted to vote, or who publicly voiced opposition to the Democratic Party experienced an increased vulnerability to mob violence. It could also be possible that this vulnerability was dampened or enhanced in specific political climates. Although we did not find a consistent relationship between the individual measures that we do have access to, like literacy or racial categorization, perhaps the risk of mob violence was conditioned by the local strength of the Democratic Party only for those men who dared to become politically active.

We also do not have the kind of information that would allow us to determine whether men who played leadership roles in indigenous black southern religious groups were more or less likely to be targeted by mob violence in communities with more hegemonic religious structures. These men may have experienced heightened risk, for example, if they engaged in faith-based activities that had emancipatory content, such as adult literacy programs or cooperative economic programs designed to help fund migration to the North, but the present data do not allow us to explore these possible relationships. We also lack data on specific economic factors that might be directly related to those we investigated in these analyses. Although we have information on farm ownership (for some census years), occupational status, and employment sector, we do not know how a particular farmer's crop yield compared to that of his neighbors, or whether a family was sufficiently prosperous to own working livestock or to hire extra labor, regardless of whether they owned or rented their land, or how those individual factors might have been moderated by stress in the local economy. Access to these additional characteristics for specific lynch victims would offer a much stronger test of the conditioning influence of the local context of danger than we were able to conduct and report on in chapter 6.

Before moving on from the discussion of the importance of contextual conditions for moderating the relationship between personal attributes and the likelihood of targeting by southern mobs, it is useful to speculate about their consequences for southern black men—the typical victim of lynching. As the decades of the lynching era passed by and the toll of mob violence mounted, an atmosphere of hypervigilance emerged within the southern black community. African American parents, wives, and sisters recognized the precarious and perilous existence of young black men. Formal and informal advice was given to black males to avoid relationships and encounters that might direct the spotlight of white antipathy on them. Even if it meant adopting subservient behaviors and postures toward all whites or forgoing potential enjoyment or success, black men were encouraged to strive for social invisibility. Some strategies for remaining inconspicuous were obvious. Polite and deferential interaction with all whites, under all circumstances, was one strategy. Avoiding even the hint of a romantic interest in a white woman was another. Shunning avenues for upward social mobility was still another. Although these strategies required sacrifices by black men, they were easily identifiable and even somewhat logical, given the prevailing racial state. Most important, their successful execution could help African American men escape the crosshairs of the southern mob.

To those obvious risk factors and their concomitant avoidance strategies, well known throughout the African American community, add the individual traits that we have identified here: being an interstate migrant, an agricultural worker, or an unmarried head of household; having a mixed racial background; being able to read and write; or owning a farm. The southern battleground for survival by black men suddenly became more complicated and difficult to navigate. But, for the sake of argument, let us assume that these additional individual-level correlates of victimization were recognized by southern black men. And let us assume further that their behavioral strategies to avoid targeting by lynch mobs took *all of these factors* into account, as implausible as that might be. Now, include the fact that the operation and strength of these risk factors for lynching varied across the South according to their concentration in the local population. Even a rational, calculating southern black man would have had no way to detect the contextual conditioning of personal characteristics that we have documented. Therefore, even with full knowledge of many of the personal behaviors and characteristics that increased his probability of victimization, the lives (and deaths) of southern black men were affected by the uncertainty associated with environmental conditions that were likely undetectable by them and certainly outside of their control.

We know less about the ways in which female and white male victims' characteristics may have affected the degree to which they were targeted for mob violence. Because we lack a sufficiently large number of victims from either of these demographic categories to enable us to systematically compare them to the members of their home communities, we can only speculate as to how their individual characteristics might have made them vulnerable to the bloody goals of lynch mobs. The age distribution does not resemble what one would expect to find in a "natural" population for either group of victims and also diverges considerably for each group when compared to black and mixed-race male victims, suggesting that women and white men experienced the greatest risk of victimization at specific moments across the life course. Women who were more embedded in their communities appear to have been at greater risk, relative to black and mixed-race male victims, as evidenced by the higher percentage of female victims who were homeowners and either heads of their households or relatives of the householder. Given the small number of linked female and white male victims in our database, however, we view the evidence presented in chapter 7 regarding the personal profiles of female and white male victims, and their selection from among the general female and white male populations, to be a preliminary step that sets the stage for more in-depth future investigations of mob violence directed against those two population groups.

Are similar environmental conditioning effects influencing the strength of discrimination and violent responses to minority or vulnerable populations in the United States today? To be sure, considerable research has been aimed at determining whether the relative size of minority groups in local areas influences a variety of outcomes such as income, employment, interpersonal violence, and arrests (Branch and Hanley 2011; Eitel, Stolzenberg, and D'Allesio 2005; Liska and Bellair 1995; McCall 2001). However, the question we are posing refers to a somewhat different phenomenon than the aggregate relationship between relative group size and discrimination. Rather, it proposes that specific characteristics of, or behaviors by, some segment of the minority group population have a differential likelihood of triggering discriminatory or violent responses from majority members of the community, based on the prevalence of those characteristics or behaviors in the area. For example, do interracial couples encounter more negative responses in communities where there are fewer interracial couples? Are public displays of affection by lesbian or gay couples more likely to generate disapproving reactions in places where such behaviors are less common among members of the LGBT community? Are there more attacks against panhandling homeless persons where the public presence of homelessness is less conspicuous? If we think of interracial relationships, public expressions of affection by gay or lesbian couples, and begging by the homeless as potential risk factors for negative or punishing community responses, then it seems quite possible that the same type of conditioning effect of the local context that we observed for southern mob violence would also pertain. The extent to which the processes that we have observed for the targeting of southern lynch victims apply to other forms of victimization, past and present, remains a question for future research.

By linking hundreds of southern lynch victims to their census records, we have been able to partially transform their figurative silhouettes to fuller portraits. The brief biographical details for the victims that we have woven throughout all of the previous chapters, coupled with the statistical analyses based on the full set of successfully linked victims, have restored at least a portion of their identities and a hint of their humanity. Furthermore, by comparing the victims to a sample of non-victims, we have learned that both social marginality and social standing influenced the targeting of lynch victims by southern mobs, though the size and direction of their effects depended on the nature of the local context. Finally, we provided suggestive evidence that the lynching of atypical victims—women and white men—followed somewhat different patterns from those of the lynching of black men. With respect to the two primary objectives that motivated our research into this subject, pure scientific discovery and social justice, we feel justified in claiming substantial success—success not only for ourselves but also on behalf of future scholars interested in investigating this terrible chapter of American history.

Despite these important contributions, we fully realize that the census data to which we have linked the victims is frustratingly limited, both in its scope and in its detail. By necessity, therefore, the portrait of lynch victims that we have been able to paint has important blank spots. We also readily acknowledge that much more can be done with the quantitative and qualitative evidence that is contained in the linked database that we have relied on so heavily for this research. For example, we have not fully explored temporal patterns in the characteristics of victims or in the process of victim selection. Nor have we attempted a systematic qualitative analysis of the materials contained in the archival component of the database. These, too, remain objectives for future research.

In addition to compiling more information about the victims, we see two major objectives for future scholarship on southern mob violence. Like the personal characteristics of lynch victims had been before the creation of the linked victim-census database, there are two missing pieces of the puzzle that have frustrated researchers of southern lynching for a very long time. First, little systematic information exists about the members of southern lynch mobs. Bits and pieces of information about the composition of mobs can be gleaned from original newspaper articles for a few lynching incidents and from the evidence that has been compiled for specific case studies. This scattered information, however, is neither extensive nor representative. Perhaps we never will have an inventory of mob members to complement our inventories of victims, or a linked "mob member–census" database that provides identities for a large number of mob members. But the extreme challenge of that possibility alone is not sufficient cause to remove this objective from the radar of lynching students and scholars.[5]

Second, the scholarship on southern lynching has long suffered from a lack of systematic information about those cases in which mob violence was threatened but thwarted—either because of the intercession of authorities or through the action of civilians.[6] We have lacked information even with which to form conclusions about the scope of the phenomenon of averted lynchings, not to mention its details. On this front, the future for lynching scholarship is looking more promising. Through years of careful and tedious archival newspaper research, E. M. Beck (2015) of the University of Georgia has compiled an inventory of prevented or averted mob violence that can be used in tandem with the inventory of the victims of successfully completed lynchings. Those data remain to be fully analyzed. However, Professor Beck's inventory indicates that the numbers of prevented and "successful" lynching incidents during the lynching era (1882–1930) were roughly equal. When taking into consideration the level of threat associated with each potential lynching incident, Beck estimates that, without the intervention of southern citizens and authorities, the volume of lynching during this period would have been 50 percent greater than the level that is represented in the inventories of lynchings that mobs were able to complete. It is, of course, too early to draw any definitive conclusions from this promising new evidence regarding averted lynchings. It is perhaps not premature, however, to predict that, when combined with the existing lynching databases, this new data source has the potential to contribute to a paradigm shift in our knowledge and understanding of southern mob violence.

During the last thirty years, social scientists of many disciplines have made great strides toward helping us better understand the sad history of mob violence in the United States during the lynching era. As a result, we know much more than ever before about the level of the carnage, the structural correlates of the temporal and spatial distribution of the phenomenon, and, now, the victims of southern mob violence themselves. But there is much additional work to do. It is our hope that this book has both contributed to the body of knowledge and helped to identify potentially fruitful avenues for future inquiry.

APPENDIX

Table A.2.1 Information Recorded in Census, by Year of Enumeration

Information	Year of Census Enumeration			
	1880	1900	1910	1920
Age	X	X	X	X
Sex	X	X	X	X
Race (general)	X	X	X	X
Mixed-race status	X		X	X
Marital status	X	X	X	X
Relationship to head of household	X	X	X	X
Occupation	X	X	X	X
Industry of Employment			X	X
Literacy	X	X	X	X
Place of birth (state/country)	X	X	X	X
Home ownership		X	X	X
Residence on a farm		X	X	X

Table A.2.2 Percentage of Successful Matches and Subjective Probability by Gender, Race, Decade, and State

	Total successful matches	Single high	Single medium	Multiple matches: one medium	Two matches: equally likely
DEMOGRAPHIC CATEGORY					
Black males (N = 1,837)	44.7%	28.9%	7.1%	5.9%	2.8%
White males (N = 218)	54.6%	37.2%	8.3%	4.6%	4.6%
Women (N = 63)	55.6%	38.1%	4.8%	6.3%	6.3%
DECADE					
1882–89	51.9%	36.6%	7.7%	5.0%	5.7%
1890–95	39.4%	22.5%	8.2%	6.4%	4.2%
1900–1909	44.2%	26.9%	5.8%	6.5%	3.8%
1910–19	45.5%	29.1%	7.0%	5.5%	4.3%
1920–29	56.6%	44.4%	6.5%	4.6%	2.3%
STATE					
Alabama	46.7%	25.8%	12.9%	5.8%	2.2%
Arkansas	44.4%	22.2%	12.9%	5.8%	3.5%
Florida	40.0%	26.3%	4.7%	5.3%	3.7%
Georgia	53.1%	34.5%	4.2%	9.5%	4.8%
Kentucky	42.3%	28.7%	6.1%	4.3%	3.7%
Louisiana	41.5%	26.4%	5.8%	7.0%	2.3%
Mississippi	47.4%	32.9%	6.6%	5.6%	2.3%
North Carolina	48.9%	27.2%	6.8%	9.1%	5.7%
South Carolina	43.0%	28.9%	7.0%	3.9%	3.1%
Tennessee	51.1%	37.5%	5.7%	7.4%	6.3%

Table A.3.1 Age Distribution of Lynch Victims by Demographic Category

	< 20	20–24	25–29	30–34	35–39	40–44	45–49	50–54	55–59	≥ 60
White male	5.43	14.73	17.83	11.63	17.05	11.63	8.53	6.98	2.33	3.88
Female	21.05	10.53	10.53	5.26	13.16	5.26	13.16	10.53	7.89	2.63
Black male	19.65	20.53	18.33	12.62	8.23	5.38	5.38	4.06	3.18	2.63

Table A.3.2 Percentage of Victims and Black Male Comparison Sample with Key Characteristics, by Demographic Category

	Black Male Non-victims	Black Male Victims	White Males	Females
INDICATORS OF SOCIAL MARGINALITY				
Born out of state	18.4	21.3	29.7	16.1
Enumerated in county of lynching	N/A	54.9	59.3	58.1
Occupation				
Agricultural sector	62.1	62.0	64.9	35.9
Nonagricultural sector	27.4	28.6	23.9	13.2
Not in the labor force	10.5	9.0	11.2	50.9
Household location				
Head of household	46.0	45.0	57.0	64.7
Child or grandchild of head	36.5	38.6	32.9	33.8
Other relative	4.6	5.1	4.2	1.5
Not related	12.9	11.2	5.9	0
INDICATORS OF SOCIAL STANDING				
Literate	46.9	44.8	74.2	45.5
Occupation				
Higher-status worker	32.1	25.8	57.4	1.6
Lower-status worker	57.4	63.4	31.8	47.5
Not in the labor force	10.5	10.9	11.2	50.9
Homeowner	17.9	22.8	39.1	45.0
Farm residence	62.0	54.0	50.0	69.1
Owner	17.7	27.2	58.3	41.4
Renter	82.3	72.8	41.7	58.6
Nonfarm residence	38.0	43.7	50.0	46.9
Owner	18.2	17.3	18.2	54.6
Renter	81.8	82.7	81.8	45.4
Enumerated "mulatto"	14.1	11.0	N/A	9.3

Table A.3.3 Migration of Victims and Comparison Sample

	Black Male Victims	Comparison Sample
Percentage enumerated outside state of birth	21.28*	18.43
N	834	19,915

*Difference between victims and non-victims significant at the $p < .05$ level

Table A.3.4 Percentage of Victims by Location of Lynching

County of enumeration	54.80
Adjacent county	31.85
Same state	12.28
Different state	1.07

* * *

Explanation of Occupational Classification

We classified occupations of victims and non-victims in two ways. First, we determined whether those individuals who were recorded as participating in the labor force worked within the agricultural sector or outside of it. Second, we identified higher-status and lower-status workers.

Determining whether a victim worked in the agricultural sector was quite simple for the comparison sample, because all census records for individuals reporting an occupation have already been assigned an industrial code (variable name IND1950). Determining whether a person was an agricultural worker was also relatively simple for the victims we located in either the 1910 or 1920 census. In those years, the census enumerator recorded each person's occupation as well as the industry in which he or she was employed.

Victims who were enumerated in either the 1880 or the 1900 census needed to have their industry assigned by hand. In most instances, this was a fairly straightforward process. For example, someone listed as a "farm hand" or "tenant farmer" clearly worked in the agricultural sector, while someone whose occupation was "bootblack" or "minister" clearly did not. However, a large proportion of the victims were enumerated as "laborers" or "day laborers" without additional information that might have helped us determine whether they were agricultural workers. In these cases, we reviewed the original census manuscript pages where each victim had been recorded and made a determination based on the occupations of others on the page, as well as on the apparent urban or rural character of the community. For example, a "laborer" living in a town or city where other men on the page were listed as carpenters, waiters, and wagon drivers was assumed to be working outside of the agricultural sector and coded as such. Men whose occupation was recorded as "laborer" who were located living in rural environments where the other men on the page were enumerated as farmers or field hands were classified as working in the agricultural sector.

Determining whether a worker had a higher-status or a lower-status job proved a bit more challenging. This was partly because the occupations that were available to black and mixed-race men, who made up most of the people whose information was in our data, were fairly limited. Certainly those recorded as laborers or servants or as doing odd jobs were lower status. People recorded as ministers, planters, or revenue collectors were likely of higher status. We determined that skilled or semiskilled occupations, such as carpenters, blacksmiths, or brick masons, were higher status. Jobs that required domestic or personal service, such as nurses or waiters, or had hazardous, physically demanding, or particularly unpleasant working conditions, such as mining or chopping wood, were classified as being lower status. In some cases, for those individuals enumerated in the 1910 or 1920 census, the industry of record also helped us determine the level of status associated with a particular occupation.

All occupational classifications were created by the first-listed author and confirmed by the second-listed author. We include examples of our classification scheme, drawn from the black and mixed-race male victims in our data, in Table A.3.5.

Table A.3.5 Example Occupations, by Agricultural Sector and Higher or
Lower Status

AGRICULTURAL OCCUPATIONS	
Higher Status	*Lower Status*
Farmer/farming	Day hand
Farm Operator	Day laborer
Horse trainer	Farm hand/farmhand
Planter	Field hand/works in field
	Farmer help
	Farm labor/farm laborer/farm lab
	General Farm
	Laborer
	Laborer of the field/laborer in oat field
	Laborer on farm/labor(s) on farm
	Tenant/tenant farmer
	Tobacco
	Turpentine/turpentine laborer
	Wages—farm
	Working on farm/work(s) in farm

NONAGRICULTURAL OCCUPATIONS	
Higher Status	*Lower Status*
Bar Keeper	Axe Man
Barber	Bartender
Blacksmith	Bellman
Carpenter	Bootblack
Clerk/Clerk in Store	Bus Driver/Jitney Driver
Miller	Butler
Mason	Carriage [Driver]
Minister	Coal Miner/Miner/Phosphate Miner
Moulder	Common Laborer
Preacher	Cook/Cook's Helper
Revenue Collector	Drayman/Drives Dray Wagon
Shoemaker	Driver in Coal Mine/Truck Driver

Table A.3.5 (*continued*)

Higher Status	Lower Status
Soldier	Engineer
	Hauling Mill Laborer
	Mechanic
	Nurse
	Odd Jobs
	Porter
	Presser
	Prisoner/Convict
	RR Labor/RR Road/RR [Serving] Hand
	Saw Mill
	Servant
	Ships Boxes
	Teamster
	Tie Maker
	Tin Chopper
	Waiter/Waiter in Hotel
	Works in Blacksmith Shop
	Works in Brick Yard
	Works in Shop

Table A.4.1 Likelihood of Being a Lynch Victim by Social Embeddedness and Marginality, Black and Mixed-Race Men, 1882–1929

	Model 1	*Model 2*	*Model 3*	*Model 4*
Born out of state	−0.270**			−0.120
	(0.100)			(0.110)
Agricultural worker		0.092		0.096
		(0.096)		(0.098)
Not in the labor force		0.169		−0.055
		(0.216)		(0.226)
Nonmarried head of household			0.510***	0.532***
			(0.150)	(0.150)
Relative of householder			0.753***	0.773***
			(0.137)	(0.139)
Not related			−0.090	−0.051
			(0.148)	(0.151)
Age at lynching	0.189***	0.234***	0.284***	0.287***
	(0.014)	(0.022)	(0.024)	(0.024)
Age squared	−0.002***	−0.003***	−0.003***	−0.003
	(0.000)	(0.000)	(0.000)	(0.000)
Number of black men	−0.027***	−0.026***	−0.026***	−0.026***
	(0.002)	(0.002)	(0.002)	(0.002)
1890–1895	−0.691***	−1.518***	−1.466***	−1.450***
	(0.115)	(0.155)	(0.162)	(0.163)
1900–1909	−0.907***	−1.136***	−1.114***	−1.112***
	(0.111)	(0.130)	(0.138)	(0.138)
1910–1919	−0.972***	−1.253***	−1.253***	−1.258***
	(0.117)	(0.138)	(0.146)	(0.147)
1920–1929	−0.939***	−1.124***	−1.120***	−1.112***
	(0.133)	(0.151)	(0.157)	(0.157)
Intercept	−4.319***	−5.429***	−6.593***	−6.698***
	(0.216)	(0.383)	(0.464)	(0.478)
AIC	6343.515	4580.614	4511.525	4514.823
Weighted *N*	20,745	15,681	15,677	15,677

Note: Coefficients presented first, with standard errors in parentheses. Models 2, 3, and 4 restricted to include only those observations at least 12 (Model 2) or 16 (Models 3 and 4) years old at the time of census enumeration.

** $p < 0.01$

*** $p < 0.001$.

Table A.5.1 Likelihood of Being a Lynch Victim by Indicators of Social Standing, Black and Mixed-Race Men, 1882–1929

	Model 1	Model 2	Model 3	Model 4	Model 5	Model 6	Model 7
Literate	0.054 (0.083)				0.104 (0.094)	0.166 (0.114)	0.126 (0.150)
Higher status		−0.591*** (0.100)			−0.541*** (0.101)	−0.446*** (0.121)	−0.346 (0.249)
Not in labor force		−0.048 (0.206)			−0.017 (0.219)	−0.010 (0.260)	−0.245 (0.657)
Mulatto			−0.378* (0.147)			−0.376* (0.170)	
Farm owner				0.281 (0.218)			0.242 (0.220)
Nonfarm owner				0.067 (0.287)			−0.192 (0.338)
Nonfarm renter				0.313† (0.162)			0.014 (0.263)
Age	0.233*** (0.016)	0.250*** (0.022)	0.270*** (0.020)	0.096* (0.038)	0.247*** (0.023)	0.284*** (0.028)	0.098* (0.038)
Age squared	−0.003*** (0.000)	−0.003*** (0.000)	−0.003*** (0.000)	−0.002* (0.000)	−0.003*** (0.000)	−0.003*** (0.000)	−0.001* (0.000)

Number of local black men	-0.026*** (0.002)	-0.025*** (0.002)	-0.025*** (0.002)	-0.026*** (0.003)	-0.024*** (0.002)	-0.023*** (0.002)	-0.026*** (0.003)
1890–1895	-1.226*** (0.135)	-1.458*** (0.155)	-1.333*** (0.137)		-1.523*** (0.160)	-1.631*** (0.163)	
1900–1909	-1.008*** (0.119)	-1.019*** (0.131)			-1.094*** (0.136)		
1910–1919	-1.094*** (0.127)	-1.111*** (0.139)	-1.181*** (0.127)	-0.073 (0.165)	-1.211*** (0.147)	-1.349*** (0.153)	-0.097 (0.166)
1920–1929	-1.093*** (0.145)	-1.033*** (0.151)	-1.179*** (0.143)	0.158 (0.178)	-1.158*** (0.161)	-1.323*** (0.168)	0.092 (0.183)
Intercept	-5.215*** (0.263)	-5.649*** (0.377)	-5.784*** (0.318)	-4.542*** (0.776)	-5.710*** (0.408)	-6.405*** (0.491)	-4.335*** (0.809)
AIC	5550.370	4545.215	3961.421	1829.564	4777.373	3034.467	1827.199
N	19,683	15,681	13,896	7,638	14,938	10,390	7,637

Note: Weighted coefficients are presented first, with standard errors in parentheses.

† $p < 0.10$
* $p < 0.05$
** $p < 0.01$
*** $p < 0.001$

Table A.7.1 Distribution of Black Male, White Male, and Female Victims by State and Decade, 1882–1930

	1882 to 1889	1890 to 1899	1900 to 1909	1910 to 1919	1920 to 1929	1930
Alabama						
Black Males	34	103	61	52	8	1
White Males	4	15	0	1	4	0
Females	0	8	2	0	0	0
Arkansas						
Black Males	16	67	41	35	20	0
White Males	20	17	6	4	1	0
Females	0	1	3	1	0	0
Florida						
Black Males	18	65	47	42	41	0
White Males	4	3	4	4	3	1
Females	0	0	1	3	1	0
Georgia						
Black Males	52	117	95	117	35	5
White Males	4	9	2	3	2	0
Females	2	0	3	6	2	0
Kentucky						
Black Males	30	47	29	12	4	0
White Males	19	16	3	2	1	0
Females	0	2	2	0	0	0
Louisiana						
Black Males	44	112	81	49	10	0
White Males	9	32	7	1	4	0
Females	1	3	1	1	0	0
Mississippi						
Black Males	103	129	135	60	55	3
White Males	11	5	3	1	2	0
Females	0	6	4	6	2	0
North Carolina						
Black Males	26	13	17	11	11	1
White Males	6	6	1	0	0	0
Females	1	0	0	1	2	0
South Carolina						
Black Males	28	50	32	20	10	2
White Males	2	3	1	0	0	0
Females	0	3	1	1	1	0
Tennessee						
Black Males	30	70	40	22	6	0
White Males	12	16	5	0	3	0
Females	3	3	2	0	0	0

Table A.7.2 Offenses Used as Reasons for Lynching, by Category

---

OFFENSES CATEGORIZED AS VIOLENT

Altercation	Kidnapping
Assault	Manslaughter
Assault & prison escapee/robbery/ burglary	Murder & arson/robbery/stealing/ insurrection/theft/train wrecking
Assaulting boy/man/officer	Murderous assault/Murder
Assisting murder	Murderous assault & robbery
Attacking man and woman/teacher	Plot to kill
Attempting assassination/murder/ murder & robber/train wrecking	Poisoning well water
	Shooting at farmer/officer/man
Biting off man's chin	Shooting boy/man/men/officer/
Child abuse	sheriff/woman
Conspiracy to kill/murder	Slapping white boys
Cutting white boy	Spouse abuse/Wife-beating
Flogging white boy	Theft & murder
Implicated in murder	Threat/s to kill
Injuring girl	Train wrecking
Intent to murder	Wounding deputy/men

OFFENSES CATEGORIZED AS SEXUAL

Adultery	Harassing white woman
Assault & attempted rape	Hiding in girl's room/under bed
Assault (rape)	Improper advances to girl
Assault (rape) & robbery	Improper remark to woman
Attack (rape)	Improper with white girl/white
Attempted assault (rape)	woman/woman
Attempted attack (rape)	In company of white woman
Attempted criminal assault (rape)	In girl's/white woman's (bed)room
Attempted rape	Incest
Attempted rape & arson/robbery/ murder	Indecent proposals (to girl/s)
	Intent to rape
Attending white girl	Intimate with white woman
Being in girl's room	Invading girl's chamber
Breaking into woman's room	Jilting girl
Cohabitation	Keeping/living with white woman
Criminal assault/attack (rape)	Making indecent remarks
Eloping with white girl	Maltreatment of woman
Entering woman's/girl's/lady's (bed) room	Miscegenation
	Murder & attempted rape
Enticement	Murder & rape
Flirting with white girl	Obscene phone call
Frightening woman/women/girls	Operating bordello

Table A.7.2 (continued)

Outrage (rape) of girl/young girl	Robbery & sexual assault/rape
Peeping Tom/Peeping into window	Sexual assault
Planning rape	Sexual assault & murder
Plotting against white woman	Sexual molestation
Proposals to white women	Shooting man & adultery
Rape	Trying to enter girl's room
Rape & assault/burglary/murder	Writing to white woman

OFFENSES CATEGORIZED AS "CONNECTIONS"

Accessory/Accomplice to murder	Father of arsonist/murderer
Advising murder	Knowledge of theft

Aided criminal/escape/fugitive/
    larcenist/murder/murderer/
    outlaw/rapist
	Mother of arsonists

	Refusing to aid lynch posse
	Resisting mob
Brother of murderer	Son of murderer
Complicity in murder/rape	Wife of murderer
Daughter of murderer	Witness to murder
Defending rapist	

OFFENSES CATEGORIZED AS PROPERTY CRIMES

Attempted burglary	Larceny
Burglary	Robbery
Counterfeiting	Robbery & arson/kidnapping
Extorting debt	Stealing
Fraud	Swindling
Grave robbery	Theft
Horse theft	

OFFENSES CATEGORIZED AS "CHARACTER" VIOLATIONS

Acting suspiciously	Lawlessness
Bad character/reputation	Moonshining
Dangerous character	Obscene language
Desperado	Voodooism
Indolence	

Table A.7.2 (continued)

OFFENSES CATEGORIZED AS CHALLENGING ESTABLISHED ORDER

Angering Klan
Arguing with white men
Arresting whitecappers
Arson
Arson & burglary/theft
Attempted arson
Barn burning
Being offensive to whites
Boasting about race riot
Colonizing Negroes
Conflict over fishing rights
Conspiracy/Conspiracy to revolt
Criticizing mob
Cursing white woman
Cutting levee
Disorderly conduct
Disputing men
Dynamiting/Dynamiting house
Fighting with white man
Giving evidence/information
Incendiarism/Incendiary language
Inciting arson/race riot/riot
Informer/Informing
Injuring mule/livestock
Insolent letter to woman
Insulting girls/white man/white
    woman
Insulting notes to white woman
Insulting remarks

Insulting white women/women
Insurrection
Making seditious utterance
Making threats
Might testify
Offending white man
Poisoning boys/horses/mules
Political activity/causes/prejudice/
    reasons
Quarrelling with white man
Race hatred/prejudice/troubles
Racial disturbance
Refusing information/to move
Reporting moonshiners
Reproving white youth
Rioting
Strike activity/striking railroad
Suing white man
Terrorism
Testifying
Threatening man/to give evidence
Threats/Threats against whites
To prevent evidence
Trouble with white man
Turning state's evidence
Unwise remarks
Violating contract
Voting Democratic
Writing insulting note

OFFENSES CATEGORIZED AS MISCELLANEOUS

Aiding in lynching
Arresting a coal miner
Being foreign worker
Entering house
Jailbreak
Mistaken identity

No offense
Outrageous acts
Praising murderer
Preaching Mormonism
Unknown
Violating a ferry law/quarantine

NOTES

Chapter 1

1. This reference to the weekly frequency of lynching is based on the confirmed inventory of victims compiled by Beck and Tolnay that includes the years 1882 to 1930 and the ten southeastern states of Alabama, Arkansas, Florida, Georgia, Kentucky, Louisiana, Mississippi, North Carolina, South Carolina, and Tennessee.

2. In his book *American Lynching*, Rushdy (2012) refers to these years as "the age of lynching."

3. Historian Roberta Senechal de la Roche (2004) uses a somewhat different definition of lynching in her theoretical work that is referenced later in this chapter. Her definition further requires that the victim was accused of some type of offense, often a crime.

4. Lawrence Cranford is included in the inventories of Georgia lynch victims constructed by Brundage (1993) and Tolnay and Beck (1995). The latter inventory indicates that Cranford's lynching was "uncertain."

5. The ten states included in the Beck-Tolnay inventory (2010) are Alabama, Arkansas, Florida, Georgia, Kentucky, Louisiana, Mississippi, North Carolina, South Carolina, and Tennessee. The omission of some states in which a large number of lynchings occurred—for example, Texas and Oklahoma—reflects the difficulty of obtaining historical newspaper sources for those areas at the time the original Beck-Tolnay inventory was created in the late 1980s, well before the availability of online and searchable archives. Other researchers have constructed inventories for additional states or regions (e.g., Brundage 1993; Carrigan 2006; Gonzalez-Day 2006; Leonard 2002; Pfeifer 2004).

6. Since it was created in the late 1980s, the Beck-Tolnay inventory of lynching has become generally accepted as the highest quality enumeration of lynching incidents and victims for these ten states between 1882 and 1930. It has been cited in many published articles and books and was the original source for the inventory of lynchings that is publicly available through Project HAL (Historical American Lynching) at http://people.uncw.edu/hinese/HAL/HAL%20Web%20Page.htm.

7. A few cases of lynchings with nonblack victims can be considered "spectacle" lynchings. For example, the lynching of Leo Frank, a white Jewish man, in Marietta, Georgia, in 1915 fits the description (see Dinnerstein 1968).

8. The U.S. Postal Service prohibited mailing images of lynchings, such as those on postcards, in 1908 as part of its enforcement of the Comstock Laws.

9. The correlation coefficient mentioned by Raper in this quotation is the

measure of the strength of the relationship between two variables—in this case the number of lynchings and the price of cotton. The correlation coefficient can range from +1.0 to –1.0, with 0 suggesting no relationship and values further from 0, in either a positive or a negative direction, indicating a stronger relationship. The correlation referred to by Raper, –0.532, describes a moderately strong negative relationship—higher cotton prices tended to be associated with fewer lynchings.

10. Quoted in Logue and Dorgan (1981, 49) (*Congressional Record*, 55th Congress, 1st Session, 2245, 3224).

11. Ayers (1984) also noted that transients were most vulnerable to being lynched.

Chapter 2

1. Vital registries were adopted unevenly within the United States across several decades. The southern region in general and rural areas within the South most particularly were late adopters of public registration of births and deaths. See Shapiro (1950) for an excellent discussion.

2. An initiative by the Integrated Public Use Microdata Series project at the University of Minnesota seeks to make all information gathered during the 1790 through 1940 U.S. Censuses (with the notable exception of 1890, due to the destruction of the original enumerators' manuscripts in a fire in the U.S. Commerce Building in Washington, D.C., in 1921) available to researchers in electronic form. Access to these "complete count" electronic and searchable census files will greatly facilitate future record linkage projects such as ours.

3. The original research notes that documented James Clark's lynching for the Beck-Tolnay inventory appear in the online supplemental material for this book (https://csde.washington.edu/lynching).

4. The most comprehensive collection of photographs of lynch victims is found in *Without Sanctuary* by James Allen, John Lewis, Leon F. Litwick, and Hilton Als, published in 2000. Of the fifty-three photographs of lynchings with known dates and locations in *Without Sanctuary*, only twenty-two were taken in the ten states included in the Beck-Tolnay inventory for 1882–1930. That is less than 1 percent of the 2,805 incidents included in the Beck-Tolnay inventory.

5. The page from the 1920 census enumerators' manuscripts on which the records for James Clark and his family appear can be found in the online supplemental materials for this book, at https://csde.washington.edu/lynching.

6. It should be noted that the information that we obtained from the original census records refers to the time that the census was taken, usually in January, April, or June of the census year. When we report the ages of victims and their family members, we use their ages at the time of the lynching. It is likely that other characteristics also changed between the time of the census and the time of the lynching. Those changes, of course, are unknown to us. In a sense, then, we have "frozen in time" the characteristics of victims for the time period between census enumeration and the lynching. This assumption is less problematic for lynchings that occurred shortly after the census was taken. Unfortunately, because

the U.S. Census is conducted only every ten years, we have no alternative to making this assumption.

7. We use the example of a jury verdict for illustrative purposes only. Our intent is not to equate lynch mobs with legitimate authoritative bodies, nor to suggest that victims were, in fact, guilty of the crimes or transgressions they were accused of having committed.

8. We are grateful to Professor Steven Ruggles, University of Minnesota, for his suggestion that we use the 1880 census enumerators' manuscripts to search for victims who were lynched during the 1890s.

9. Two researchers independently searched for each victim in the census that immediately preceded the lynching.

10. E. M. Beck, one of the principal investigators on the original study, conducted a subsequent review of newspaper reports for all cases of individuals lynched in Georgia and supplied supplementary information regarding many of these cases. We are grateful to Professor Beck for sharing information from his searches with us.

11. Estimates suggest that between 88 percent and 98 percent of eligible men were registered (Capozzola 2008, 27–30), making draft registration coverage of prime-age black men far more complete than census records (Coale and Rives 1973).

12. For the vast majority of the lynch victims who were African American, at the time we were compiling this data source, this required conducting multiple searches for each name, as individuals may have been listed as belonging to any of various racial categories used by the Census Bureau in a given decade, including "Black," "Mulatto," "Negro," or "Colored." This functionality has been streamlined somewhat in the current user interface for Ancestry.com.

13. Soundex is a coding scheme that relies on consonants to identify surnames based on how they sound rather than on how they are spelled (National Archives and Records Administration 2003).

14. Once the searching was completed, a "Search Documentation Form" was prepared to record our initial results and identify the pool of candidate matches. The search documentation form for James Clark is included in the online supplemental material for this book (https://csde.washington.edu/lynching).

15. Additionally, county-level political boundaries may have changed throughout the half century under investigation, meaning that a small minority of lynchings occurred in counties that did not exist in the year of census enumeration or whose borders may have changed between the time of census enumeration and the date of the lynching. Because of this, when a lynching occurred in a county that experienced boundary changes, we used separate adjacency criteria that reflected county boundaries at the time of the census and at the time of lynching for all searches (Horan and Hargis 1995). The spatial search area for this small minority of cases, then, may encompass a somewhat larger geographic area than that for other cases.

16. Because these attempts at forward linkage utilized a variety of information

available from the earlier census record—including age, literacy, marital status, co-resident family members, state of birth for the individual and both parents, and occupation—we generally were able to have a high level of confidence judging possible forward census matches. Unfortunately, young children who were co-resident with their parents in the earlier census have few distinguishing characteristics on which to base a between-census match. Therefore, in most cases this forward record linking strategy was used only for individuals who were at least in their mid- to late-teenaged years when enumerated in the earlier census. If a child had some distinguishing characteristic that might facilitate a match, we attempted a forward match. Such characteristics might include having been born out of state, having a parent who was born out of state, or having a disability.

17. The form documenting our decision on selecting a match for James Clark appears in the online supplementary material for this book (https://csde .washington.edu/lynching).

18. In chapters 3 through 6, we compare the characteristics of black and mixed-race male lynch victims with the characteristics of other similar men living in counties where lynchings occurred. Our data for this comparison sample are discussed at length in chapter 3. We expected the same patterns of selective census undercount to also apply to this sample of non-victims, so we did not expect underenumeration to seriously influence our comparison of victims and non-victims.

19. Complete tables reporting the results of our record linkage effort by race/ethnicity, time period, and state are included in Table A.2.2 in the appendix for this book.

Chapter 3

1. This number represents the individuals identified in the census manuscript records as possible "high likelihood" and "medium likelihood" matches for people in the inventory of victims. For most victims, only a single high likelihood or medium likelihood match is included. For seventy-five victims, we identified two matches who were considered to be equally likely and so have included both candidate matches. In these instances, each match is assigned a weight of 0.50.

2. As stated in previous chapters, the individuals profiled in this chapter were lynched between 1882 and 1929 in one of ten southern states: Alabama, Arkansas, Florida, Georgia, Kentucky, Louisiana, Mississippi, North Carolina, South Carolina, and Tennessee.

3. The victim's age at the time he was lynched was calculated based on the age that was reported for him in the census manuscripts and the date of the lynching. For example, if someone was reported as being age twelve in the 1900 census and was lynched in 1905, we estimated that his age at the time of lynching would have been seventeen ($12 + 5 = 17$). Absent additional information that suggested that a victim was a very young child, we omitted cases where the matches we located had seemingly implausible ages: 9 in 1880; .5 (an infant under the age of one year) and

1.0 for 1900; 2.5, 5, 8, and 9 for 1920. These unlikely ages are probably the result of age misreporting in the census, which was not uncommon in those decades. Still, it was not impossible for infants or small children to be the victims of mob violence, usually in conjunction with the lynching of their parents or another adult. However, none of the victims for whom we located plausible matches in the original census enumerators' manuscripts fell into these categories.

4. The mean age was three years higher at 32 years. That the mean is larger than the median tells us that the distribution of victims' ages is skewed to the right. By this, we mean that the difference between the median age (29) and the oldest age (76) is much greater than the difference between the median age (29) and the youngest age (11). This suggests that victims are "bunched" in the ages between 11 and 29 and spread out more thinly across the ages 29 to 76.

5. The seventy-six-year-old Ben Smith is one of two candidate matches, both of whom we considered to be equally likely to have been the person who was lynched. The other potential match would have been sixty-six years old when he was lynched. Both are included in our data and weighted at 0.50.

6. We are grateful to Professor E. M. Beck for providing us with this article reporting the lynching of Benjamin Smith and with many additional newspaper reports of specific lynching events. The article we refer to here appeared on the front page of the *Abbeville Chronicle*.

7. For additional details about the lynching of the Gillespies in 1902 and 1906 near Salisbury, North Carolina, see the excellent case study of racial violence in Rowan County, North Carolina, by Claude A. Clegg III titled *Troubled Ground: A Tale of Murder, Lynching, and Reckoning in the New South* (2010).

8. It is certainly possible, indeed likely, that individuals older than Benjamin Smith and younger than James Gillespie were lynched in the South during this time period. However, they are the oldest and youngest victims that we were able to link with their census records with an adequate level of confidence.

9. The single-year age distributions contained in Figure 3.1 have been smoothed by taking moving three-year averages. As a result, the first and last elements in the distribution are not represented. Despite the smoothing procedure, the evidence of "age heaping" at ages that end in "0" and "5" is apparent. Age heaping is a form of "rounding" that is well known to demographers and survey researchers. Age heaping means that people report their approximate age rather than their exact age. So, for example, someone who is nineteen might report their age as twenty, or someone who is twenty-seven might report that they are twenty-five. Appendix Table A.3.1 contains more detailed information on the age of victims.

10. The 1880 instructions for census enumerators were more detailed regarding the "mulatto" category than those in 1910 or 1920, which were nearly identical. The latter read as follows: "*Color or race.—Write 'W' for white; 'B' for black; 'Mu' for mulatto; 'In' for Indian; 'Ch' for Chinese; 'Jp' for Japanese; 'Fil' for Filipino; 'Hin' for Hindu; 'Kor' for Korean, for all persons not falling within one of these classes, write 'Ot' (for other), and write on the left-hand margin of the schedule the race of the person so indicated.*" In the census records for 1910 and 1920 we found a small number

of cases enumerated as "colored." This was not an official racial category used by the Census Bureau for those decades and likely represents enumerator error. We have combined those cases with "black" or "Negro," which were official racial categories. Along with information about census enumerator instructions, census forms and census data themselves are available from the Integrated Public Use Microdata Series (IPUMS) website at the University of Minnesota Population Center, http://usa.ipums.org/usa/index.shtml.

11. A table containing detailed information about the demographic and socioeconomic characteristics of lynch victims is included in the online supplementary material for this book (https://csde.washington.edu/lynching).

12. In Figure 3.2 a dagger symbol (†) is used to denote differences between victims and non-victims that are statistically significant at $p < .10$. A single asterisk (*) denotes differences that are statistically significant at $p < .05$. To be "statistically significant" means that the difference between the samples for the two groups is large enough to indicate that it did not arise from chance alone. Rather, it suggests that the distribution or concentration of the characteristic in question really differs between the population of victims and the population of non-victims. The probability of making a mistake in drawing this conclusion is only 10 percent for a p-value of .10 and 5 percent for a p-value of .05. Put another way, a p-value of .10 means that at least 90 percent of the time that we observe differences between groups of that magnitude, it will be because the two groups *really do* differ on that measure. A p-value of .05 means that 95 percent of the time, differences as large as those that we observe identify real differences between the two groups.

13. Individuals residing in institutions or group quarters settings at the time of census enumeration were not considered to be a member of a "household" as we have defined it for the classification scheme used in this chapter.

14. In creating this typology of households, we also classified as nuclear families married couples living without children and single-parent families with children. We did not distinguish among biological, step-, and adopted children.

15. The 1910 census is the only one included in our linkage efforts that recorded information about the number of times an individual had been married. Without that information, it is impossible to distinguish first marriages from remarriages for the vast majority of our sample.

16. There were relatively small differences between these two categories of tenancy status. Sharecroppers brought essentially no resources to the arrangement other than their capacity for labor, while share tenants supplied some of their own tools and other supplies. There were additional categories of farm tenants as well. For example, cash renters did not split the proceeds from their crop with the landowner; rather, they paid a fixed cash rent and supplied their own tools and animals. It is possible to sort these different types of status into a hierarchy from more to less advantageous. However, the most important consideration is that none of them included ownership of the farmland itself. For more information see Daniel (1972), Mandle (1992), and Ransom and Sutch (2000). Note also that the population census does not allow us to distinguish between different types

of farm tenancy. Population census records do include numeric codes that would allow the interested researcher to link household records to the agricultural census, which includes detailed information on the circumstances and economic relations involved in agricultural production.

17. Despite initially having been granted the right to vote and hold elected office, blacks were systematically disenfranchised throughout the South in the years following the dismemberment of federal Reconstruction programs. See Kousser (1974) for an excellent discussion of this process.

18. A table detailing the information presented in Figure 3.3 is included in Appendix Table A.3.2.

19. The IPUMS version of the 1880 census has imputed information for farm residence for any household that included an individual with the occupation of "farmer." We have not adopted that strategy in Figure 3.3 because not all individuals who worked in the agricultural sector lived on farms and because we also directly examined the reported occupations for lynch victims.

20. We use the end of the Civil War as the beginning of "freedom" for southern African Americans rather than the date of the Emancipation Proclamation in 1863. Many slaves were not affected by President Lincoln's proclamation, and most were in no position to take advantage of the benefits of freedom until after hostilities ended in 1865.

21. According to Gibson and Jung (2002, Table 4) there was a total of 4,097,111 blacks residing in the South in 1860. Of that total, 3,838,765 were slaves and 258,346 were free.

22. We deliberately use the terms "higher-status" and "lower-status," rather than the alternative "high status" and "low status," in order to avoid the implication that even the more privileged group of southern African American workers should be considered of high occupational status on any kind of objective scale that might be applied to all workers in the United States during this time period. Social scientists have developed a number of more or less objective criteria to determine the relative status of a variety of occupations. The most utilized of these is the Duncan SEI (or socioeconomic index), which indicates the status of occupations, based on the average educations and incomes of individuals with those occupations in 1950, ranging from a low of 4 (for woodchoppers) to a high of 96 (for dentists). Indeed, when the Duncan SEI is used to summarize the occupational prestige of the sample of non-victims, we find averages (means) of 10.74 and 11.46—and medians of 14 and 8—for the agricultural and nonagricultural sectors, respectively. The extreme values of the SEI for the sample of non-victims are 4 and 93. Note that we have not translated the occupations of victims into SEI scores and so do not have comparative numeric summaries for lynch victims.

23. A fuller description of how we constructed these occupational categories from the information contained in the census manuscripts for different decades is provided in the Appendix on pages 223–24.

24. Authors' calculations from the 1870 and 1930 Public Use Microdata Samples are available from the Minnesota Population Center's IPUMS-USA archive.

25. We have opted for a definition of literacy that includes the ability to both read and write. It was rare for individuals to report that they could do one but not the other. Only 6.6 percent of the victims reported that they could read but could not write; 0.3 percent were able to write but not read, a seemingly impossible combination of abilities.

26. As described in chapter 2, it is possible for a "contiguous" county to be located in a different state from the one in which the lynching occurred.

27. That is, the county in which the lynching occurred and county in which the victim was enumerated were in the same state but were not contiguous.

28. This category does not include cases in which the two counties were contiguous but in different states.

29. It should be noted that we cannot know whether the victims lynched in a county different from the one in which they had been enumerated had actually moved to the former county before they died or if the mobs simply killed them in a county that was different from their county of residence.

30. It is possible that the evidence in Figure 3.4 reflects a greater likelihood that victims who had not moved were considered to have been successfully linked to their census records. We must admit to such a possibility. A potential bias in favor of linking individuals who were enumerated in a location that was closer to the site of the lynching could have been introduced through our searching and selection procedures described in chapter 2. For example, when presented with equally likely matches in the county of lynching and in a different state, we typically favored the more geographically proximate option. More common, however, was a situation in which our alternative matches resided in the county of lynching and a contiguous county. Furthermore, as described in chapter 2, we considered a number of factors in our effort to identify successful matches and in assigning levels of confidence in those cases for which we had multiple possible matches. Our best guess, and it must remain a guess, is that this type of bias could slightly inflate the proportion of cases in which the county of lynching and county of enumeration were the same while understating the proportion of victims who were killed in a county that was contiguous to their county of enumeration. Even in light of such possible bias, however, the general conclusion that most victims were lynched close to home remains valid.

31. In this chapter we did not exploit the sequential enumeration of households by census workers to describe the neighbors of the victims, as we did for James Clark in chapter 2. However, extension is possible because the case files that we are publicly disseminating at csde.washington.edu/lynching include electronic images of the census page on which the victim's records were found, as well as the reel and line number of the original image.

Chapter 4

1. See the *Macon Telegraph* article "Two Counties Hunt Killer. Tom Ray Will Never be Jailed if Caught, Members of Posses Threaten," June 23, 1920, 1.

2. This information about the Tommy Ray case was drawn from the following newspaper articles: *Macon Telegraph*, "Murderer Held in Detroit. Michigan Governor Refuses to Deliver Negro to Georgia Sheriff," October 17, 1920, 10; *Flint [MI] Journal*, "Halt Extradition of Negro Slayer. Groesbeck Reopens Case of Confessed Georgia Murderer," June 21, 1921, 18; *Augusta Chronicle*, "Wilkinson County Justly Indignant Over the Tommy Ray Case," August 6, 1921, 4; *Washington Bee*, "Michigan Governor Releases Ray. Great Victory for Race and Justice; Blow to Lynching," August 27, 1921, 6. We are grateful to Professor E. M. Beck for locating these newspaper articles for us.

3. We are grateful to Professor E. M. Beck for pointing out these possible alternative explanations for why some lynch victims were unnamed in newspaper accounts of their deaths.

4. By "state-decade time periods," we mean all lynchings that occurred in a given state within a specific decade—for example, all of the lynchings that occurred in Tennessee between 1900 and 1909.

5. This positive inflation is due to the fact that interstate migration and age are negatively correlated, while age is also negatively related to the risk of victimization. If this indirect pathway connecting interstate migration and the likelihood of being lynched is not considered, the associated positive pathway (i.e., a negative correlation times a negative effect of age) will be subsumed in the positive relationship between interstate migration and the likelihood of victimization.

6. We include both the person's age and the square of his age, because we know that the age profile of lynch victims is curvilinear. That is, it increases from late childhood through early adulthood, reaching a peak at around age twenty-one, and then declines in later adulthood. Note that the peak age for risk of lynching *does not* reflect the same concept as the median age at lynching.

7. Controlling for the age of the victim and the decade when he was lynched allows us to account for the possibility that the individual measure of social marginality varied by age and over time. By controlling for the number of adult black men in the county of lynching, we adjust the overall likelihood of lynching (i.e., the model intercept) for the simple fact that the size of the sample of *non-victims* will be a direct result of the size of the black population within a locale.

8. Demonstrating a "causal" relationship between two variables with cross-sectional statistical evidence is challenging. Although, when discussing our empirical findings, we occasionally use language that suggests causation, we readily admit that our statistical methodologies fall short of the threshold required for inferring causation. A more cautious interpretation of our findings is that they describe "relationships" or "associations" between variables, not necessarily the causal impact of one variable on another.

9. While this result might appear to contradict the evidence presented in chapter 3 of a positive relationship between interstate migration and the likelihood of being lynched, it is important to recognize that the naive relationships described in Figure 4.6 include statistical controls for age, the number of adult black and

mixed-race men living in the county, and the decade of observation. Finding this negative relationship, then, means that age, which is negatively related to the probability of being lynched (the risk of victimization declines with age), is also negatively related to the likelihood of having been born out of state.

10. An alternative explanation, in line with much research on migration, could also be that men who were able to effect long-range geographic mobility were possessed of substantial enough social and financial resources that they represented an advantaged stratum within the black community.

11. For example, the multiplicative interaction term for percentage born out of state would be derived by multiplying the individual-level indicator (scored "1" for men who were enumerated outside their state of birth and "0" for men who were enumerated in the same state where they were born) by the percentage of the adult black male population that was born out of state (a continuous measure). For more detail about the use of interaction terms, see Jaccard and Turrisi (2003).

12. A percentile score indicates the percentage of cases in a distribution that occur at or below a particular value. So, for a county at the 25th percentile for the percentage of black and mixed-race men who were born out of state, 25 percent of counties would have a smaller proportion who were born out of state.

13. In order to derive the estimated relationship between the individual-level characteristic and the likelihood of lynching at different levels of the contextual characteristic, the latter variable was "centered" at the three specific values of the 25th, 50th, and 75th percentiles for the appropriate decade. All other county-level variables were centered at their 50th percentiles.

14. Deciles make up the set of percentiles that divides a distribution into ten equal parts. For example, the lowest decile is the value in the distribution (e.g., percentage of black adult males that possess a specific characteristic) below which 10 percent of all cases fall; the highest decile is the value below which 90 percent of cases fall, and so on.

15. The relationship between being an unmarried head of household and the likelihood of lynching was not statistically significant at the 80th and 90th percentiles.

16. The percentiles used to derive the information presented in Table 4.2 are specific to the decade in which the victim was lynched, and the sample of non-victims was extracted from the PUMS files. The 30th percentile for the percentage of the black adult male population that was born out of state ranges from 3 percent in 1910 to 10 percent in 1890.

17. Because the sample sizes are reduced when lynch victims are disaggregated by type of offense, we restricted these supplementary analyses to bivariate comparisons between victims and non-victims. These results are available in the online supplementary materials for this book, at https://csde.washington.edu/lynching.

Chapter 5

1. Reprinted in Ames 1942 from Nordyke 1939.

2. This would be true whether "mulattos" enjoyed higher socioeconomic status *because* of their racial classification or whether successful individuals were more likely to be enumerated as mulatto in the census.

3. Note that because "black" and "mulatto" were not included as separate racial categories in the 1900 census, when we use this measure we restrict our analyses to the decades of 1880, 1890, 1910, and 1920.

4. Recent scholarship has cast a somewhat different light on the public and private positions that Booker T. Washington took on these matters (e.g., Brundage 2004; Norell 2009). We are grateful to Professor Mark Schultz for bringing this to our attention.

5. The difference for higher-status occupations in the nonagricultural sector reported in chapter 3 was not statistically significant at the $p < .05$ level. But the difference was in the same direction as in the agricultural sector, with a p-value of .18. Given the relatively smaller number of workers in the nonagricultural sector—particularly higher-status workers—and the generally similar difference between victims and non-victims, we decided to pool the sectors for the analyses in this chapter.

6. This account of the lynching and subsequent events in Forsyth County, Georgia, draw heavily from the very thorough history of the case provided by Elliot Jaspin in chapter 7 of his book *Buried in the Bitter Waters* (2007).

7. Because some measures are not available for all decades, we obtained the refined estimates by using information from all of the decades for which we had data. The refined estimates for literacy and occupational status use data from all decades but do not include controls for "mulatto" status or home ownership. Refined estimates for "mulatto" status use data from all decades except 1900 and do not include controls for home ownership. Refined estimates for home ownership exclude 1880 and 1890 and do not include controls for "mulatto" status.

8. Note also that percentiles are calculated separately for each decade. This is important in light of, for example, the increase in the rate of literacy over time. Failing to use these time-specific references when constructing percentile measures would confound the relationship between victimization and local context.

9. These supplemental analyses are available in the online appendixes for this book, which may be found at https://csde.washington.edu/lynching.

10. Because information about "mulatto" status and home ownership is available only in some decades, when they are included in the robustness tests for the indicators of social marginality (available in all census years) the number of cases is reduced sharply—by nearly one-third in the case of "mulatto" status and by nearly two-thirds in the case of home ownership. This reduces the utility of the robustness tests because they are based on substantially different samples than were the original analyses. For that reason, in our description of the robustness

tests for the effects of social marginality on the likelihood of being lynched, we emphasize the findings from those models that included literacy and occupational status as measures of social standing.

Chapter 6

1. This is not to imply that Montgomery County had a history unstained by mob violence. Our records indicate that the county endured five lynchings between 1895 and 1910. We thank E. M. Beck for reminding us of this important fact.

2. Details on the life of S. S. Mincey were compiled based on newspaper reports (*Atlanta Constitution*, July 29, 1930), census documents, and an accounting of his lynching that appeared in *The Tragedy of Lynching* by Arthur Raper ([1933] 1969).

3. Historians, perhaps most notably Steven Hahn (1983), have presented evidence that localized power arrangements *within* the Democratic Party, rather than competition from other political challengers, represented an important arena for political struggles and may have had greater effects on the local community.

4. Tolnay and Beck actually consider the strength of the local Republican Party in their empirical analyses and find a negative relationship with the intensity of lynching. However, in the large majority of areas, for most elections, the Democratic Party was the major alternative to the Republican Party. Therefore, it is reasonable to infer a positive relationship between lynching and the strength of the Democratic Party from their evidence.

5. In light of Hahn's observation (1983) that white religious denominations largely reflected particular social class positions, the presence of multiple denominations may also signal divisions within the white community.

6. Note that in communities with less intensive agricultural production, reflected in a lower percentage of workers engaged in farmwork, agricultural workers were also more marginal. We do not, however, control for the strength of the local agricultural sector in the analyses presented in this chapter.

7. The original manuscripts of the agricultural census are available for all years covered by our current research, allowing analyses that focus on individual farmers and their families. Numerical codes are included in both the population census and the agricultural census; these codes allow the two information sources to be linked. Because our interest here is in testing the relationship between individual characteristics and the contextual measures that earlier work has found to predict the incidence of lynching, we focus on the aggregated, county-level measures here. A fruitful avenue for future work could utilize the individual-level agricultural records in conjunction with county-level tabulations of agricultural production.

8. The bivariate correlation between the race-specific measures of farm tenancy approximated 0.70 in each of the three decades they were available, and were highly significant ($p < .01$).

9. Data are also available for congressional elections, which are held every two years rather than every four years, thus providing measures of the local

political environment with a more direct temporal link to local political alliances. However, throughout the five decades covered by our research, a large number of counties have missing information on the distribution of voters by political party for congressional elections—particularly in years when there was not also a presidential election. Because of missing data on congressional elections, we have opted to focus on returns for presidential elections, for which there is only a single county with unreported election statistics, despite the fact that presidential elections are somewhat less frequent than congressional elections.

10. We explored the possibility that the conditioning effect of Democratic Party strength on the association between individual-level risk factors and the likelihood of victimization was nonlinear by also including a squared term for party strength. One might argue, for example, that the most politically dangerous communities for black men were those in which the Democratic Party's dominance was most vulnerable—or where the percentage of Democratic presidential votes hovered around 50 percent. In contrast, where the party's strength was very low or very high, political competition would have played a less prominent role in shaping the local atmosphere of danger. We found no evidence of a nonlinear conditioning effect.

11. Bailey and Snedker (2011) also incorporated additional material from denominational histories and other scholarly work. We have used, with permission, their coding structure for religious variables included here.

12. Note that having a mixed-race membership did not mean that blacks and whites necessarily worshiped in the same congregations or that blacks were afforded leadership opportunities within the institutional structure. Indeed, in many instances, even when blacks and whites were allowed to join the same local congregations, black members were required to sit in separate parts of the sanctuary during worship services.

13. To emphasize, the denominator here is *not* the total county population but is the total number of members claimed by all religious bodies.

14. Here, note that the denominator *is* the total number of black residents reported in a county. Because so few institutional structures were available to southern blacks, the degree of control blacks had over organizational religious resources had particular import for the organizational resources available to the black community.

15. For example, "If 90 percent of the religious adherents in an area belong to one group and 5 percent belong to each of two other groups, the situation is quasi-monopolistic and pluralism is low $(1 - [.90^2 + .05^2 + .05^2] = .185)$. If three denominations were of equal size, pluralism would be much higher $(1 - [.33^2 + .33^2 + .33^2] = .67)$. Pluralism also increases with the number of denominations; if there were not 3 but 10 groups of equal size, the pluralism index would be .90" (Voas, Olson, and Crockett 2002, 214).

16. We have relied on the "County Longitudinal Template, 1840–1990," created by Horan and Hargis (1995) for information on county boundary changes.

17. A reduction in the effect of "mulatto" status on the likelihood of being lynched may seem to contradict the "+" reported in Table 6.2. However, because the main effect of being "mulatto" is negative, the positive interaction indicates that this negative effect grows smaller, or shrinks, as the level of cotton dominance increases.

18. One might argue that a more thorough investigation of the issues examined in this chapter should include testing for second-order interactions between the relevant individual-level and county-level characteristics. For example, a model considering whether the conditioning influence of cotton dominance on the relationship between "mulatto" status and victimization varied by the concentration of "mulattos" in the county might include a multiplicative second-order interaction term of the following form: "mulatto" status × percentage "mulatto" in county × cotton dominance in county. All first-order interactions terms would also appear on the right-hand side of an equation that contained such a second-order interaction—"mulatto" status × percentage "mulatto" in the county, "mulatto" status × cotton dominance in the county, percentage "mulatto" in the county × cotton dominance in the county. We have not explored such second-order interactions because the complexity of the required model specifications, combined with the distributions for many of the individual-level characteristics, places excessive demands on the number of lynch victims contained in our analytic models, especially when considering "mulatto" status and farm ownership.

19. According to the Beck-Tolnay inventory of confirmed lynch victims, 10.6 percent of all victims whose race was known were not black and 2.8 percent of all victims whose sex was known were females (Tolnay and Beck 1995, 269).

Chapter 7

1. Home ownership was not recorded in the 1880 census.

2. We obtained death certificates for only a very small number of lynch victims, meaning that these vital records did not serve as a useful source of information for the vast majority of attempted linkages between victims and their census records. However, in some of the cases for which we do have access to death certificates—such as Ella Mays Wiggins's—they can provide useful information about the deceased. As with World War I draft registration documents, the death certificates that *are* available tend to be from the latter years of our inventory. Vital registries were adopted gradually across the South in the late nineteenth and early twentieth centuries, with earlier implementation in urban areas and later implementation in more rural communities (Shapiro 1950).

3. Because we were unable to locate in the census enumerators' manuscripts more than a few victims whose racial categorization was not either black or white (e.g., Chinese or Native American), and in light of the great diversity in their circumstances, we restrict the discussion of male victims in this chapter to include only white men.

4. Recall that a successful linkage indicates that either we identified a single potential match in whom we had a reasonable level of confidence or that we identified more than one possible match but had at least 50 percent confidence in one of them.

5. Information on the spatial and temporal distribution of female and white male victims is included in the appendix. See Table A.7.1.

6. Newspaper reports also list his name as E. R. Romeo. The census listing for the Romey family and the Florida death index for 1929 that includes both Fannie and Nola are consistent in their usage of the name Nola Romey, so we use that name here.

7. The categorization of crimes we developed is included in the appendix. See Table A.7.2.

8. Barn burning, as an act of social resistance and class conflict, is beautifully illustrated in William Faulkner's short story "Barn Burning."

9. Other classifications of the alleged offenses of lynch victims have been used by Brundage (1993) and Tolnay and Beck (1995). When referring to the reported offenses of victims, it is important to remember that, in most cases, the person who was killed was not convicted in a court of law.

10. A table including the information presented in this graphic is included in Table A.3.1 in the appendix to this book.

11. The historical census manuscripts followed the patriarchal convention of considering the male householder as the "head" and assigning a subsidiary status to his wife, if he was married. For households headed by a married couple, in this current classification we have opted to classify both the husband and wife as "head of household." Note that the significance of this decision mainly affects female victims, in that had we chosen to adhere to the original classifications in the census manuscripts, the only women who would have been designated as heads of household would have been widowed or divorced women or unmarried women who were living independently.

12. The specific data that this graphic is based on are presented in Table A.3.2 in the appendixes to this book.

13. The reader is referred to pages 223–24 in the Appendix for details on the occupational classification scheme we developed.

14. Recall that these percentages include all victims aged twelve and older at the time of census enumeration, regardless of whether they were reported as having participated in the paid labor force.

15. The percentage of female victims who are recorded as being literate is actually somewhat higher for black women than it is for white women, suggesting that white women of extraordinarily low status may have been the only ones singled out for mob violence.

16. The data underlying this graphic presentation are presented in Table A.3.2 in the appendixes to this book.

Chapter 8

1. For this presentation, Raper uses the number of lynchings between 1900 and 1920 per ten thousand population (Raper [1933] 1969, 483).

2. Raper also argued that the personal characteristics of mob members contributed to the frequency of lynching in the South. According to Raper, the typical mob member was unschooled, unchurched, and uncultured. He proposed expanded education as one important approach to eliminating mob violence. H. L. Mencken, the Baltimore newspaper editor and a contemporary of Raper's, held a similar view of the general southern population, which he articulated in his scathing essay "The Sahara of the Bozart" (1917).

3. In principle, the county-level information for measuring the strength of the Democratic Party, the dominance of the cotton economy, the extent of farm tenancy, and the nature of the local religious environment was available in the 1930s. However, analyzing these data for more than a small number of counties at a time would have been extremely difficult without the aid of modern computing technology and software.

4. Another example of the important contribution of technological innovations to sociohistorical scholarship can be found in the pathbreaking work of Roger Ransom and Richard Sutch in their book *One Kind of Freedom*, published originally in 1977. The revised and updated version of *One Kind of Freedom* published in 2000 includes an extensive appendix in which Ransom and Sutch conduct additional analyses that were not possible in 1977 because of computational limitations.

5. See Franzosi, De Fazio, and Vicari (2012) for an interesting and intriguing description of the use of Quantitative Narrative Analysis (QNA) to analyze the dynamics surrounding lynching incidents. QNA identifies the sequential actions performed by various participants in the lynching incident as reported in newspaper articles about the incident. When this type of interactive information is available for several lynching incidents, QNA can lead to generalizable conclusions about the agency of mobs. Griffin (1993) has also proposed an analytic strategy based on narrative accounts and the examination of sequences of events during lynching incidents to better understand the underlying causal mechanisms.

6. Interestingly, Appendix C in Arthur Raper's *The Tragedy of Lynching* includes an estimate of the number of lynchings that were "prevented" in the United States from 1914 through 1932. A note at the bottom of the table informs readers that Raper obtained his information from "The Negro Year Book, 1931–32" and with the assistance of the Department of Records and Research at the Tuskegee Institute. According to Raper's sources, there were 715 lynchings and 704 prevented lynchings during this eighteen-year period.

REFERENCES

Alderson, Arthur S., and Stephen K. Sanderson. 1991. "Historic European Household Structures and the Capitalist World Economy." *Journal of Family History* 16 (4): 419–32.

Alexander, Michelle. 2010. *The New Jim Crow: Mass Incarceration in the Age of Colorblindness.* New York: New Press.

Allen, James, John Lewis, Leon F. Litwack, and Hilton Als. 2000. *Without Sanctuary: Lynching Photography in America.* Santa Fe, N.M.: Twin Palms.

Ames, Jessie Daniel. 1942. *The Changing Character of Lynching: Review of Lynching, 1931–1941, with a Discussion of Recent Developments in this Field.* Atlanta: Commission on Interracial Cooperation.

Anderson, James D. 1988. *The Education of Blacks in the South, 1865–1930.* Chapel Hill: University of North Carolina Press.

Ayers, Edward L. 1984. *Vengeance and Justice: Crime and Punishment in the Nineteenth-Century American South.* New York: Oxford University Press.

Bailey, Amy Kate, and Karen A. Snedker. 2011. "Practicing What They Preach? Lynching and Religion in the American South, 1890–1929." *American Journal of Sociology* 117 (3): 844–87.

Bailey, Amy Kate, Stewart E. Tolnay, E. M. Beck, and Jennifer D. Laird. 2011. "Targeting Lynch Victims: Social Marginality or Status Transgressions?" *American Sociological Review* 76 (3): 412–36.

Bailey, Amy Kate, Stewart E. Tolnay, E. M. Beck, Alison Renee Roberts, and Nicholas H. Wong. 2008. "Personalizing Lynch Victims: A New Database to Support the Study of Southern Mob Violence." *Historical Methods* 41: 47–61.

Beck, E. M. 2015. "Judge Lynch Denied: Combating the Mob in the American South, 1877–1950." *Southern Cultures* (in press).

Beck, E. M., and Stewart E. Tolnay. 1990. "The Killing Fields of the Deep South: The Market for Cotton and the Lynching of Blacks, 1882–1930." *American Sociological Review* 55: 526–39.

———. 2010. "Confirmed Inventory of Southern Lynch Victims, 1882–1930." Machine-readable data file available from authors.

Beckett, Katherine, and Theodore Sasson. 2004. *The Politics of Injustice: Crime and Punishment in America.* Thousand Oaks, Calif.: Sage.

Blackmon, Douglas A. 2009. *Slavery by Another Name: The Re-enslavement of Black People in America from the Civil War to World War II.* New York: Doubleday Press.

Blokland, Arjan A. J., and Paul Nieuwbeerta. 2005. "The Effects of Life Circumstance on Longitudinal Trajectories of Offending." *Criminology* 43 (4): 1203–40.

Branch, Enobong Hannah, and Caroline Hanley. 2011. "Regional Convergence in Low-Wage Work and Earnings, 1970–2000." *Sociological Perspectives* 54 (4): 569–92.

Brundage, W. Fitzhugh. 1993. *Lynching in the New South: Georgia and Virginia, 1880–1930*. Urbana: University of Illinois Press.

———, ed. 1997. *Under Sentence of Death: Lynching in the South*. Chapel Hill: University of North Carolina Press.

———, ed. 2004. *Booker T. Washington and Black Progress: Up from Slavery 100 Years Later*. Gainesville: University of Florida Press.

Capozzola, Christopher Joseph Nicodemus. 2008. *Uncle Sam Wants You: World War I and the Making of the Modern American Citizen*. New York: Oxford University Press.

Carrigan, William D. 2006. *The Making of a Lynching Culture: Violence and Vigilantism in Central Texas, 1836–1916*. Urbana: University of Illinois Press.

Clegg, Claude A., III. 2010. *Troubled Ground: A Tale of Murder, Lynching, and Reckoning in the New South*. Urbana: University of Illinois Press.

Cloward, Richard A., and Lloyd E. Ohlin. 1960. *Delinquency and Opportunity: A Theory of Delinquent Gangs*. New York: Free Press.

Clubb, Jerome M., William H. Flanigan, and Nancy H. Zingale. 2006. "Presidential and Congressional Races, 1840–1972." Computer file ICPSR08611-v1. Inter-university Consortium for Political and Social Research, Ann Arbor, Mich. (distributor). http://doi:10.3886/ICPSR08611.

Coale, Ansley J., and Norfleet W. Rives. 1973. "A Statistical Reconstruction of the Black Population of the United States, 1880–1970: Estimates of True Numbers by Age and Sex, Birth Rates, and Total Fertility." *Population Index* 39: 3–36.

Cohen, Lawrence E., and Marcus Felson. 1979. "Social Change and Crime Rate Trends: A Routine Activity Approach." *American Sociological Review* 44 (August): 588–608.

Cunningham, David, and Benjamin T. Phillips. 2007. "Contexts for Mobilization: Spatial Settings and Klan Presence in North Carolina, 1964–1966." *American Journal of Sociology* 113 (3): 781–814.

Daniel, Pete R. 1972. *The Shadow of Slavery: Peonage in the South*. Urbana: University of Illinois Press.

———. 1985. *Breaking the Land: The Transformation of Cotton, Tobacco, and Rice Cultures since 1880*. Urbana: University of Illinois Press.

Dinnerstein, Leonard. 1968. *The Leo Frank Case*. New York: Columbia University Press.

Dozier, Howard Douglas. 1920. *A History of the Atlantic Coast Line Railroad*. Boston: Houghton Mifflin.

Eitel, David, Lisa Stolzenberg, and Stewart J. D'Allesio. 2005. "Police

Organizational Factors, the Racial Composition of the Police, and the Probability of Arrest." *Justice Quarterly* 22 (1): 30–57.

Elkins, Stanley M. 1959. *Slavery: A Problem in American Institutional and Intellectual Life*. Chicago: University of Chicago Press.

Engerman, Stanley L. 1977. "Black Fertility and Family Structure in the U.S., 1880–1940." *Journal of Family History* 2 (2): 117–38.

Evans, Ivan. 2009. *Cultures of Violence: Lynching and Racial Killing in South Africa and the United States*. Manchester, UK: Manchester University Press.

Farrington, David P. 1986. "Age and Crime." *Crime and Justice* 7 (20): 189–250.

Feimster, Crystal. 2009. *Southern Horrors: Women and the Politics of Rape and Lynching*. Cambridge, Mass.: Harvard University Press.

Ferrie, Joseph P. 1996. "A New Sample of Males Linked from the Public Use Microdata Sample of the 1850 U.S. Federal Census of the Population to the 1860 U.S. Federal Census Manuscript Schedules." *Historical Methods* 29: 141–56.

Franzosi, Roberto, Gianluca De Fazio, and Stefania Vicari. 2012. "Ways of Measuring Agency: An Application of Quantitative Narrative Analysis to Lynchings in Georgia (1875–1930)." *Sociological Methodology* 42: 1–42.

Frazier, E. Franklin. 1964. *The Negro Church in America*. New York: Schocken.

Frederickson, George M. 2002. *Racism: A Short History*. Princeton: Princeton University Press.

Garland, David. 2010. *Peculiar Institution: America's Death Penalty in an Age of Abolition*. Cambridge, Mass.: Harvard University Press.

Gibson, Campbell, and Kay Jung. 2002. "Historical Census Statistics on Population Totals by Race, 1790 to 1990, and by Hispanic Origin, 1970 to 1990, for the United States, Regions, Divisions, and States." Working Paper Series No. 56, Population Division, U.S. Census Bureau, Washington, D.C.

Godoy, Angelina Snodgrass. 2006. *Popular Injustice: Violence, Community, and Law in Latin America*. Stanford: Stanford University Press.

Gonzales-Day, Ken. 2006. *Lynching in the West, 1850–1935*. Durham: Duke University Press.

Gottfredson, Michael R., and Travis Hirschi. 1990. *A General Theory of Crime*. Redwood City, Calif.: Stanford University Press.

Grant, Donald L. 1975. *The Anti-lynching Movement, 1883–1932*. San Francisco: R and E Research.

Griffin, Larry J. 1993. "Narrative, Event-Structure Analysis, and Causal Interpretation in Historical Sociology." *American Journal of Sociology* 98: 1094–133.

Guest, Avery M. 1987. "Notes from the National Panel Study: Linkage and Migration in the Late Nineteenth Century." *Historical Methods* 20: 63–77.

Gullickson, Aaron. 2005. "The Significance of Color Declines: A Re-analysis of Skin Tone Differential in Post–Civil Rights America." *Social Forces* 84 (1): 157–80.

———. 2010. "Racial Boundary Formation at the Dawn of Jim Crow: The

Determinants and Effects of Black/Mulatto Occupational Differences in the United States, 1880." *American Journal of Sociology* 16: 187–231.

Gullickson, Aaron, and Florencia Torche. 2014. "Patterns of Racial and Educational Assortative Mating in Brazil." *Demography* 51 (3): 835–56.

Hahn, Steven. 1983. *The Roots of Southern Populism: Yeoman Farmers and the Transformation of the Georgia Upcountry, 1850–1890*. New York: Oxford University Press.

Hall, Jacqueline Dowd. 1993. *Revolt against Chivalry: Jessie Daniel Ames and the Women's Campaign against Lynching*. New York: Columbia University Press.

Harlow, Catherine Wolf. 2005. *Hate Crime Reported by Victims and Police*. Bureau of Justice Statistics, Special Report, National Crime Victimization Survey and Uniform Crime Reporting, Washington, D.C., November.

Hashima, Patricia Y., and David Finkelhor. 1999. "Violent Victimization of Youth versus Adults in the National Crime Victimization Survey." *Journal of Interpersonal Violence* 14 (8): 799–820.

Hines, Elizabeth, and Eliza Steelwater. 2013. *Project HAL: Historic American Lynching Data Collection Project*. http://people.uncw.edu/hinese/HAL/HAL %20Web%20Page.htm.

Hirschi, Travis. 1969. *The Causes of Delinquency*. Berkeley: University of California Press.

———. 1977. "Causes and Prevention of Juvenile Delinquency." *Sociological Inquiry* 47: 322–41.

Hoffman, Frederick L. 1896. *The Race Traits and Tendencies of the American Negro*. New York: Macmillan for the American Economic Association.

Hofstadter, Richard. 1955. *Social Darwinism in American Thought*. Boston: Beacon Press.

Horan, Patrick M., and Peggy G. Hargis. 1995. "County Longitudinal Template, 1840–1990." Computer file ICPSR06576-v1. Inter-university Consortium for Political and Social Research, Ann Arbor, Mich. (distributor). http://doi.org/10.3886/ICPSR06576.v1.

Horney, Julie, D. Wayne Osgood, and Ineke Haen Marshall. 1995. "Criminal Careers in the Short Term: Intra-individual Variability in Crime and Its Relation to Local Life Circumstances." *American Sociological Review* 60 (5): 655–73.

Inter-university Consortium for Political and Social Research. 2001. "Historical, Demographic, Economic, and Social Data: The United States, 1790–1970." Computer file ICPSR00003-v1. Inter-university Consortium for Political and Social Research, Ann Arbor, Mich. (distributor). http:// doi:10.3886/ICPSR00003.

Inverarity, James. 1976. "Populism and Lynching in Louisiana, 1889–1896: A Test of Erikson's Theory of the Relationship between Boundary Crises and Repressive Justice." *American Sociological Review* 41: 262–80.

Jaccard, James J., and Robert Turrisi. 2003. *Interaction Effects in Multiple Regression*. 2nd ed. Thousand Oaks, Calif.: Sage.

Jacobs, David, Jason T. Carmichael, and Stephanie L. Kent. 2005. "Vigilantism, Current Racial Threat, and Death Sentences." *American Sociological Review* 70 (4): 656–77.

Jacobs, David, Chad Malone, and Gale Iles. 2012. "Race Relations and Prison Admissions: Lynchings, Minority Threat, and Racial Politics." *Sociological Quarterly* 53: 166–87.

Jaspin, Elliot. 2007. *Buried in the Bitter Waters: The Hidden History of Racial Cleansing in America.* New York: Basic Books.

King, Ryan D., Steven F. Messner, and Robert D. Baller. 2009. "Contemporary Hate Crimes, Law Enforcement, and the Legacy of Racial Violence." *American Sociological Review* 74 (2): 291–315.

Kousser, Morgan J. 1974. *The Shaping of Southern Politics: Suffrage Restrictions and the Establishment of the One-Party South.* New Haven: Yale University Press.

Lamb, Chris. 2004. *Blackout: The Untold Story of Jackie Robinson's First Spring Training.* Lincoln: University of Nebraska Press.

Lauritsen, Janet L., and Robin J. Schaum. 2004. "The Social Ecology of Violence against Women." *Criminology* 42: 323–57.

Lee, Everett S., Ann R. Miller, Carol P. Brainerd, and Richard A. Easterlin. 1957. *Population Redistribution and Economic Growth, United States, 1870–1950.* Vol. 1. Philadelphia: American Philosophical Society.

Leonard, Stephen J. 2002. *Lynching in Colorado, 1859–1919.* Boulder: University Press of Colorado.

Liska, Allen E., and Paul E. Bellair. 1995. "Violent Crime Rates and Racial Composition: Convergence over Time." *American Journal of Sociology* 101 (3): 578–610.

Logue, Cal M., and Howard Dorgan, eds. 1981. *The Oratory of Southern Demagogues.* Baton Rouge: Louisiana State University Press.

Mandle, Jay R. 1978. *The Roots of Black Poverty: The Southern Plantation Economy after the Civil War.* Durham: Duke University Press.

———. 1992. *Not Slave, Not Free: The African American Economic Experience since the Civil War.* Durham: Duke University Press.

Margo, Robert A. 1990. *Race and Schooling in the South, 1880–1950: An Economic History.* Chicago: University of Chicago Press.

Marteleto, Leticia J. 2012. "Educational Inequality by Race in Brazil, 1982–2007: Structural Changes and Shifts in Racial Classification." *Demography* 49 (1): 337–58.

Mathews, Donald G. 2000. "The Rite of Human Sacrifice." *Journal of Southern Religion* 3.

McAdam, Doug, Kaisa Snellman, and Yang Su. 2013. "'Burning Down the House': Race, Politics, the Media, and the Burning of Churches in the U.S., 1996–2001." Unpublished manuscript.

McCall, Leslie. 2001. "Sources of Racial Wage Inequality in Metropolitan Labor Markets: Racial, Ethnic, and Gender Differences." *American Sociological Review* 66 (4): 520–41.

McClure, Helen. 2013. "'Who Dares to Style This Female a Woman?': Lynching, Gender, and Culture in the Nineteenth-Century U.S. West." In *Lynching beyond Dixie: American Mob Violence outside the South*, edited by Michael J. Pfeifer, 21–53. Urbana: University of Illinois Press.

McGovern, James R. 1982. *Anatomy of a Lynching: The Killing of Claude Neal.* Baton Rouge: Louisiana State University Press.

McVeigh, Rory. 2009. *The Rise of the Ku Klux Klan: Right-Wing Movements and National Politics.* Minneapolis: University of Minnesota Press.

Mencken, H. L. 1917. "The Sahara of the Bozart." *New York Evening Mail.*

Merton, Robert King. 1957. *Social Theory and Social Structure: Toward the Codification of Theory and Research.* New York: Free Press.

Messner, Steven F., Robert D. Baller, and Matthew Z. Zevenbergen. 2005. "The Legacy of Lynching and Southern Homocide." *American Sociological Review* 70 (4): 633–55.

Miller, Robert Moats. 1957. "The Protestant Churches and Lynching, 1919–1939." *Journal of Negro History* 42 (2): 118–31.

Montgomery, William E. 1992. *Under Their Own Vine and Fig Tree: The African American Church in the South, 1865–1900.* Baton Rouge: Louisiana University Press.

National Archives and Records Administration. 2003. *Census Soundex.* Pamphlet.

National Association for the Advancement of Colored People. 1919. *Thirty Years of Lynching in the United States, 1889–1918.* New York: Negro Universities Press.

Nordyke, Lewis T. 1939. "Ladies and Lynching." *Survey Graphic* 28.

Norrell, Robert J. 2009. *Up from History: The Life of Booker T. Washington.* Cambridge, Mass.: Belknap Press of Harvard University Press.

Pfeifer, Michael J. 2004. *Rough Justice: Lynching and American Society, 1874–1947.* Urbana: University of Illinois Press.

———, ed. 2013. *Lynching beyond Dixie: American Mob Violence outside the South.* Urbana: University of Illinois Press.

Piquero, Alex R., John M. MacDonald, and Karen F. Parker. 2002. "Race, Local Life Circumstances, and Criminal History." *Social Science Quarterly* 83 (3): 654–70.

Porter, Jeremy, Frank M. Howell, and Lynn M. Hempel. 2013. "Old Times Are Not Forgotten: The Institutionalization of White-Flight Segregationist Academies in the American South." Unpublished manuscript.

Ransom, Roger L., and Richard Sutch. 2000. *One Kind of Freedom: The Economic Impact of Emancipation.* 2nd ed. New York: Cambridge University Press.

Raper, Arthur. (1933) 1969. *The Tragedy of Lynching.* Montclair, N.J.: Patterson Smith.

———. 1936. *Preface to Peasantry.* Chapel Hill: University of North Carolina Press.

Reed, John Shelton, G. Doss, and J. Hurlburt. 1987. "Too Good to Be False: An Essay in the Folklore of Social Science." *Sociological Inquiry* 57 (Winter): 1–11.

Remillard, Arthur. 2011. *Southern Civil Religions: Imagining the Good Society in the Post-Reconstruction Era.* Athens: University of Georgia Press.

Robinson, W. S. 1950. "Ecological Correlations and the Behavior of Individuals." *American Sociological Review* 15 (3): 351–57.

Rosenwaike, Mark E., Samuel H. Preston, and Irma T. Elo. 1998. "Linking Death Certificates to Early Census Records: The African American Matched Records Sample." *Historical Methods* 31: 65–74.

Ruggles, Steven, Matthew Sobek, J. Trent Alexander, Catherine A. Fitch, Ronald Goeken, Patricia Kelly Hall, Miriam King, and Chad Ronnander. 2008. Integrated Public Use Microdata Series: Version 4.0 (machine-readable database). Minneapolis: Minnesota Population Center (producer and distributor).

Rushdy, Ashraf H. A. 2012. *American Lynching.* New Haven: Yale University Press.

Sampson, Robert J., and John H. Laub. 1990. "Crime and Deviance Over the Life Course: The Salience of Adult Social Bonds." *American Sociological Review* 55: 609–27.

Saperstein, Aliya, and Aaron Gullickson. 2013. "A 'Mulatto Escape Hatch' in the United States? Examining Evidence of Racial and Social Mobility during the Jim Crow Era." *Demography* 50 (5): 1921–42.

Schultz, Mark. 2005. *The Rural Face of White Supremacy: Beyond Jim Crow.* Urbana: University of Illinois Press.

Senechal de la Roche, Roberta. 1996. "Collective Violence as Social Control." *Sociological Forum* 11: 97–128.

———. 1997. "The Sociogenesis of Lynching." In *Under Sentence of Death: Lynching in the South,* edited by W. Fitzhugh Brundage, 48–76. Chapel Hill: University of North Carolina Press.

———. 2001. "Why Is Collective Violence Collective?" *Sociological Theory* 19: 126–44.

———. 2004. "Modern Lynchings." In *Violence: From Theory to Research,* edited by Margaret A. Zahn, Henry H. Brownstein, and Shelly J. Jackson, 213–26. Cincinnati: Anderson Publishing.

Shapiro, Herbert. 1988. *White Violence and Black Response: From Reconstruction to Montgomery.* Amherst: University of Massachusetts Press.

Shapiro, S. 1950. "Development of Birth Registration and Birth Statistics in the United States." *Population Studies* 4 (1): 86–111.

Sitton, Thad, and James H. Conrad. 2005. *Freedom Colonies: Independent Black Texans in the Time of Jim Crow.* Austin: University of Texas Press.

Smead, Howard. 1986. *Blood Justice: The Lynching of Mack Charles Parker.* New York: Oxford University Press.

Soule, Sarah H. 1992. "Populism and Black Lynching in Georgia, 1890–1900." *Social Forces* 71: 431–49.

Spiro, Jonathan Peter. 2009. *Defending the Master Race: Conservation, Eugenics, and the Legacy of Madison Grant.* Burlington: University of Vermont Press.

Steckel, Richard H. 1988. "Census Matching and Migration: A Research Strategy." *Historical Methods* 21: 52–60.

Telles, Edward E. 2004. *Race in Another America: The Significance of Skin Color in Brazil.* Princeton: Princeton University Press.

Theobald, Delphine, and David P. Farrington. 2009. "Effects of Getting Married on Offending: Results from a Prospective Study of Males." *European Journal of Criminology* 6 (6): 496–516.

Tolnay, Stewart E. 1999. *The Bottom Rung: African American Family Life on Southern Farms.* Urbana: University of Illinois Press.

———. 2004. "The Living Arrangements of African American and Immigrant Children, 1880–2000." *Journal of Family History* 29: 421–45.

Tolnay, Stewart E., and E. M. Beck. 1992. "Racial Violence and Black Migration in the American South, 1910 to 1930." *American Sociological Review* 57: 103–16.

———. 1995. *A Festival of Violence: An Analysis of Southern Lynchings, 1882–1930.* Urbana: University of Illinois Press.

Tolnay, Stewart E., Glenn Deane, and E. M. Beck. 1996. "Vicarious Violence: Spatial Effects on Southern Lynchings, 1890–1919." *American Journal of Sociology* 102(3): 788–815.

Truman, Jennifer, Lynn Langton, and Michael Planty. 2013. *Criminal Victimization, 2012.* Washington, D.C.: Bureau of Justice Statistics.

U.S. Bureau of the Census. 1894. *Statistics of Churches: Eleventh Decennial Report of the Census, 1890.* Washington, D.C.: Government Printing Office.

———. 1906. *Census of Religious Bodies.* Pts. 1 and 2. Washington, D.C.: Government Printing Office.

———. 1916. *Census of Religious Bodies.* Pts. 1 and 2. Washington, D.C.: Government Printing Office.

———. 1926. *Census of Religious Bodies.* Pts. 1 and 2. Washington, D.C.: Government Printing Office.

Vandiver, Margaret. 2006. *Lethal Punishment: Lynchings and Legal Executions in the South.* New Brunswick, N.J.: Rutgers University Press.

Voas, David, Daniel V. A. Olson, and Alasdair Crockett. 2002. "Religious Pluralism and Participation: Why Previous Research Is Wrong." *American Sociological Review* 67 (2): 212–30.

Wacquant, Loïc. 2000. "America's New 'Peculiar Institution': On the Prison as Surrogate Ghetto." *Theoretical Criminology* 4 (3): 380.

Western, Bruce, and Becky Pettit. 2005. "Black-White Wage Inequality, Employment Rates, and Incarceration." *American Journal of Sociology* 111: 553–78.

Wexler, Laura. 2003. *Fire in the Cane Break: The Last Mass Lynching in America.* New York: Scribner.

White, Walter. (1929) 1969. *Rope and Faggot: A Biography of Judge Lynch.* New York: Arno Press.

Wilkes, Donald E., Jr. 1997. "The Last Lynching in Athens." *Flagpole Magazine*, September 10, 8.

Wilson, James Q., and Ricard J. Herrnstein. 1985. *Crime and Human Nature: The Definitive Study of the Causes of Crime*. New York: Free Press.

Wood, Amy Louise. 2009. *Lynching and Spectacle: Witnessing Racial Violence in America, 1890–1940*. Chapel Hill: University of North Carolina Press.

Woodward, C. Vann. 1956. *The Strange Career of Jim Crow*. New York: Oxford University Press.

INDEX

Note: Information in figures and tables is indicated by *f* and *t*.